THE HOME FRONT

Implications of
Welfare Reform
for Housing Policy

THE URBAN INSTITUTE PRESS
Washington, D.C.

THE URBAN INSTITUTE PRESS
2100 M Street, N.W.
Washington, D.C. 20037

Library of Congress Cataloging in Publication Data

The Home Front: Implications of Welfare Reform for Housing Policy /
Sandra J. Newman, editor.

Includes bibliographic references and index.

1. Public housing—United States—Congresses. 2. Housing subsidies—United States—Congresses. 3. Poor—Housing—Government policy—United States—Congresses. 4. Housing policy—United States—Congresses. 5. Welfare recipients—Employment—Government policy—United States—Congresses. 6. Public welfare—Law and legislation—United States—Congresses. I. Newman, Sandra J. II. Title: Implications of welfare reform for housing policy.

| HD7288.78.U5H655 | 1999 | 98-48887 |
| 363.5'85'0973—dc21 | | CIP |

ISBN 0-87766-685-7 (paper, alk. paper)
ISBN 0-87766-684-9 (cloth, alk. paper)

Printed in the United States of America

Distributed in North America by
University Press of America
4720 Boston Way
Lanham, MD 20706

THE URBAN INSTITUTE is a nonprofit policy research and educational organization established in Washington, D.C., in 1968. Its staff investigates the social and economic problems confronting the nation and public and private means to alleviate them. The Institute disseminates significant findings of its research through the publications program of its Press. The goals of the Institute are to sharpen thinking about societal problems and efforts to solve them, improve government decisions and performance, and increase citizen awareness of important policy choices.

Through work that ranges from broad conceptual studies to administrative and technical assistance, Institute researchers contribute to the stock of knowledge available to guide decision-making in the public interest.

Conclusions or opinions expressed in Institute publications are those of the authors and do not necessarily reflect the views of staff members, officers or trustees of the Institute, advisory groups, or any organizations that provide financial support to the Institute.

For Jack
". . . the best man I know."
(H. Hunt, 1998)

PREFACE AND ACKNOWLEDGMENTS

This book is an effort to develop a better understanding of the inter-relationship between housing and welfare policy. Although the diffi-culties of this interrelationship have been lurking in the background of debates about the proper goals of housing assistance since the earliest days of housing policy development, they have only begun to move to the foreground in the last 15 years. And there is little wonder why. This was a period of intensified interest in reforming the welfare system, which prompted all parts of the safety net to reconsider their goals and strategies.

Housing has always had an uneasy relationship with the rest of the social welfare safety net. Part of the explanation is that housing has never been strictly a poverty issue, with the largest government hous-ing subsidies flowing not to the poor but to the middle class and affluent through the mortgage interest deduction. But even the housing assistance system for the needy has always used more liberal defini-tions of income eligibility than welfare programs, most recently re-lying on a standard that is about 30 percent higher than the poverty line but has reached up to three times the poverty line in the heyday of subsidies to developers of low-income housing. Thus, unlike in-come assistance policy, conversations about housing policy have never been synonymous with conversations about the poor. And for part of the history of housing programs, the profile of housing assistance recipients was a mix of the lower middle class and the working poor along with the most disadvantaged. This profile changed dramatically in the 1980s, as larger and larger proportions of very poor recipients were given housing assistance priority. There is also some evidence that the poorest households were channeled into public housing, fur-ther exacerbating the concentration of very disadvantaged households in this part of the housing assistance system.

The increasing share of housing assistance recipients who are very disadvantaged, and the growing overlap between households who re-ceive both housing assistance and income assistance, mean that welfare reform is going to affect housing assistance recipients and, ultimately, housing policy in important ways.

This book is a first effort to critically analyze what we know about this issue and what we need to know to fashion a coherent social policy. The book evolved from a symposium on the implications of welfare reform for housing held at Johns Hopkins University in July 1997. I would like to thank the Fannie Mae Foundation for sponsoring the symposium and for its support throughout the production of this book. I am also enormously grateful to the Ford Foundation, and particularly to Mark Elliott, formerly a project officer at Ford, for supporting our attempts to simulate the quantitative impacts of welfare reform on the housing assistance system, which resulted in the chapter I coauthored with Joe Harkness.

By definition, an edited book is a joint effort and this project is certainly no exception. I am very grateful for the outstanding contributions of everyone involved—the authors, the funders, the symposium participants from the worlds of welfare as well as housing, and the production team at the Urban Institute Press. This was truly a dream team. Last but hardly least, my heartfelt thanks to Sally Katz, who has been my right and left hand at Johns Hopkins for more than 11 years and who always makes me look better than I am.

CONTENTS

What effect is welfare reform likely to have on Americans' ability to afford decent housing? We don't know. Even more surprising, the question was ignored in the policy debates surrounding welfare reform. One immediately wonders why: After all, housing costs account for a major portion of most people's income, and having a home is essential to one's well-being.

The answer, in large part, is that housing assistance recipients and welfare recipients used to be virtually separate populations, a situation that has changed in the last 30 years. By the time the Personal Responsibility and Work Opportunity Reconciliation Act was passed, in 1996, more than half of U.S. households receiving housing assistance were also receiving some form of income assistance.

Of particular importance, nearly half of all families with children now living in public housing are likely to be touched by welfare reform. The authors of *The Home Front: Implications of Welfare Reform for Housing Policy* take a look at how.

They begin by observing that the same public attitudes that underlie welfare reform have prompted a rethinking of the goal of housing assistance. Instead of being simply a way of providing a decent place to live, housing assistance is being viewed as another means by which poor people can achieve economic independence. Yet there is no direct evidence on which to base this notion: Policy analysts cannot say for certain that affordable housing in a safe, stable neighborhood located near jobs and schools improves the chances that a household will achieve economic self-sufficiency. Moreover, housing administrators point out that current policy presents several disincentives to work.

The authors of this invaluable book not only examine the conceptual and policy links between welfare reform and housing (both assisted and unassisted), they also clarify what previous studies can tell us about the relation between housing assistance and economic self-sufficiency and what research needs to be done in the future.

The Urban Institute is exploring the link between welfare reform and housing as part of its *Assessing the New Federalism* program. In 1997, it surveyed a representative sample of Americans in order to establish baseline data on the affordability of housing and numerous other indicators of family well-being. The survey will be repeated this year, giving researchers an opportunity to measure changes and to begin assessing the effects of recent policies on the ability of families to afford housing.

This outstanding and timely book should spark discussion about this neglected aspect of the home front, and I am pleased that the Urban Institute will have a voice in that discourse.

William Gorham
President
The Urban Institute

Chapter One

INTRODUCTION AND OVERVIEW

Sandra J. Newman

The sea change in social welfare policy that occurred with passage of the Personal Responsibility and Work Opportunity Reconciliation Act of 1996 has appropriately been accompanied by much discussion and debate. Most of this attention focuses on work requirements and time limits, the core elements of welfare reform. But a second tier conversation has also been taking place about the roles that child care, transportation, and health care will play in enabling welfare recipients to meet the work requirements. This second tier discussion is significant not only for its substantive content but also for its symbolic value. It reflects the acknowledgment that moving recipients from welfare to work requires more than job skills and work readiness. It involves, in addition, solving the logistic problems of everyday life and satisfying very basic needs so that getting and keeping a job is possible.

What is noteworthy about this second tier discussion is that housing is not part of the conversation, even though housing policy poses two obvious questions for welfare reform. The first is whether living in a decent, affordable home in a good neighborhood improves a welfare recipient's chances of achieving self-sufficiency. Is there an argument for housing subsidies that is analogous, for example, to the argument that good and affordable child care and transportation to and from work improve the ability to get and keep a job? The second is how welfare reform will reverberate on the housing assistance system for the poor. This system, broadly defined,[1] represents a $28 billion component of the federal budget, larger than the $20 billion Aid to Families with Dependent Children (AFDC) program that welfare reform replaces.[2]

Why is housing being left out, as it has been left out of the last 20 years of angst and analysis of how the welfare system should be fixed? Part of the answer lies in the bureaucratic separation of housing and welfare in congressional committees, executive branch agencies, and delivery systems (Hornburg 1997). But much of the explanation is that the housing assistance system has been preoccupied with its own major transformation, which has been unfolding over the last two decades but, unlike welfare reform, is still very much in process. Two to three decades ago—when only a relatively small proportion of households receiving housing assistance also received welfare—it was reasonable that the housing assistance system consciously, even proudly, distinguished itself from the welfare system. The fact that the housing assistance system has always been only one small part of a very large housing sector and, therefore, only one focus of U.S. housing policy, made this separation seem even more justifiable.[3] Indeed, during this period, inclusion of the housing assistance system in the welfare debate would have been not only unexpected but unwelcome by many in the housing sector.

Today, the situation is substantially different. Even though the welfare and housing systems were originally designed to assist different clienteles, there is now substantial overlap (Newman and Schnare 1992). The proportion of households living in assisted housing that also receive assistance from one of the three main income assistance programs (AFDC, Supplemental Security Income [SSI], and General Assistance) has more than doubled since 1966, now reaching more than 50 percent.[4] Similar increases have occurred in the proportion of income assistance recipients who also receive housing assistance. Between 1981 and 1995, for example, this fraction increased from about one-fifth to one-third.[5] The overlap is even greater when AFDC recipients alone are considered. In the mid-1990s, for example, nearly 50 percent of households with children living in public housing were receiving AFDC.[6] Thus, nearly half of all families with children who live in public housing are potentially affected by welfare reform. Taken together, these changes have moved a significant part of housing policy squarely into the safety net.

This transformation has been furthered by the shift in public opinion regarding the principles that ought to govern all assistance programs for the poor. The assistance programs developed in the New Deal era had the basic goal of income replacement. The social values and attitudes undergirding current welfare reform efforts—most prominently, that economic independence and self-sufficiency are the ultimate goals, and that there are reciprocal obligations between recipients and government—logically apply to housing assistance as well.

The cumulative effect of all these changes has been a rethinking of the goals of housing policy for the poor and the tools for achieving those goals. While the debates continue, strong arguments are now being made for a new orientation, in which helping poor people live in decent housing—the traditional goal of housing policy for the poor over its more than 50-year history—is no longer viewed as an end in itself, but as a means to economic independence.

Housing has been left out of the welfare reform conversation, then, because it hasn't been ready to participate. One important measure of not being ready is not having much hard information to bring to the table about how welfare policy does—and how it should—interact with housing assistance policy. This book begins to provide that information. It has three specific goals: (1) to present new research on the projected impacts of welfare reform on housing; (2) to distill the most important lessons learned from past research and demonstration programs, in both the housing and welfare arenas, aimed at moving recipients to self-sufficiency; and (3) to identify the special challenges welfare reform presents to low-income housing practitioners and researchers, and promising approaches to addressing these challenges. The immediate issue of the ripple effects of welfare reform on housing, the focus of this book, can best be addressed within a broader agenda of questions that must be answered if we are to advance our knowledge of the role of housing in helping move poor people into the economic mainstream.

DOES DECENT HOUSING IMPROVE THE CHANCES OF ACHIEVING ECONOMIC INDEPENDENCE?[7]

The most compelling evidence for providing a role for housing policy in welfare reform would show that decent, safe, and affordable housing in a decent neighborhood actually increases the ability of the poor to achieve sustained economic self-sufficiency. To answer this question definitively would require a controlled experiment in which otherwise similar sample members were assigned to an experimental "decent housing" group, and a control group who were not. Since the two groups would be the same except for their housing situation, any difference in subsequent income, employment, welfare receipt, and so on, could be confidently attributed to the housing difference. Unfortunately, no such experiment has been undertaken, forcing us to rely on more indirect evidence.

At the low-quality extreme, of course, are the homeless. Although studies suggest that 20–30 percent of the homeless have jobs, most observers take it as self-evident that being homeless increases the difficulty of pursuing education or job training, or getting and keeping a job. But, given that one does have housing, does the quality of that housing—measured by such characteristics as affordability, physical adequacy, location (e.g., accessibility to training, work, or school; safety or other conditions of the neighborhood; quality of the environment for children), and stability—make a difference to one's chances of achieving economic independence? The three major housing dimensions that have been studied in this connection are proximity to attainable jobs (the "spatial mismatch" hypothesis), housing quality, and neighborhood quality more generally.

THE SPATIAL MISMATCH HYPOTHESIS

The spatial mismatch hypothesis holds that unemployment (and therefore welfare use) is high in inner cities because there are no entry-level jobs in the areas where the poor can afford to live.[8] At this writing, the accumulated evidence from the most rigorous studies of this topic suggests that spatial mismatch plays some role in employment, though the size of its influence on getting and keeping a job remains in dispute (Cutler and Glaeser 1995; O'Regan and Quigley 1996; Raphael 1998; Ihlanfeldt 1997; Holzer 1991; Kain 1992). Nonetheless, on at least the implicit assumption that these effects are large enough to present real impediments to work, transportation subsidies have been included in many states' welfare reform plans. But we do not know the relative benefits and costs of such subsidies relative to the benefit-cost picture for subsidizing housing in the vicinity of available work.

Some observers question whether "dispersal," such as through housing opportunities outside inner-city poverty areas can, in fact, make much difference to long-term economic independence (e.g., Hughes 1987). They argue that the basic problem facing poverty area residents is lack of job qualifications, which housing does not affect. The work of Case and Katz (1991) supports this view. They find that neighborhood influences (peer criminal activity, substance abuse, teen pregnancies) were important even in the tight labor market in which they did their research. None of these researchers address the relative advantages and disadvantages of developing those qualifications while surrounded by various neighborhood constraints, however. Such constraints characterize a significant fraction of assisted housing developments.

THE HOUSING QUALITY HYPOTHESIS

One version of the housing quality hypothesis holds that housing quality affects health, and that health affects one's chances of achieving economic independence. The proven deleterious effects of lead-based paint on children is a clear example of such a link. Except for extreme housing dilapidation and infestation, analysts have generally not found a direct connection between housing and health (Kasl 1976; Wilner 1962; Weicher 1980, 1982). But much of this research is nearly two decades old or older and methodologically primitive when judged against current standards for testing complex hypotheses.

Housing quality may also mean a more spacious dwelling (in which each resident can find a quiet place to read or study), a more comfortable dwelling (with adequate heat in winter and air conditioning in summer), the presence of appropriate furnishings and perhaps time-saving amenities (such as a dishwasher, washing machine, and dryer). Here, again, there is little systematic research. Mayer's (1997) recent work suggests that there is some effect, but the measures of physical quality used in this research are difficult to evaluate.[9]

THE NEIGHBORHOOD QUALITY HYPOTHESIS

The neighborhood quality hypothesis argues that high rates of drug abuse, other criminal activity, unemployment, and teenage pregnancy affect a resident's willingness and ability to work toward economic independence in the mainstream economy. The research literature offers different conceptualizations of how this hypothesized link might operate (Jencks and Mayer 1990; Ginther et al. 1993) which, for simplicity, I collapse into two broad categories. The first holds that childrens' perceptions of appropriate values, norms and behavior—both good and bad—are influenced by their peers and adult role models (Wilson 1987; Crane 1991; Clark 1992). For example, children who see successful adults who are hardworking are more likely to form the opinion that hard work pays off. Children who grow up in "good" neighborhoods are, therefore, more likely to adopt mainstream values and behaviors than those who grow up in problem neighborhoods. The second broad conceptualization is the very different notion that growing up in a "good" neighborhood may actually be detrimental. According to this view, children judge their success by comparing themselves with their peers. Research has shown that, other things equal, children from poor families do worse academically than those from more affluent backgrounds. Depending on many factors (including an individual's psychological makeup), the response to growing up in a neighborhood in which the majority of families are more affluent, or attending a school in which the majority of students are from more affluent families, may be to work harder. But it may also be to give up, which is the response hypothesized by this second view.

Findings about the effects of neighborhood quality are inconsistent. Wilson's research on the ghetto poor established a convincing theoretical case for the negative effects of isolation and concentration on aspirations and achievement. The empirical studies of Datcher (1982), Brooks-Gunn et al. (1993), Case and Katz (1991), Crane (1991), Clark (1992), and Aaronson (1995) all suggest that growing up in a more affluent neighborhood has positive influences on a variety of outcomes for adolescents from poor families—including educational attainment, criminal behavior, drug abuse, and labor force participation. It is not clear, however, that beneficial effects of good neighborhoods have a direct counterpart in deleterious effects of bad neighborhoods. Some of these same researchers, for example, find that the positive effect of middle-income neighbors is more powerful than the detrimental effect of poor neighbors. But male adolescents who are black and poor appear relatively less affected by the presence of middle-class neighbors than other groups (Duncan 1994), although they become responsive when the middle-class neighbors themselves are black. And Corcoran et al. (1991), Evans et al. (1992), Plotnick and Hoffman (1993) and Ginther et al. (1993) find few, if any, neighborhood effects.

It is important to note that even the research that reports significant neighborhood effects finds the size of these impacts, at least on child outcomes, to be modest. In probably the most rigorous study to date, Aaronson (1995) found that a 10 percent increase in the rate of neighborhood poverty would reduce the likelihood of graduating from high school by 7 percent. The Gautreaux program provides the most direct test of neighborhood effects to date. This program resulted from a successful court case charging the Housing Authority of the City of Chicago with racial discrimination in provision of public housing to its minority population. Under the *Gautreaux* decision, the Chicago housing authority provided housing certificates and housing counseling to public housing families to help them move out of inner city Chicago to the suburbs. Research on the program suggests overwhelmingly positive effects for those who moved out of the inner city compared to those who remained in the city. Suburban movers were 25 percent more likely than city dwellers to have a job after their move, and school dropout rates were much lower for the suburban group of households (Rosenbaum 1991). The lack of a true experimental design, no follow-up data on dropouts, and other methodological questions, however, indicate caution in interpreting the results.

Both the methodological and substantive questions raised by the Gautreaux program will potentially be addressed by the Moving to

Opportunity (MTO) Demonstration Program, which the U.S. Department of Housing and Urban Development (HUD) launched in six metropolitan areas around the country in 1994. MTO used an experimental design, randomly assigning public housing tenants to either an experimental group, who were given Section 8 certificates and housing counseling to help them locate a unit in a low-poverty neighborhood and to refer them to other assistance they might need, or to one of two control groups. One of these groups received a certificate but no housing counseling, the other received neither a certificate nor housing counseling.[10] Participating households are to be tracked for 10 years. MTO represents the best opportunity to date for disentangling the effects of neighborhood characteristics from the effects of parental and family characteristics.[11]

IS ASSISTED HOUSING LINKED TO DECENT HOUSING AND NEIGHBORHOODS?[12]

Households living in assisted housing confront both a macroenvironment comprising all the units in the development and surrounding neighborhood, and the microenvironment of their individual housing unit. According to the most recent empirical evidence, the macroenvironment of assisted housing is bad. Public housing is disproportionately located in neighborhoods where incomes are very low, unemployment and poverty rates are high, and the quality of the surrounding housing stock is poor. And neighborhoods surrounding other project-based developments are roughly equivalent to the neighborhoods of welfare households who do not receive housing assistance (Newman and Schnare 1997). Thus, roughly 75 percent of all assisted housing units are located in distressed neighborhoods. Some research suggests that, for a sizable fraction of residents living in large public housing developments, venturing out into the neighborhood is rare, and the orbit of activity is restricted to the development itself (Shlay and Holupka 1991). These are also the developments that have large concentrations of households with very low incomes, high welfare dependency rates, and low educational achievement (Newman and Schnare 1993). If the concentration of disadvantaged neighbors has a negative effect on child outcomes, then both components of the macroenvironment of much assisted housing—the surrounding neighborhood and the development itself—suggest that children growing up there are likely to experience worse outcomes than other children.

How about the microenvironment? One element of the microenvironment is the quality of the dwelling. Because assisted housing regulations require that all dwellings meet housing quality standards, the overall physical adequacy of these units should be higher than for comparable households who do not receive assistance. This expectation is generally borne out by recent empirical evidence (Newman and Schnare 1993), although the General Accounting Office's review of a sample of dwellings rated by housing inspectors as meeting the housing quality standards of HUD found that "some properties clearly violated" these standards (U.S. General Accounting Office 1994). The quality of furnishings and other material possessions in the dwelling should also be greater because assisted housing residents pay only 30 percent of their income for rent (a smaller proportion than that paid on average by nonassisted poor households), but there is no empirical evidence about these expenditures. On balance, then, assisted housing environments may be more physically adequate than other low-income rental properties. Whether this difference matters for a range of outcomes is not yet known.

A second element of the microenvironment is the family. As alluded to earlier, previous research suggests that family background characteristics are closely related to a number of child outcomes such as educational attainment (e.g., Aaronson 1995; Duncan 1994). It is also plausible that such characteristics are related to adult outcomes, such as work activity. In public housing, which constitutes about one-fifth of all assisted housing, somewhat less than half of all household heads have a high school education, nearly 90 percent of households are headed by a single female, and nearly half receive welfare. The profile is slightly less disadvantaged among certificate and voucher users, and substantially so among those living in private developments that receive housing subsidies (the group that accounts for the largest share of all assisted housing). On balance, then, in assisted housing as a whole there may be modest positive effects, at best, on such behavioral outcomes as labor force participation or educational attainment.

Another element of the microenvironment is how the household responds to the housing subsidy. As noted in chapter 2, there are plausible arguments for expecting both more positive, and more negative, effects on behavioral outcomes. If the receipt of a housing subsidy allows the family to increase the consumption of necessities that are forgone when housing cost burdens are very high, the effects may be positive. But to the extent that the housing subsidy acts as a disincentive for the parent(s) to engage in work or other activities to move to self-sufficiency, the effects on achievement by both children and adults may be negative. Such disincentive effects of housing assistance are discussed further below.

DOES ASSISTED HOUSING ACT AS A BONUS OR ENHANCER?[13]

Beyond its direct effects on behavioral outcomes, housing subsidies could be used as a "bonus" to spur welfare recipients to comply with the requirements of welfare reform. Compared to transportation allowances, Medicaid, or even day care, housing assistance provides a substantial, tangible, and immediate reward. Such a bonus effect could be a powerful argument for linking housing assistance to welfare reform. Many states are reporting that sizable fractions of recipients are not showing up for the required orientation sessions and some are not complying with other new rules (Holcomb et al. 1998; Pavetti et al. 1995). While the reasons for the high rate of no-shows and noncompliance are not yet understood, one possibility is lack of motivation among some welfare recipients which, in turn, will reduce the effectiveness of welfare reform. Providing a large bounty like housing assistance might make a difference.

A second way in which housing might combine with services to increase self-sufficiency is if increased housing security made the impact of other services stronger. For example, in the welfare-to-work demonstrations, those with the most persistent dependency experienced smaller gains in employment and earnings than the somewhat less dependent (Burtless 1989; Holcomb et al. 1998; Pavetti et al. 1997; Friedlander and Burtless 1995). This has prompted speculation that more intensive services might be more effective (Burtless 1989; Friedlander and Burtless 1995) in making welfare reform a success.

HUD demonstrations have tried both approaches, although methodological weaknesses in the associated evaluations prevent us from learning much about the behavioral effects of combining housing and services. (Chapter 5 reviews some of these demonstrations, chapter 6 summarizes the major lessons from the welfare-to-work demonstrations, and chapter 7 critiques some of them.) In addition to formal federal demonstration programs, elements within the housing assistance system itself have been moving in the direction of combining housing with services. For example, many public housing authorities[14] have either implemented supportive service programs in some of their public housing projects or are running demonstration programs of this kind. And many housing managers have cobbled together supportive services in their privately owned, federally subsidized developments. Unfortunately, there has not been much support available to systematically evaluate these initiatives. For example, research on a family-oriented social service intervention in Baltimore public housing reported limited effects across a wide range of outcomes including income, education, and social and behavioral characteristics. But since the evaluation was conducted early in the intervention, no information will be available on long-term effects (Shlay and Holupka 1991). There has been one rigorous evaluation of the effects of child care centers located in public housing projects, although not on exit rates from public housing, and the results are positive. The proximity to such centers was associated with increases in the probability of being employed, increased earnings, increased work hours, and decreased welfare rates (Robins 1988). Not surprisingly, these effects were particularly strong for parents with preschool children.

IS HOUSING ASSISTANCE ITSELF A DISINCENTIVE?[15]

Although survey data indicate that welfare recipients who also receive housing assistance have lower employment rates than those who do not receive housing assistance, these differences may be the result of administrative decisions, such as preference rules for housing programs that gave priority to the most disadvantaged—not the result of the disincentive effect of housing assistance, per se.

Theoretically, there are plausible arguments for expecting both more positive, and more negative, effects. Because housing assistance provides a stable and affordable residence, housing assistance may be a springboard into the job market and, therefore, success under welfare reform. On the other hand, by offering housing security, housing assistance may dull the incentives to work or cushion the risk of noncompliance with welfare reform requirements, thereby contributing to negative outcomes. Perhaps a more significant way housing assistance may have the negative outcome of discouraging work is the housing assistance system's 30 percent tax rate on income. The tenant rent contribution is set at 30 percent of adjusted gross income. Thus, every dollar increase in income is effectively taxed at 30 percent. Housing assistance benefits decline as income rises and phase out entirely when income rises beyond a certain point. Under the certificate and voucher programs, for example, when 30 percent of income has been greater than or equal to the rent for six months, the tenant is no longer eligible for a subsidy. Since this rule is equivalent to a tax on earnings, it should be a work disincentive, other things equal.

What are the likely effects of this rule under welfare reform, which requires recipients to work and, presumably, to have earnings? Past research on the effects of employment and training programs for welfare recipients and on state work-welfare programs indicates only a modest short-run net gain in earnings (between $560 and $1500 a year) (Cottingham 1989; Burtless 1989; Ellwood 1989; Gueron and Pauly 1991; Friedlander and Burtless 1995; Nightingale and Holcomb 1997; Strawn 1998). If welfare reform follows this pattern, the earnings impact would not be enough to make most recipients lose eligibility for housing assistance. Even if incomes rose to the poverty line, housing affordability problems would still be pervasive.

There are no data on the longer-term impacts of housing programs on earnings, however, leaving unanswered the question of a recipient's motivation to increase earnings when the housing assistance payment is either reduced or lost as a result. By contrast, earnings effects of cash welfare have received great attention. Research on the Seattle-Denver Income Maintenance Experiment, for example, showed "substantial and significant reductions" in annual earnings for both males and females (SRI International 1983). These effects established the rationale for introducing more rigorous work requirements into welfare programs (Aaron 1984). It is unclear how these findings relate to the case of housing, however. Prior to welfare reform, the AFDC program had a tax rate on additional income that was more than double that for housing assistance.[16] The most that can be said about housing is that, since the income eligibility cutoffs for housing assistance are roughly 33 percent higher than the poverty line, housing benefits continue over a substantial earnings range. Since the total loss of a housing benefit is unlikely for this reason, the disincentive may not be very large. This conclusion would change, of course, if housing policy either neutralized the disincentive effects by reducing or eliminating the tax on earnings for some period of time or, alternatively, eliminated the automatic reduction in out-of-pocket rent payments for those not in compliance with the welfare reform requirements.

One other feature of housing assistance may also play a direct role in employability: neighborhoods. Even though the empirical evidence is not unambiguous, neighborhood conditions are likely to have some effect on access to education and jobs (as demonstrated by chapter 4), and the absence of suitable role models in distressed neighborhoods may discourage individual initiative and integration with the broader community. The sobering findings regarding the neighborhoods of public housing and, to a lesser extent, private developments built and operated with federal subsidies suggest that housing assistance may be hurting rather than helping these recipients achieve economic independence.

THE REST OF THE BOOK

Part 1 scopes out the problem and addresses such basic questions as: What kinds of impacts will welfare reform have on housing? How large are these impacts on numbers and characteristics of people affected, and on government budgetary outlays? And what is the geography of these impacts? Will some geographic areas feel the housing impacts more acutely than others, and why? In fact, geography is another way to think about the first part of this volume: We begin with a national level analysis, then narrow in to examine a sample of metropolitan areas, and then look intensively at one city and its surrounding region.

Part 2 reviews the policies and programs that the housing sector has tried in the past to improve the economic independence of housing assistance recipients. A thorough description of these efforts is followed by a critical assessment from each of two perspectives: their structure and implementation, using the lessons learned from welfare-to-work demonstration programs as the standard; and the policy value of research on these policies and programs more generally. The goal of both critiques is to assess whether any useful information can be salvaged from existing programs, and, perhaps more importantly, to suggest improvements in the design, implementation, and analysis of future programs.

Part 3 examines welfare reform from the housing program practitioner's vantage point. One source of concern is the incompatibility or inconsistency of welfare reform and housing policies and programs. The "mixed signals" to housing assistance recipients on AFDC noted earlier in this first chapter are causing problems both for recipients and for program practitioners. Several examples of such incompatibilities are reviewed, as are other tensions between the "new" welfare thrust and the "old" housing rules. Where the base of experience and research evidence is strong, suggestions are offered for addressing these tensions. Where it is not, a practitioner-oriented research agenda emerges that is largely similar to the policy researcher's agenda implicit in the first two sections of this volume.

Part 1

CHAPTER 2

The implications of the new work requirements, work incentives, and time limits on the work effort, earnings, and housing cost burden of welfare recipients in assisted housing are the subject of chapter 2. Since federal welfare reform only became law in 1996, and states are still at varying stages of implementing their new programs to comply with these federal requirements, Sandra J. Newman and Joseph Harkness used evidence from states that instituted welfare reform waiver programs similar to Temporary Assistance for Needy Families (TANF) (the component of the welfare reform law that eliminates the AFDC system) to simulate the likely effects of TANF on housing assistance recipients. Four such programs were chosen on the basis of two criteria. First, the programs had to reflect a range of stringency with regard to the key elements of welfare reform—time limits, work requirements, and sanctions. Second, there had to be some impact data available. The states chosen are Florida and Virginia at the stringent end of the spectrum, Michigan in the middle, and Vermont at the liberal end. These waiver-based estimates provide the first quantitative evidence on how welfare reform is likely to affect recipients of housing assistance.

Assisted households turn out to be particularly vulnerable to welfare reform. More of them are not working, they have less outside income on average, and they have been on welfare for longer periods than nonassisted households. The potential impact of the cumulative duration on welfare could be particularly dramatic. If the waiver programs in Virginia and Florida had been in full operation in 1994, for example, the more than 75 percent of assisted households who had received AFDC for 24 months or longer at that time could have been dropped from the welfare rolls.

According to the simulation results, welfare reform is likely to lead to modest net increases in the proportions of households that are not exempt from work requirements who receive housing assistance under each waiver program. This increase could be as high as 14 percent (about 119,000 households nationwide) in Vermont, the most liberal waiver state in the sample. The proportion of assisted households working in unsubsidized jobs would also increase in all four states. But these simulated increases in employment vary widely, from 25 percent under Michigan's policy (which has no time limit on welfare receipt) to 151 percent under Virginia's. The proportion of assisted cases exempt from work requirements would shrink under all waivers, from about half of all cases prewaiver to between one-third and one-sixth post-waiver. The simulated effects on the incomes of assisted households also vary widely. Under the Michigan and Vermont waivers, average incomes would rise by 2–4 percent, reflecting work incentives that are somewhat more enticing than those under the old AFDC program and no time limits on assistance. Under the Florida and Virginia waivers, in contrast, average incomes for assisted renters would fall (by 8 and 21 percent, respectively), indicating that gains in income for those in subsidized employment while on welfare will be more than offset by losses in income for those who do not find such jobs and have their benefits reduced by sanctions or eliminated due to hitting the time limit.

The estimated impact on the HUD budget for assisted housing indicated by these simulations varies with the overall income impacts. But the simulated savings under the Michigan and Vermont reforms (less than one-half of one percent of HUD's budget) are not enough to offset the 1.2 percent budget increase associated with Florida- and Virginia-type policies. Finally, none of the waiver programs has a large average effect on housing burdens. For those hitting time limits, however, the simulated national impacts are substantial. The worst cases are under the Virginia waiver program. The one-third of assisted renters hitting the time limit and not working will experience more than a 50 percent decline in income, triggering HUD expenditures of over $400 million. For the one-fifth of unassisted welfare recipients hitting the time limit, housing cost burdens will rise by more than 50 percent, almost certainly necessitating a move to lower quality dwellings.

CHAPTER 3

A three-pronged thesis undergirds the chapter by G. Thomas Kingsley and Peter Tatian: The response of the assisted housing sector to federal welfare reform—if it is to be maximally effective—should be strongly influenced by the degree of overlap in the two recipient populations in a specific area, the importance of HUD presence in an area, and the predominant form that presence takes. If urban areas differ substantially along these dimensions, in other words, no "one size fits all" approach makes much sense.

Their analysis of a major new HUD data set, A Picture of Subsidized Households (APSH), takes a first step in providing the relevant data for assessing such differences. The authors focus on the 100 largest metropolitan areas, which together account for 58 percent of the U.S. population, 60 percent of all assisted households in public housing and publicly assisted housing, and 53 percent of those receiving tenant-based assistance. The authors include only areas for which APSH response rates are at least 60 percent, a limitation that forces them to drop some major metropolises from at least parts of their analysis.

Wide variations are revealed in patterns of housing assistance and in the welfare/housing assistance overlap. A major reason is that some cities have been much more aggressive than others in seeking HUD assistance. In addition, HUD's allocation procedures have enabled them to reallocate funds initially designed for some areas to other areas with more projects ready in the pipeline. Among these largest metropolitan areas, the proportion of low-income renter households receiving housing assistance varies from a low of 8 percent to a high of 50 percent. The share of assisted households ranges from 0 to 60 percent in public housing, 0 to 74 percent in publicly assisted housing, and 0 to 97 for tenant-based assistance. The share of HUD-assisted households whose dominant source of income is welfare ranges from 11 percent to 36 percent overall, and reaches a high of 44 percent for tenant-based assistance and 50 percent for public housing.

As for how initiatives to help these "overlap" households move toward self-sufficiency should be tailored to different types of geographic concentration, the authors have several general points to make. Obviously, opportunities for community-building approaches and intensive support services are greatest within the project environment. They could also work well in publicly assisted housing if the prior required step of motivating project owners to cooperate is successful. In a metropolis where most housing assistance is tenant-based, more individualized self-sufficiency initiatives will be required. Where a large proportion of local welfare recipients are HUD-assisted, partnerships with other local services agencies should be central to the overall response to welfare reform. But where housing assistance is minor and the economy weak, counteracting the danger of major increases in homelessness because of welfare reform may need strong interventions in the supply side of the local housing market. In areas with high unemployment and few new jobs, public employment strategies may be needed before any linkages with other local agencies can make a difference.

CHAPTER 4

Major mismatches between the areas where the jobs are and the areas where low-income city residents live have been much discussed as a cause of joblessness in the inner city. Whether the new welfare emphasis on moving recipients out and into the regular job market is successful will depend in good part on availability of jobs within commuting distance of the neighborhoods in which they live. Claudia Coulton, Laura Leete, and Neil Bania examine how welfare recipients' locations match low-skill job openings and availability of affordable rental housing for the City of Cleveland—using county welfare program records for recipient residence information, decennial census data on occupational characteristics, Ohio Bureau of Employment Services data on job openings, published bus schedules and estimated automobile commute times from the Northeast Ohio Area Coordinating Committee, and decennial census data on affordable rental housing availability in the Cleveland/Akron labor market.

Welfare recipients in Cleveland, according to this detailed analysis, will not have an easy time finding jobs they can get to. First, they typically live in the inner city. The inner city is the only major source of low-wage jobs within striking distance of where they live. But a large proportion of welfare recipients can only find jobs there by displacing existing workers in the city. All other major jobs sources are long automobile commutes from the inner city and not well served by public transportation. Overcoming the current public transit problems looks difficult, since half of the forecast job openings are served by transit authorities other than the one that serves inner-city Cleveland residents. The likelihood of moving to where the jobs are is not high, because housing affordable by low-wage workers is hard to come by outside the center city. Even if welfare recipients do move to the suburbs where the jobs are, transportation problems will remain, because public transit within those areas is much less frequent and pervasive than in the inner city.

Part 2

In the past 20 years, there have been numerous studies of the impact of programs to move low-income individuals into jobs and welfare recipients into work, but far less attention has been paid to the connection between housing assistance and self-sufficiency.

Chapter 5

Amy Bogdon describes the design, implementation, and findings of three major HUD programs that have used housing assistance to encourage recipients to become economically self-sufficient: Project Self-Sufficiency, Operation Bootstrap, and Family Self-Sufficiency.

Project Self-Sufficiency (PSS) was designed to encourage communities to develop mechanisms for integrating public and private support services for the participants. HUD provided participating housing authorities with a special allocation of Section 8 certificates but no additional funding for support services, making involvement of the community a key design feature. HUD required the programs to follow the same basic model, but communities were given substantial flexibility within that model. A total of 154 communities were selected to participate in the PSS demonstration, with selection based on public housing authority (PHA) diversity, past PHA performance, and program resources and planning. The target group was low-income single-parent households from the Section 8 waiting lists, with programs encouraged to select motivated participants.

Operation Bootstrap was very similar to Project Self-Sufficiency, the major difference being inclusion of two-parent families, a requirement that participants develop individual action plans, and even more local flexibility under Bootstrap. Almost 12,000 Section 8 certificates were awarded to 353 communities. The Family Self-Sufficiency program (FSS) was similar in some respects to the other two initiatives but had different PHA selection criteria, participant eligibility, incentives, and sanctions. In the first two program years, PHAs were selected through an award process. In the third year, participation became mandatory for all PHAs receiving incremental Section 8 or public housing units. Screening for motivation was still permitted, but the participation of individual families was limited to current holders of Section 8 certificates or vouchers or current residents of public housing. For the first time, participants faced sanctions for failure to comply with their contract of participation, and participants deposited rent increases resulting from increased earnings into an escrow savings account for later use in purchasing a house. As Bogdon notes, none of the three followed the type of experimental design necessary to assign causation. Participants were not randomly selected, most sites screened out less motivated participants, and some even used previous educational attainment or job experience as a screen. Design and implementation flexibility across sites also prevented outcomes from being compared across sites.

Even so, Bogdon argues, the outcomes tell us some things that are useful. People did volunteer for self-sufficiency programs and are making progress toward self-sufficiency. Receipt of Section 8 certificates did improve housing outcomes for many participants, and local programs have been reasonably successful in coordinating a wide range of services to assist participants. However, few participants have become completely independent of all types of assistance; there have been difficulties in recruiting participants, particularly for programs with sanctions; and dropout rates are considerable. Bogdon concludes that understanding the potential role of housing assistance in the process of attaining self-sufficiency requires that future programs be designed so that their impacts, and not just their outcomes, can be measured. She also recommends improving program standardization, introducing experimental or quasi-experimental designs, and improving data collection.

The next two chapters are considerably more pessimistic about whether anything can be learned about the impact of housing programs designed to promote self-sufficiency from these HUD initiatives, because there is no way to measure the counterfactual—what would have happened in the absence of those programs.

CHAPTER 6

Starting from his view that the programs Bogdon describes cannot tell us about program effectiveness, James Riccio reviews what the large-scale social experiments that have evaluated welfare-to-work and job training programs, including Jobs Training Partnership Act (JTPA) programs, can tell us about whether at least the assumptions underlying the housing/self-sufficiency programs are plausible. He then describes an ambitious new employment initiative for public housing residents, the Jobs-Plus Initiative, that will be subject to rigorous evaluation.

Two assumptions are shared by all three of the housing/self-sufficiency programs described in chapter 5: (1) that support services should give priority to education and training activities before encouraging participants to enter the labor market, and (2) that program effectiveness is enhanced by choosing participants selectively. An additional assumption of the third demonstration, FSS, is that stronger financial incentives for residents to work help achieve that goal, and that an escrow savings plan is an effective incentive. The overall message from the rigorous evaluation literature is that some welfare-to-work strategies have been effective (and cost-effective) in increasing employment and earnings and reducing welfare payments. But these gains are modest, none of the programs has had much success in reducing poverty, and the problem of high job turnover has not been resolved.

With respect to the three particular assumptions Riccio highlights, he has the following responses: (1) The housing programs' approach to selecting participants who show particular motivation may not be the most effective strategy. It is at least as plausible that recipients who do not show individual initiative are the ones that self-sufficiency programs must try to reach if they are to be effective in moving large numbers of residents into work. (2) Evidence from the welfare-to-work and JTPA evaluations indicates that putting up-front job search and work-based strategies ahead of education and training in the program participation sequence, and combining them with substantial resources into job development efforts, are more effective in moving participants into the job market than those that stress more general development of human capital. (3) There is some evidence that financial incentives can increase earnings when combined with strong work requirements. But diverting rent increases into escrow accounts may be too distant, and too restrictive, a payoff to be an effective inducement to change behavior.

The Jobs-Plus Initiative Riccio goes on to describe is an ambitious undertaking, designed to build on the successes of past welfare-to-work initiatives within the public housing context and within a rigorous evaluation design. In seven cities, eight public housing developments have been selected to form new partnerships—collaboratives—of residents, welfare departments, JTPA and other employment and training agencies, and private sector employers. The evaluators and a team of consultants are assisting the PHAs in building their collaboratives. In addition, the strategies the Jobs-Plus communities must follow include work incentives and requirements built into the PHA rent and welfare rules, best practices in preparing residents for sustained employment and linking them with jobs, and enhanced community support for work (through promoting social networks that support work both inside and outside the development). The target group encompasses all working-age residents in the PHA hosting the program—providing an opportunity to test whether a comprehensive, intensive, place-based employment intervention can transform housing developments into communities of workers and, in turn, improve their quality of life.

Since place-based interventions cannot be studied with a random assignment design, the initiative builds in several other methodological approaches. First, the sites' implementation strategies and experiences will be a major focus of the research so that the interventions will be rigorously delineated. Second, groups of similar housing developments were identified. One of these was randomly selected to be a Jobs-Plus host and the other(s) served as comparison sites. Data will include administrative records and survey information spanning five years before and five years after the start of Jobs-Plus. As Riccio puts it, "Dramatic change requires bolder interventions that can draw only partial guidance from past research. Jobs-Plus will carefully test an employment initiative created by committed local stakeholders (with guidance from national partners). And it will provide a scope and intensity of assistance to public housing residents that is unprecedented. Success is not guaranteed, of course, but the stakes are too high not to make bold efforts to outperform programs of the past."

CHAPTER 7

Craig Thornton, Robert G. Wood, and Pamela M. Jones discuss how the policy value of demonstration research on housing and self-sufficiency can be increased. On the issue of whether anything can be salvaged from the three demonstrations described by Bogdon, they conclude that "the impact estimation methods and supporting data cannot provide evidence that would persuade skeptics about the value of housing-based self-sufficiency programs." They follow this verdict with a discussion of two housing-related self-sufficiency studies— Jobs-Plus, as discussed in Chapter 6, and Moving to Opportunity (MTO).

They agree with Riccio that the Jobs-Plus evaluation design was innovative and a great step forward from previous housing/self-sufficiency studies. Their main concern is that the broad program design flexibility given to each community may produce such different programs that evaluators will not be able to pool the impact results across sites. If so, the power of the evaluation will be substantially reduced.

The MTO seeks to improve economic outcomes for public housing residents by offering them Section 8 certificates on condition that they use them to obtain private housing in low-poverty neighborhoods. The program also provides housing search assistance and counseling. The evaluation involves five cities and will collect 10 years of data. It also includes random assignment of MTO applicants to (1) a primary treatment group receiving the full MTO treatment, (2) a secondary treatment group receiving Section 8 certificates that can be used anywhere but no housing search or counseling services, and (3) a control group not receiving a certificate or services.

This research design is powerful and will provide clear and reliable results on the effects of the housing initiative being tested. But it has two limitations. First, it can only provide information on a voluntary program. Second, to the extent that the programs differ across cities, analysts may have to treat each as a separate program, which will reduce effective sample size. Differences across sites may be useful in helping identify which parts of the treatment caused which impacts, however. This concern can also be addressed by comparing outcomes for the primary treatment group with outcomes for the secondary treatment group.

Part 3

CHAPTER 8

The housing practitioners who staff the more than 3,000 local PHAs view welfare reform and its impacts on housing assistance from the unique vantage point of implementation. Newman's last chapter looks at their views for the hypotheses they generate about the role of assisted housing in achieving economic independence. She finds practitioners concerned about a wide variety of disincentives in current housing policy with respect to fostering self-sufficiency.

The first of these—discussed in earlier chapters from the analysts' perspective—is the disincentive to work provided by the sliding scale rent calculations for housing assistance recipients. This implicit tax on earnings, particularly since housing assistance is not an entitlement and has long waiting lists, constitutes a powerful work disincentive. It can also be expected to discourage tenants from reporting income, as required by housing program regulations. There is no systematic information on either receipt of underground income or the extent to which it is investigated by PHAs. But administrators quote substantial evidence that tenants often reduce work as they approach the six-month limit on eligibility for those earning above the income limit in the certificate and voucher programs. And PHAs who investigate fraud allegations report large numbers of cases of unreported earnings. Many PHAs do not pursue fraud, however, because the investigative costs are likely to be higher than the back rent to be collected from the effort.

One strategy for encouraging recipients to work, and to report earnings, is the earned income disregard. Such disregards have been required in housing programs since 1990. But few PHAs have implemented them. PHAs may be unwilling to implement such a policy because they risk the loss of operating subsidies—calculated prospectively as estimated revenues minus estimated costs over the next year. If only earned income above the level used to project rents is disregarded, the PHAs are not at risk. But if all earnings are to be disregarded—which is the case for tenants participating in any HUD-funded or JTPA employment/training program—operating subsidies are affected, at least in the short run. For Section 8 certificate and voucher programs, operating subsidies are not relevant. The risk for them is that the subsidy slots vacated as families earn their way out of the program will not be replaced and the total subsidies available will, therefore, shrink. PHAs may also be deterred from implementing earned disregards because they would no longer be able to recapture any income increases through increased rent.

Because HUD has been almost continuously in the throes of reorganization, reinvention, and downsizing throughout the 1990s, it would not be surprising if the many PHAs who have not implemented the earned income disregard requirement have been betting that HUD would not detect such violations. It is also very likely—since the relevant regulations were not published until four years after the statute was passed, and HUD has yet to train PHAs in how to interpret and implement them—that PHAs chose not to implement because of confusion about the interpretation of the requirement. The historical record of many features of housing assistance is replete with such examples of unclear regulations—including core elements such as how rents are set, how income is calculated, and what percentage of income is to be paid as rent. Such confusion suggests that there is probably much more variation in the implementation of housing programs across the country than is commonly recognized—with attendant complications for analysts trying to isolate the impact of housing assistance on economic independence.

How would housing practitioners fix housing programs? Their consistent answer is that government should greatly increase the PHAs' flexibility to run their programs as they see fit. The Moving-to-Work demonstration (MTW), launched in 1997, is doing just that by allowing participating PHAs to combine their different streams of HUD subsidies for use in any way they think will best encourage tenants to work. MTW provides no additional monies but allows PHAs to keep any savings they can generate. Unfortunately, research goals played no role in MTW site designs or implementation decisions, drastically limiting what can be learned from the effort about impacts on self-sufficiency generally or about the relative promise of different strategies.

*   *   *

Although this volume takes an important first step in presenting new analytical and critical thinking about the implications of welfare reform for housing, it goes without saying that it is only a first step, and much, much more needs to be done. For example, we need to understand the responses of housing assistance recipients to welfare reform using a dynamic, behavioral model, not a static cross-sectional model. We also need to learn whether assisted housing residents respond differently to welfare reform from those who do not receive housing assistance, and the causes, nature, and magnitude of those differential responses. In addition, because housing policy is also undergoing major changes, we need to carefully analyze the interactions between these changes and welfare reform. And to be of assistance to federal policy development, we need to generate solid national-level impact estimates, albeit reflecting important local variations in both housing and welfare administration and implementation.

But as valuable as such research would be to the particularly timely issue of welfare reform and its effects on housing, it still leaves the most fundamental questions about the impacts of housing, such as those noted earlier, largely unanswered. We have the research tools to study these questions. And as the final chapter in this volume makes clear, practitioners and researchers agree on the questions. But support for housing research of any kind is modest, and for research of the kind suggested here, nearly nonexistent. Unless such support is forthcoming, we will continue to lament our perpetual inability to answer fundamental questions about housing, and our exclusion from the "big debates" about social policy. Our state of knowledge about whether housing is a route to independence will continue to be, as the title of a paper I wrote 10 years ago put it, "A Case That Has Yet to Be Made."

Notes

1. Throughout this book, "housing assistance" refers to federal housing subsidy programs for the poor. Included here are public housing, private developments that receive federal subsidies through either the U.S. Department of Housing and Urban Development or the Internal Revenue Service in the form of low-income housing tax credits, and certificates and vouchers that allow recipients to rent modest, affordable apartments in the private rental market and to pay no more than 30 percent of income for rent.

2. All estimates are for FY1996 to capture pre–welfare reform levels. The housing assistance estimate includes subsidies for rental housing ($25 billion) plus the revenue loss associated with the low-income housing tax credit ($2.6 billion) (U.S. House of Representatives 1998; Budget of the U.S. Government, FY1998, 1997; Pedone 1998). AFDC numbers reflect the federal and state share of benefit outlays (administrative costs are excluded). (Numbers expressed in 1996 dollars.)

3. The universal scope of housing policy will always distinguish housing assistance from other safety net programs.

4. Figures range from 53 percent in the Panel Study of Income Dynamics–Assisted Housing Database for 1993 to 61 percent from Burke (1995).

5. Author's tabulations from the 1981 and 1995 national American Housing Surveys.

6. Figures range from 45 percent in the Panel Study of Income Dynamics–Assisted Housing Database for 1993 to 48 percent from Burke (1995).

7. This section draws heavily from Newman and Schnare (1994) and Newman and Harkness (1998).

8. As first stated by Kain (1968), this hypothesis referred to black central city residents. More recent work has extended it to low-skilled white workers (Ihlanfeldt and Sjoquist 1989).

9. For example, several key items on Mayer's physical quality index were collected through interviewer observations, which often have reliability problems.

10. High-poverty tracts are those with poverty rates of at least 40 percent. Low-poverty tracts are those with poverty rates of less than 10 percent.

11. Because children in the MTO experimental groups will have moved not only from high- to low-poverty areas but also from public housing to private rental housing with a Section 8 certificate, it may be difficult to disentangle the effects of the change in neighborhood, the change in housing, and the move itself.

12. This section is based on Newman and Harkness (1998).

13. This section is based on Newman and Schnare (1994).

14. Public housing authorities are quasi-governmental units vested with the responsibility for managing federal housing subsidies for public housing and for Section 8 certificates and vouchers.

15. This section is based on Newman and Schnare (1994).

16. The welfare rules were complex. During the first four months of employment, the earnings tax was equal to one-third of earnings minus $30; after the first four months, only the $30 disregard applied and earnings were taxed dollar for dollar. However, other benefits continued (e.g., Medicaid, reimbursement for work-related expenses such as child care).

References

Aaron, H. 1984. "Six Welfare Questions Still Searching for Answers," *The Brookings Review* (Fall): 12–17.

Aaronson, D. 1995. "Using Sibling Data to Estimate the Impact of Neighborhoods on Children's Educational Outcomes." Northwestern University. Photocopy.

Brooks-Gunn, J., et al. 1993. "Do Neighborhoods Influence Child and Adolescent Development?" Educational Testing Service, Columbia University, and University of Michigan. Mimeo.

Burke, Paul. 1995. *A Picture of Subsidized Households in June 1995.* Washington, D.C.: U.S. Department of Housing and Urban Development, Office of Policy Development and Research, October 3.

Burtless, G. 1989. "The Effect of Reform on Employment, Earnings, and Income." In *Welfare Policy for the 1990's*, edited by P. Cottingham and D. Ellwood (103–140). Cambridge, Mass.: Harvard University Press.

Case, A., and L. Katz. 1991. "The Company You Keep: The Effects of Family and Neighborhood on Disadvantaged Youth." *NBER Working Paper Series*, No. 3705. Cambridge, Mass.: National Bureau of Economic Research.

Clark, R. 1992. "Neighborhood Effects on Dropping Out of School Among Teenage Boys." *Population Studies Center Discussion Paper Series*. Washington, D.C.: The Urban Institute.

Corcoran, M., et al. 1991. "The Association Between Men's Economic Status and Their Family and Community Origins." *Journal of Human Resources* 27(4): 575–601.

Cottingham, P. 1989. "Introduction." In *Welfare Policy for the 1990's*, edited by P. Cottingham and D. Ellwood (1–9). Cambridge, Mass.: Harvard University Press.

Crane, J. 1991. "The Epidemic Theory of Ghettos and Neighborhood Effects on Dropping Out and Teenage Childbearing." *American Journal of Sociology* 96(5): 1226–1259.

Cutler, D., and E. Glaeser. 1995. "Are Ghettos Good or Bad?" *NBER Working Paper Series*, No. 5163. Cambridge, Mass.: National Bureau of Economic Research.

Datcher, L. 1982. "Effects of Community and Family Backgrounds on Achievement." *Review of Economics and Statistics* 64: 32–41.

Duncan, G. 1994. "Families and Neighbors as Sources of Disadvantage in the Schooling Decisions of White and Black Adolescents." Ann Arbor, Mich.: University of Michigan, Survey Research Center. Mimeo.

Ellwood, D. 1989. "Conclusion." In *Welfare Policy for the 1990's*, edited by P. Cottingham and D. Ellwood (269–289). Cambridge, Mass.: Harvard University Press.

Evans, W., et al. 1992. "Measuring Peer Group Effects: A Study of Teenage Behavior." *Journal of Political Economy* 100(5): 966–991.

Friedlander, Daniel, and Gary Burtless. 1995. *Five Years After: The Long Term Effects of Welfare-to-Work Programs*. New York: Russell Sage Foundation.

Gueron, Judith, and Edward Pauly. 1991. *From Welfare to Work*. New York: Russell Sage Foundation.

Ginther, D., et al. 1993. "Neighborhood Characteristics as Determinants of Children's Outcomes: How Robust are the Relationships?" Paper presented at the Fifteenth Annual Association for Public Policy Analysis and Management Research Conference, Washington, D.C., Oct. 28–30.

Holcomb, Pamela, LaDonna Pavetti, Caroline Ratcliffe, and Susan Riedinger. 1998. *Building an Employment-Focused Welfare System: Work First* and Other Work-Oriented Strategies in Five States. Washington, D.C.: U.S. Department of Health and Human Services.

Holzer, H. 1991. "The Spatial Mismatch Hypothesis: What Has the Evidence Shown?" Urban Studies 28(1): 105–122.

Hornburg, Stephen. 1997. "The Implications of Welfare Reform for Housing." Introductory remarks at the Fannie Mae Foundation–Johns Hopkins University Housing Policy Roundtable, Evergreen House, Baltimore, Md., July 18.

Hughes, M. 1987. "Moving Up and Moving Out: Confusing Ends and Means About Ghetto Dispersal." Urban Studies 24(6): 503–517.

Ihlanfeldt, Keith. 1997. "The Geography of Economic and Social Opportunity within Metropolitan Areas." Paper prepared for the Committee on Improving the Future of U.S. Cities through Improved Metropolitan Area Governance, National Research Council/National Academy of Sciences, February.

Ihlanfeldt, Keith, and David Sjoquist. 1989. "The Impact of Job Decentralization on the Economic Welfare of Central City Blacks." Journal of Urban Economics 26: 110–130.

Jencks, C., and S. Mayer. 1990. "The Social Consequences of Growing Up in a Poor Neighborhood." In Inner-City Poverty in the United States, edited by L. Lynn and M. McGeary (111–186). Washington, D.C.: National Academy Press.

Kain, John. 1968. "Housing Segregation, Negro Employment, and Metropolitan Decentralization." Quarterly Journal of Economics 82(2): 175–197.

Kain, John. 1992. "The Spatial Mismatch Hypothesis: Three Decades Later." Housing Policy Debate 3(2): 371–460.

Kasl, S. 1976. "Effects of Housing on Mental and Physical Health." National Housing Policy Review: Housing in the Seventies, Working Papers 1: 286–304. Washington, D.C.: U.S. Government Printing Office.

Mayer, S. 1997. What Money Can't Buy. Cambridge, Mass.: Harvard University Press.

Newman, S., and J. Harkness. 1998. "The Implications of Welfare Reform for Housing: A National Analysis." Paper presented at the midyear meeting of the American Real Estate and Urban Economics Association, Washington, D.C., May.

Newman, S., and A. Schnare. 1997. ". . . 'And a Suitable Living Environment': The Failure of Housing Programs to Deliver on Neighborhood Quality." Housing Policy Debate 8(4): 703–741.

————. 1994. "Back to the Future: Housing Assistance Policy for the Next Century." In New Beginnings Project: A First Report (1–24). Washington, D.C.: Center for Housing Policy.

————. 1993. "Last in Line: Housing Assistance for Households with Children." Housing Policy Debate 4(3): 417–455.

_____. 1992. *Beyond Bricks and Mortar: Reexamining the Purpose and Effects of Housing Assistance*. Washington, D.C.: The Urban Institute.

Nightingale, Demetra, and Pamela Holcomb. 1997. "Alternative Strategies for Increasing Employment." *The Future of Children: Welfare to Work* 7(1): 52–64.

O'Regan, K., and J. Quigley. 1996. "Teenage Employment and the Spatial Isolation of Minority and Poverty Households." *Journal of Human Resources* 31(3): 16–92.

Pavetti, LaDonna, Pamela Holcomb, and Amy-Ellen Duke. 1995. *Increasing Participation in Work and Work-Related Activities: Lessons from Five State Welfare Reform Demonstration Projects*. Washington, D.C.: U.S. Department of Health and Human Services, September.

Pavetti, LaDonna, Krista Olson, Demetra Nightingale, Amy-Ellen Duke, and Julie Isaacs. 1997. *Welfare-to-Work Options for Families Facing Personal and Family Challenges: Rationale and Program Strategies*. Washington, D.C.: The Urban Institute, August.

Pedone, Carla. 1998. Special tabulations using Congressional Budget Office data, July 7.

Plotnick, R., and S. Hoffman. 1993. "Using Sister Pairs to Estimate How Neighborhoods Affect Young Adult Outcomes." Paper presented at the Fifteenth Annual Association for Public Policy Analysis and Management Research Conference, Washington, D.C., Oct. 28–30.

Raphael, S. 1998. "The Spatial Mismatch Hypothesis and Black Youth Joblessness: Evidence from the San Francisco Bay Area." *Journal of Urban Economics* 43: 79–111.

Robins, P. 1988. "Child Care and Convenience: The Effects of Labor Market Entry Costs on Economic Self-Sufficiency Among Public Housing Residents." *Social Science Quarterly* 69(1): 122–136.

Rosenbaum, J. 1991. "Black Pioneers—Do Their Moves to the Suburbs Increase Economic Opportunity for Mothers and Children?" *Housing Policy Debate* 2(4): 1179–1213.

Shlay, A., and S. Holupka. 1991. "Steps Toward Independence: The Early Effects of the Lafayette Courts Family Development Center." Baltimore, Md.: Johns Hopkins University Institute for Policy Studies. Mimeo.

SRI International. 1983. *Final Report of the Seattle-Denver Income Maintenance Experiment*. Menlo Park, Calif.: Author.

Strawn, Julie. 1998. *Beyond Job Search or Basic Education: Rethinking the Role of Skills in Welfare Reform*. Washington, D.C.: Center for Law and Social Policy (CLASP), April.

U.S. General Accounting Office. 1994. *Federally Assisted Housing: Condition of Some Properties Receiving Section 8 Project-Based Assistance Is*

Below Housing Quality Standards. GAO/T-RCED-94-273. Washington, D.C.: Author.

U.S. Government Printing Office. 1997. Budget of the U.S. Government, FY1998. Analytical Perspectives. Washington, D.C.: U.S. Government Printing Office.

U.S. House of Representatives, Committee on Ways and Means. 1998 Green Book. Washington, D.C.: U.S. Government Printing Office.

Weicher, J. 1982. "Urban Housing Programs: What Is the Question?" Cato Journal 2(2): 411–436.

————. 1980. Housing: Federal Policies and Programs. Washington, D.C.: American Enterprise Institute for Public Policy Research.

Wilner, D., et al. 1962. The Housing Environment and Family Life. Baltimore, Md.: Johns Hopkins University Press.

Wilson, W. 1987. The Truly Disadvantaged. Chicago: University of Chicago Press.

Chapter Two

THE EFFECTS OF WELFARE REFORM ON HOUSING: A NATIONAL ANALYSIS

Sandra J. Newman and Joseph Harkness

The welfare reform legislation President Clinton signed into law on August 22, 1996, the Personal Responsibility and Work Opportunity Reconciliation Act of 1996 (PRWORA) (Public Law 104-193), makes major changes in federal welfare programs (Congressional Budget Office [CBO] 1996). Title I of the act, Temporary Assistance for Needy Families (TANF), completely overhauls the Aid to Families with Dependent Children (AFDC) program, which has been the nation's primary approach to providing cash assistance to children in poverty and their guardians. Such assistance is now time-limited, recipients must engage in work after two months of welfare receipt, and legal immigrants are no longer eligible. Perhaps most importantly, states now have much greater control over the specific design of their welfare programs. As long as the state fulfills the "maintenance of effort" requirement,[1] it has considerable discretion about who will be assisted, for how long, and under what conditions. For example, states may decide to impose family caps, set more restrictive time limits on welfare receipt than the 60-month limit required by TANF, and sanction (cut or eliminate) benefits if work requirements are not fulfilled. Key changes under other titles of PRWORA include restriction of eligibility of legal aliens for welfare, modification of eligibility rules and benefit levels for the Food Stamp Program, and tightened eligibility requirements for disabled children under Supplemental Security Income (SSI).

Because PRWORA, in general, and TANF, in particular, represent a radical departure from past welfare policy, they have been and will continue to be the objects of policy discussion and analysis. However, neither the policy debate nor the studies now underway have considered the effects of welfare system changes on recipients' housing.

As noted in chapter 1, about 25 percent of welfare recipients also receive housing assistance, and nearly 50 percent of households with children in public housing receive welfare benefits.[2] All these assisted housing residents will be affected by TANF to the extent that their incomes change. Those whose incomes increase will receive lower housing subsidies; those whose incomes decline (due to sanctions or time limits) will require higher housing subsidies if they remain in assisted housing. TANF will also affect the ability of unassisted households on welfare to maintain affordable housing, because those who are unable to meet the TANF work or other requirements will lose their formerly guaranteed AFDC payment.

This chapter presents a preliminary examination of the implications of welfare reform on the profile of housing assistance recipients ("assisted households"), U.S. Department of Housing and Urban Development (HUD) budgets for housing subsidies, and poor households who do not receive housing assistance ("unassisted households"). We use microsimulation and other statistical techniques to answer four policy questions:

1. How is welfare reform likely to affect the proportion of AFDC households who will be required to work under welfare reform and who also receive housing assistance?
2. What is the magnitude of welfare reform's impact on the employment of AFDC households receiving housing assistance?
3. What is the magnitude of welfare reform's impact on the income of AFDC households receiving housing assistance and, therefore, on government budgets?
4. What is the magnitude of welfare reform's impact on the housing cost burden of AFDC households who do not receive housing assistance?

Our conceptual framework posits direct relationships among income, housing subsidies, and housing cost burdens. Applying this conceptual framework to welfare recipients whose incomes decrease, for example, we assume that the loss of benefits from other safety net programs forces the household to increase its out-of-pocket payments for basic necessities. In the short run, however, cuts in other benefits that occur while the household is still receiving AFDC will result in increases in AFDC benefits.[3] Over the longer run, when the household moves off AFDC, the implications of these reverberations differ for assisted and unassisted households. For assisted households, reductions in benefits from welfare programs (excluding food stamps) are treated as reductions in income, necessitating an increase in housing subsidies if the household is to retain its assisted housing unit.[4] For unassisted households, welfare benefit reductions require a reallocation of the household's budget, either increasing the housing cost burden or reducing the amount spent on housing.

APPROACH, DATA, AND STUDY LIMITATIONS

Because states are in the early stages of TANF implementation, and the interpretation of several features of TANF remains unclear, we simulate TANF impacts by turning to a set of programs that have actually defined welfare reform for at least the last 15 years, namely, state AFDC waiver programs.[5] As of August 1996, 43 states had implemented federally approved waivers of their AFDC rules.[6] We chose six of these for ultimate analysis, basing our selection on three primary criteria:

1. The analysis states should reflect a mix of conservative and liberal philosophies of the key elements of welfare reform—time limits, work requirements, and sanctions.
2. The waivers should include provisions that are likely to have sizable effects on income and, therefore, housing.
3. There should be at least some data available on waiver program impacts.[7]

Figure 2.1 lists the sample of states, our ranking of their philosophical bent, and our primary sources of data on their impacts.[8] While we will ultimately examine all six, this chapter is based on the four that have either generated the most public interest, or, at least in the minds of some experts, have developed programs that were likely to

Figure 2.1 STATE SAMPLE

State	Date	Name	Philosophy	Impact Data Sources
Florida	2/'94	Family Transition Program (FTP)	Conservative	MDRC;[a] state
Michigan	9/'92	To Strengthen Michigan Families (TSMF)	Moderate	Abt;[b] state
Ohio	7/'96	Ohio First	Moderate	state
Vermont	7/'94	Welfare Restructuring Program (WRP)	Liberal	MDRC;[a] state
Virginia	7/'95	Virginia Independence Program (VIP)	Conservative	state
Wisconsin	'96	Wisconsin Works (W2)	Conservative	state

a. MDRC = Manpower Demonstration Research Corporation.
b. Abt = Abt Associates, Inc.

be copied by other states: Florida's Family Transition Program (FTP); Michigan's To Strengthen Michigan Families (TSMF); Vermont's Welfare Restructuring Program (WRP); and Virginia's Virginia Independence Program (VIP). We address the following specific question: If all states in the nation adopted FTP, or TSMF, or WRP, or VIP, what would the effects be on assisted households, the HUD budget for subsidized housing, and the housing cost burdens of unassisted households, both renters and owners?

Although our primary interest is in AFDC reforms, ignoring interactions between TANF and other titles under PRWORA could lead to distorted estimates of TANF impacts. We therefore account for the effects of three major provisions from other PRWORA titles in our analysis: (a) elimination of SSI benefits for the subgroup of disabled children whose disabilities are not rated as "marked" or "severe" in at least two areas of functioning, or who manifest maladaptive behavior but no specifically listed disability;[9] (b) reduction of maximum food stamp benefits from 103 percent to 100 percent of the Thrifty Food Plan; and (c) the elimination of food stamp benefit increases in the case of income reductions associated with TANF participation.[10,11] We also added the Earned Income Tax Credit (EITC) to the incomes of families with earnings, though we did not account for other possible taxation effects.[12] In our future work, we will also account for the effects of liberalizations of welfare rules that increase the number of households on welfare.[13]

The current analysis focuses on four provisions in each waiver program: time limits, family caps (reduction or elimination of benefits for children born to households on AFDC for more than nine months), earnings disregards, and work requirements. We estimate the effects of these policy changes on the profile of assisted and unassisted households and on the budget for housing subsidies, under the assumption that a particular state's waiver program is applied nationwide and fully implemented for a period of five years.

The data come from the 1994 file of the AFDC–Quality Control (QC) database (U.S. Department of Health and Human Services 1994). They are based on a systematic probability sample of active AFDC cases in each state, and include more than 300 variables covering a full range of demographic and economic attributes of the household and each of its members. The 1994 database contains roughly 50,000 unweighted observations of AFDC households. As discussed in chapter 1, the AFDC-QC data are subject to reporting errors for receipt and type of housing assistance. However, the overall fraction reporting assisted housing receipt is approximately correct. But income and employment are underreported in the survey compared to other nongovernmental surveys such as the Panel Study of Income Dynamics. Therefore, estimates presented in this chapter are likely to overstate the extent of the problem.

Data on the waiver effects are drawn from evaluation reports for Michigan and Florida (Werner and Kornfeld 1994, 1995, 1996; Bloom et al. 1997) and from state reports for Virginia and Vermont (Virginia Department of Health and Human Resources 1996; Virginia Department of Social Services 1997; Vermont Department of Social Welfare 1997). Of particular importance is the information on the waiver impacts on employment and earnings. In the evaluations, these are measured by the differences in employment and earnings between a control group operating under traditional AFDC and an experimental group operating under the waiver. More disaggregation was possible for some states than others. For Michigan, it was possible to disaggregate impacts for the number of parents in the AFDC unit and time on the waiver. Florida provided data on differences by the imputed time limit faced by recipient, the length of time on AFDC, and race/ethnicity. The Virginia waiver impact on employment was drawn from state data on the difference between the percentage of VIP and Job Opportunities and Basic Skills (JOBS) participants with unsubsidized employment in 1996. For the impact on earnings, we deflated and compared average earnings of VIP participants to average earnings of Virginia cases with earnings in the 1994 AFDC-QC data. Under the Vermont waiver, only 20 percent of the cases were assigned to the AFDC control group, and the only comparative data available on the control and waiver groups were mean annual earnings in the first year of random assignment. We assumed that half the increase in earnings was due to more cases obtaining employment and the other half was due to those cases with work earning more.

Several limitations of the analysis need to be kept in mind (see appendix A for detail). First, data limitations made it impossible for us to simulate the effects of asset limits and sanctions in the waiver programs.[14] We also assume that AFDC households living in assisted housing will have the same behavioral responses to welfare reform as those not living in assisted housing.[15] Additionally, the four waivers we examined have been in effect for only a short time, as shown in figure 2.1; have operated in a robust economic climate; and are not statewide in all cases. Longer-term effects, and especially those generated in a less healthy economy, may look different from those presented here, although there is no serious correlation between welfare-to-work incentives that perform well and local economic conditions (Wallace and Riccio 1997).[16] Our simulations also do not model behavioral responses to each of these welfare reform packages. (Doing so requires individual-level data tracked across time, which are generally not available.) Instead, the simulations apply the aggregate behavioral responses observed in the four sample states, applying subgroup variations in responses whenever possible.

A PROFILE OF AFDC HOUSEHOLDS WITH, AND WITHOUT, HOUSING ASSISTANCE

To provide an empirical base for the policy simulations, table 2.1 presents data on selected attributes of the three groups of AFDC households of primary interest in this analysis. As a frame of reference, distributions are also provided for all AFDC households.[17]

More than three-fourths of AFDC households have three or more members. Nearly all are headed by a female who is 32 years old on average, and most are members of a racial or ethnic minority group. The AFDC households with rental assistance are smaller in size and even more predominantly minority. Owner households are larger than average, with older household heads (39 years on average). The majority of AFDC owner households are white, and the proportion headed by a male is nearly twice that for all AFDC households (and unassisted renter households) and more than three times that for assisted households.

At least 30 percent of all AFDC household heads are high school graduates; only 9 percent are employed.[18] The large majority are out of the labor force (that is, neither working nor looking for work). Another 11 percent of heads are unemployed (that is, laid off and/or looking for work). Among the 9 percent who reported being employed, at least 27 percent work less than 30 hours a week in a typical month.[19] In view of these labor force participation characteristics, it is not surprising that the outside income of these households is extremely low, averaging only about $50 per month. The large majority of AFDC households are living primarily on their benefit payments, which average $383 per month.

Interestingly, although the proportion of high school graduates is higher among the heads of both assisted households and owner households than that for all AFDC households, the two groups differ in employment status, benefit payments, and other (nonbenefit) income.

Owners are more likely to be employed (11 percent) and assisted renters are least likely to be employed (6.8 percent) than any other household group. Similarly, a higher proportion of heads of assisted households than heads of owner households (80.1 percent versus 71.3 percent) are out of the labor force.[20] On average, AFDC payments are roughly $74 higher among assisted households than among owners ($364.05 versus $290.40). Outside income of assisted households is roughly $17 per month lower than among owners ($41.16 versus $58.30), perhaps because of differences in hourly wage rates paid to these two groups or because more owners report income from members not in the AFDC unit.[21]

The duration of the current spell of assistance is more than three years for the average AFDC household, with a median of slightly less than two. Owners have slightly longer current welfare spells than average. But assisted households have current spells nearly a year longer than average. According to the cumulative number of months of AFDC receipt over the household's lifetime—the duration that triggers TANF time limits—a sizable proportion of current AFDC households, and particularly assisted households, would be affected by the national TANF time limits if they were fully in effect, and an even higher proportion by the more stringent time limits of some state waiver programs.

About 12 percent of AFDC household heads are immigrants who could be dropped from the AFDC rolls under TANF, some of whom could also be dropped from food stamps and have family members dropped from SSI under PRWORA. The proportion is lower than average among both assisted households (6.2 percent) and owners (5.2 percent). Finally, 7 percent of AFDC household heads are probably exempt from the new restrictions because they are disabled or age 60 or older. The proportion in this potentially exempt group is considerably higher for owners than for other household heads.

This profile leaves two strong impressions. First, owner households differ from other AFDC household types in several ways. Their household heads are predominantly white, older, and more likely to be male. On average they have somewhat fewer years of education and larger households. And nearly 40 percent (not shown) live in states in the lowest quintile of AFDC payments, primarily in the South.[22] Second, assisted households are particularly vulnerable to welfare reform. They have the longest average current durations of welfare receipt and by far the longest cumulative durations. If Virginia's VIP program or the 24-month time limit option of Florida's FTP were in full effect in 1994, for example, the more than 75 percent of assisted households

Table 2.1 CHARACTERISTICS OF AFDC HOUSEHOLDS: ASSISTED RENTERS, UNASSISTED RENTERS, AND OWNERS

	Assisted Renters (N = 1,126,360)	Unassisted Renters (N = 3,240,868)	Owners (N = 209,800)	Total (N = 4,577,028)
Age of head (%)				
Under 18	.5	1.3	.1	1.1
18 to 21	9.4	12.9	2.8	11.6
22 to 24	13.3	13.7	6.0	13.2
25 to 29	21.2	20.6	13.0	20.4
30 to 49	50.9	44.4	59.7	46.7
50 to 64	4.0	5.1	14.6	5.3
65+	.6	1.2	3.6	1.2
Unknown/missing	.2	.7	.1	.6
All households*	100.0	100.0	100.0	100.0
Mean age (years)	31.9	31.6	39.0	32.0
(std. dev.)	(9.2)	(10.5)	(11.9)	(10.4)
Sex of head (%)				
Male	4.9	8.0	15.8	7.6
Female	95.1	92.0	84.1	92.4
Unknown/missing	—	—	.1	—
All households*	100.0	100.0	100.0	100.0
Household size (%)[a]				
One	.4	.5	.1	.4
Two	26.3	21.6	17.1	22.5
Three	32.2	27.2	25.2	28.4
Four or more	41.2	50.7	57.6	48.7
All households*	100.0	100.0	100.0	100.0

Race/ethnicity of head (%)				
White, non-Hispanic	29.8	38.7	55.1	37.2
Black, non-Hispanic	48.3	32.7	18.8	35.9
Hispanic	16.1	21.9	22.0	20.5
Other	4.2	4.2	3.4	4.2
Unknown/missing	1.7	2.5	1.0	2.2
All households*	100.0	100.0	100.0	100.0
Education of head (%)				
Grade school or less	5.2	5.2	11.0	5.5
Some high school	18.3	15.9	15.8	16.5
High school graduate	23.9	19.9	25.0	21.1
Some college	8.3	5.8	8.8	6.5
College graduate or more	.5	.5	1.0	.5
Unknown/missing	43.9	52.7	38.4	49.9
All households*	100.0	100.0	100.0	100.0
Employment status of head (%)				
Employed	6.8	9.1	11.0	8.6
Out of labor force	80.1	76.5	71.3	77.1
Unemployed	10.9	10.7	10.5	10.8
Unknown/missing	2.2	3.8	7.2	3.5
All households*	100.0	100.0	100.0	100.0

Table 2.1 CHARACTERISTICS OF AFDC HOUSEHOLDS: ASSISTED RENTERS, UNASSISTED RENTERS, AND OWNERS (continued)

	Assisted Renters (N = 1,126,360)	Unassisted Renters (N = 3,240,868)	Owners (N = 209,800)	Total (N = 4,577,028)
Employment hours[b] of head (%)				
1-9 hrs/wk	6.7	5.2	6.9	5.6
10-19 hrs/wk	15.7	9.5	8.8	10.6
20-29 hrs/wk	12.0	10.2	7.9	10.4
30-39 hrs/wk	21.5	18.5	11.9	18.6
40 hrs/wk or more	10.0	14.9	12.3	13.8
Work hours not known	9.7	12.3	12.7	11.9
Unknown/missing	24.4	29.4	39.6	29.2
All households*	100.0	100.0	100.0	100.0
AFDC payment/month	$364.05	$395.00	$290.40	$382.59
(std. dev.)	($203.36)	($202.35)	($193.65)	($203.64)
Median	$330	$366	$250	$347
Other income/month[c]	$41.16	$54.02	$58.30	$51.05
(std. dev.)	($142.82)	($225.94)	($173.57)	($206.34)
Duration on AFDC (months)[d]				
Current spell	46.7	34.1	39.1	37.4
(std. dev.)	(46.9)	(41.1)	(47.6)	(43.2)
Median	34	20	21	22
24 months or longer	63.1	47.8	47.0	51.7
60 months or longer	30.2	19.5	23.2	22.4

Cumulative period of receipt[d]	68.5	51.7	63.0	56.4
(std. dev.)	(53.4)	(49.5)	(54.9)	(50.7)
Median	57	37	51	43
24 months or longer	78.3	62.4	70.1	66.7
60 months or longer	47.5	33.2	43.9	37.2
Disability status of head (%)				
Disabled	4.6	5.9	5.7	5.5
Not disabled, ≥ 60 yrs old	0.9	1.5	4.7	1.5
Not disabled, < 60 yrs old	91.9	88.1	81.2	88.8
Unknown/missing	2.4	4.5	8.4	4.2
All households*	100.0	100.0	100.0	100.0
Children with unmarried parents, paternity not established (%)	32.6	33.1	14.3	32.1
Immigrant status of head (%)				
Legal or illegal immigrant	6.2	14.1	5.2	11.7
Citizen	92.5	82.9	92.8	85.7
Unknown/missing	1.4	3.0	2.1	2.6
All households*	100.0	100.0	100.0	100.0

Source: Weighted estimates derived from a sample of 47,052 AFDC households as identified by the 1994 AFDC-QC data.

Note: Duration, paternity, and AFDC payment variables pertain to AFDC recipients only.

a. Household size includes the AFDC unit plus other household members not receiving AFDC.

b. Employment hours shown for those who reported some work.

c. Outside income pertains to the AFDC unit plus other household members not receiving AFDC.

d. Current spell reflects number of months since last opening; cumulative reflects total months since first receipt of AFDC. Imputation for latter based on Urban Institute's AFDC-QC model.

*Components may not add to 100.0 due to rounding.

who had received AFDC for 24 months or longer could have been dropped from the welfare rolls (assuming none were exempt). Their particularly low rates of employment and outside income also raise concern about how they will fare without public assistance.

OVERVIEW OF THE STATE WAIVERS

Key characteristics of the four state waiver programs in our sample are summarized in figure 2.2. Programs are typically placed on the conservative-to-liberal spectrum on the basis of the first four entries. By this standard, Virginia's VIP is the most conservative of the four. It imposes a two-year time limit, nonexempt recipients must begin some work activity within 90 days, the entire family benefit is sanctioned for noncompliance, and there is a family cap. Florida is also conservative because it has a 24- or 36-month time limit and sanctions by removing noncompliant adult recipients from the welfare benefit unit (although FTP does not have a family cap).[23] Florida's time limit is not as strict as Virginia's, however, because it allows for the extension of the child's portion of welfare benefits if the AFDC unit has no other income and children would be put at risk of becoming homeless.[24] Although there is no formal time requirement after which recipients must participate in employment-related activities (the time frame is established through a case management process), Bloom et al. (1997) report that participants are closely monitored, leading these analysts to describe FTP as a "tough" program [quotes in original].

Vermont is the most liberal of the four sample states. Vermont's WRP has no time limit on benefit receipt, recipients can receive welfare for more than a year before they are required to begin work-related activities, there is no family cap, and the sanction for noncompliant families is mild: Part of the grant is converted into a vendor payment (spendable only for approved services), with the remainder paid to the family by check, as usual.

Michigan's TSMF waiver is liberal because it has no time limit on welfare receipt, no family cap, and no set time frame for all recipients to participate in work-related activities. It is conservative because its sanction policies are strict. For example, both the welfare grant and food stamp allocations are reduced by 25 percent during periods of noncompliance. So, overall, it can be described as moderate.

The fifth entry in figure 2.2, earnings disregards, shows the limitations of the first four entries as defining characteristics of liberal or conservative.[25] Virginia, for example, which is the most conservative according to the first four entries, has among the most liberal earnings disregard of all waiver programs, exempting all earnings up to the federal poverty level. Thus, a three-person household with a full-time worker earning the minimum wage could retain all of her earnings and still receive welfare benefits. Vermont, the most liberal according to the first four entries, and Michigan, moderate according to the first four entries, are more conservative than Virginia on earned income disregards, allowing a fixed amount of outside earnings plus a fixed percentage to be retained. Florida is somewhere in between.[26]

The changing characterizations of these waiver programs, depending on the particular program dimension, suggests that looking at all the major waiver provisions as a package may yield a clearer sense of the state's basic strategy for achieving its welfare reform goals. Virginia's VIP's primary goals are moving recipients from welfare to work and ultimately off welfare (Virginia Department of Health and Human Resources 1996). Its strategy for achieving this is two-pronged: the financial incentive of a generous earned income disregard, which allows recipients to keep all of their earnings even if they earn somewhat above the minimum wage, combined with a strict time limit and other disincentives to remain on AFDC.

By contrast, the Michigan and Vermont waivers are designed to engage recipients in at least some activities that will improve their employability, with case-by-case variations in the form and time this will take. Both states rely on intensive case management and career counseling to achieve this individually tailored approach, and neither emphasizes financial incentives to work. The absence of a set time limit is consistent with this individualized approach, which carries with it the likelihood that some recipients may remain on welfare for a long time.[27]

Florida is a mixture. It provides relatively generous earned income and asset disregards, though not as generous as Virginia's, as incentives to find jobs. Its time limits and sanctions, though less rigid than Virginia's, are designed to move recipients off AFDC. Its child care exemption, more stringent than Virginia's or Vermont's, pertains to children six months of age or younger. Like Michigan and Vermont, Florida has adopted a case management and career counseling approach, suggesting at least the possibility of some tailoring of plans, goals, and time frames. And Florida makes subsidized jobs available

Figure 2.2 KEY FEATURES OF SELECTED STATE WELFARE REFORM WAIVERS

	Florida (FTP)	Michigan (TSMF)	Vermont (WRP)	Virginia (VIP)
Time Limits	• After accumulation of 24 months of AFDC receipt during a 60-month period • *For families with adult member <24, not a high school graduate, no work history in past year, and on AFDC for 36 of 60 months prior to FTP:* After accumulation of 36 months on AFDC receipt during a 72-month period • AFDC benefits extended for child(ren) if AFDC is only income and benefit cut would put child at risk	No time limit on AFDC receipt	No time limit on AFDC receipt (time limit applies to duration on AFDC without need to work)	After 24 months of AFDC receipt, ineligible for 24 months
Sanctions	JOBS sanctions: removal of nonexempt noncompliant person(s) from AFDC grant	• Grant reduced 25% for 12 months or until compliance, whichever is sooner; after 12 months, case closed until compliance • Food stamps reduced 25% for 12 months or until compliance, whichever is sooner • AFDC applicants in Pilot Program: Grant reduced by 25% for failure to comply with job search	• *For adults:* Failure to accept a job, quitting, or being fired without good cause results in vendor payments for housing, food, and utility expenses[a] • *For minor parent:* For non-attendance of school or JOBS, grant is converted to vendor payments for housing, food, and utility expenses[b] • Failure to comply with sanction requirements results in grant termination	3 sanction levels: 1st: suspension of family's entire AFDC benefit for one month 2nd: as above, but for three months 3rd and subsequent: as above, for six months
Family Cap	None	None	None	Yes; applies to AFDC child born >10 months after start of AFDC receipt

Work Requirement	• Within about 2 weeks, required to develop self-sufficiency plan with case manager and employability plan with career counselor • Subsidized employment for participants who have complied with requirements but can't find jobs. Earnings = min. wage + $90	Varies, set through Social Contract	• 30th month of cumulative benefits for single parent and incapacitated families with child <13 (AFDC-I) • 15th month of cumulative benefits for unemployed parent families and AFDC-I families with no children <13 • Cumulative time on AFDC reduced by 6 months for each intervening period of non-receipt lasting ≥12 months • For every 12 continuous months of earnings of >$150 from unsubsidized job, 6 months subtracted from time limit • 2 months prior to time limit, must participate in job search • Able-bodied primary wage earner in 2-parent family must obtain full-time job, unsubsidized or subsidized • Able-bodied single parent or able-bodied parent in 2-parent family where other parent incapacitated must obtain half-time job if child <13 years old or full-time job if child ≥13.	Within 90 days of initial receipt of benefits
Earnings Disregards	First $200 earned + 50% of balance	First $200 earned + 20% of balance	• First $150 earned + 25% of balance[c]	All earnings up to federal poverty level

Figure 2.2 KEY FEATURES OF SELECTED STATE WELFARE REFORM WAIVERS (continued)

	Florida (FTP)	Michigan (TSMF)	Vermont (WRP)	Virginia (VIP)
			• $90/month work expense deduction for those in community service jobs • Incentive payments for completing parenting education program or related volunteer work as part of an individualized family development plan	
Asset Limits	$5,000 + car worth $8,150	$3,000 + one car	Savings from earnings + one car	$5,000 + car worth $7,500
Exemptions[d]	• Parent with child ≥6 months born before time limit in effect • Ill or incapacitated adult • Full-time caretaker of a disabled dependent person • Caretaker relative not included in grant • Age 62 or older • <18 years old, in school, or working 30+ hours/week	• <16 years old • None others specified; negotiated through Social Contract	• Caring for child <18 months if on AFDC >30 months • Child <16 years old • Child 16-18 years old and in school or training • Permanently/chronically disabled • Nonrelative caretaker • Parent caretaker of disabled parent, spouse, or child • Parent in class 24+ hours/week working toward HS diploma or GED • Employed 30+ hours/week • 1-3 months pregnant; 4+ months pregnant only if medically necessary	• Ill or incapacitated • Age 60 or older • Ill or incapacitated family member • 4+ months pregnant • Caring for child <18 months (but if child subject to family cap, then exempt for 6 weeks only) • <16 years old or 16-19 years old and in school or training

a. Remainder of AFDC payment, if any, paid to recipient.
b. Minor parent must meet with caseworker three days each month to facilitate vendor payments, assess problems associated with non-compliance, and receive remainder of grant.
c. Also disregard certain employment and training stipends paid by JTPA.
d. In Michigan, June 1996 amendments specified exemptions closer to those in the JOBS program.

to those who cannot find private market jobs, also reflecting the desire to accommodate employability variations among recipients.

SIMULATED EFFECTS OF WELFARE REFORM

Proportions of Nonexempt Welfare Recipients Receiving Housing Assistance

Figure 2.3 displays the proportion of households who are not exempt from work requirements who live in assisted housing.[28] Michigan's program is excluded because, other than those younger than 16 years of age, exempt cases are not defined.

Assisted households do not have characteristics that would exempt them from work under the waivers. Therefore, the simulated change under the waivers is generally modest. The greatest proportional change occurs under Vermont's WRP, which induces a 14 percent increase in the proportion of households receiving housing assistance—119,000 additional households nationwide.[29] However, the largest absolute change occurs under Florida's FTP. Because exemptions are greatly curtailed under FTP, the number of assisted renters who must meet work requirements increases by 364,000.

Figure 2.3 WAIVER EFFECTS ON % NONEXEMPT IN ASSISTED HOUSING

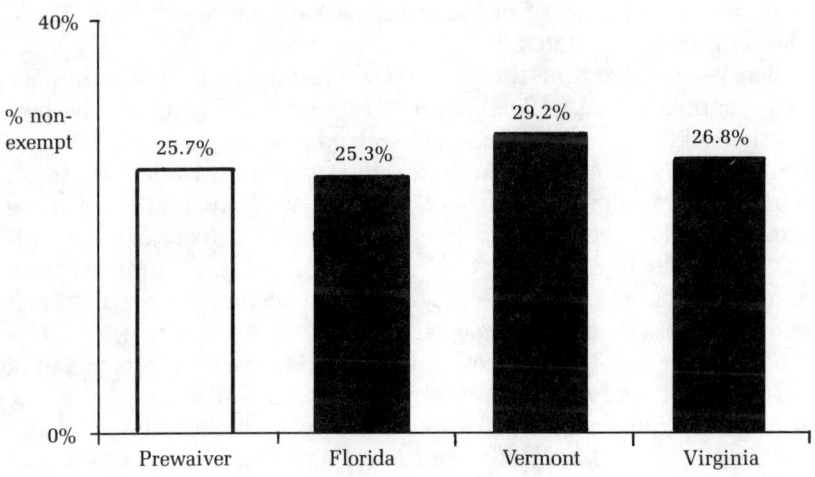

Note: Michigan largely determined by negotiation.

Employment of Assisted Households

Table 2.2 shows the employment status of housing assistance recipients five years after program implementation.[30] All four waiver programs increase the proportion (and number) of households working in unsubsidized jobs. The size of the impacts varies greatly, however. Virginia's VIP, at the high end, leads to a 151 percent increase in the proportion of assisted renters who are working—from 8 percent to 20.1 percent (from 90,008 to 263,925 assisted renters nationwide). Florida's FTP increases the proportion in unsubsidized jobs from 8 percent to 14 percent. The Michigan and Vermont waivers have a more modest effect, increasing the unsubsidized employment rate from 8 percent to 10 percent and from 8 percent to 12.5 percent—25 and 50 percent increases, respectively. The results are even more dramatic for public housing residents, with increases in the proportion of 40 percent in Michigan and 184 percent in Virginia. The relative ranking of the four waiver programs remains the same, with Virginia's VIP having the largest effect, followed by Florida, Vermont, and Michigan (appendix table 2B.1).

Even with these employment impacts, few of those working in unsubsidized jobs attain self-sufficiency and leave welfare. Interestingly, because of the explicit time limits under Virginia's and Florida's waivers, the proportion of households working while still on welfare after five years is somewhat lower than in Michigan and Vermont. The larger effects in Virginia and Florida may say something about the positive incentive effect of the more generous earned income disregards in these two states.[31]

Because the two time-limit states have varying provisions (Florida's being somewhat more flexible), it is interesting to compare the proportions of those working in unsubsidized jobs who are off AFDC and the proportions receiving welfare while working. Under Virginia's VIP, the proportion employed and off welfare is twice that of those working and on welfare (12.7 percent versus 6.7 percent). Under Florida's more flexible FTP, the two proportions are more similar—with somewhat more than half employed and on welfare (7.7 percent), and somewhat less than half employed and off welfare (5.4 percent). Under a nationwide VIP-type reform, roughly 140,000 assisted renters out of about 1.1 million who were working while on welfare would hit the time limit. Under an FTP-type reform, the comparable number would be 60,655 out of 1.1 million. Only very small proportions of households under both waivers are projected to get unsubsidized jobs and

Table 2.2 SIMULATED EFFECTS ON EMPLOYMENT STATUS OF ASSISTED HOUSEHOLDS

	Prewaiver		Changes under Waiver			
	Households	%	Florida FTP %	Michigan TSMF %	Vermont WRP %	Virginia VIP %
Employed						
Unsubsidized job, on AFDC	89,642	8.0	13.9	10.0	12.5	20.1
Unsubsidized job, off AFDC (before time limit)	89,642	8.0	7.7	10.0	12.5	6.7
Unsubsidized job, off AFDC (hit time limit)	(366)	—	<1.0	—	—	<1.0
Unsubsidized job, hit time limit	—	—	5.4	—	—	12.7
Subsidized job or work preparation, on AFDC	493,823	43.8	64.4	88.2	49.9	13.9
Not employed, hit time limit	—	—	5.9	—	—	32.5
Exemption	542,152	48.1	15.8	1.4	37.1	34.2
TOTAL	1,125,983	100.0%	100.0%	100.0%	100.0%	100.0%

Source: Authors' simulations based on 1994 AFDC-QC data.

Notes: Numbers may not add to 100 percent due to rounding. Prewaiver "unsubsidized job off AFDC" not interpretable. "—" denotes not applicable.

Prewaiver estimate of unsubsidized employment based on QC respondents reporting some earnings. This item yields a slightly higher employment rate than the question of whether the respondent is employed.

Exemptions in Michigan are limited to those younger than 16 years old. Other exemptions to be determined by Social Contract.

Neither impact evaluation data nor state data distinguish subsidized employment and employability program participation. Therefore these are combined.

A sizable proportion of those categorized as "subsidized job . . ." in Florida are those whose AFDC was extended because termination would put a child at risk. This category represents 36.6 percent of assisted renters.

attain self-sufficiency before hitting the time limit (a set of results that is similar for public housing residents).

A substantial share of households are engaged in subsidized employment or a work preparation program after 5 years under all the waivers except Virginia's. Since participation in at least some activity geared to increase self-sufficiency is the linchpin of the Social Contract under Michigan's TSMF, it is not surprising that most welfare recipients in that program are in this category.[32] Under Vermont's waiver, roughly half of housing assistance recipients are engaged in subsidized employment or work readiness. Although Florida's FTP figures are consistent with the state's commitment to providing subsidized employment for those unable to obtain unsubsidized employment, they are inflated by a factor of three because they include a group of child recipients whose benefits are extended to avoid placing the child at risk. Under Virginia's VIP, the 13.9 percent of recipients engaged in subsidized employment or work preparation is only a fraction of those under the other waivers. This low rate is consistent with VIP's primary goal of moving recipients into the regular workforce as quickly as possible.

Because the figures for unsubsidized versus subsidized work engagement are so different, particularly under Michigan's TSMF, the increase in the proportion of recipients engaged in *at least some work activity* ranges from a low of 34 percent *fewer* residents engaged in a work activity under Virginia's VIP (a drop from 51.8 percent to 34 percent) to a high of about 90 percent *more* under Michigan's TSMF (a rise from 51.8 percent to 98.2 percent). (The results are comparable for public housing residents.) Three factors underlie these results, one real and two probably artifactual. The real influence is Virginia's stringent time limit; because of it, many households are off welfare and not working. The first artifactual influence is our treatment of Florida's extension provision, under which a child's portion of the benefit may be continued if the family has no other source of income. We modeled households that would have benefits extended under this provision as engaged in subsidized work.[33] The lack of information on exempt categories under Michigan's TSMF is the second artifactual factor. It is likely that a large portion of those modeled as engaged in subsidized jobs or work training would be exempt.

The proportions of cases exempt from work requirements shrink under all waivers—from about half of all cases prewaiver to one-third under Vermont's WRP and Virginia's VIP, and to one-sixth under Florida's FTP. Vermont's WRP and Virginia's VIP are similar because both states generally adopted the rules of the JOBS program and both lowered the age of the child care exemption from three years to 18 months.[34] Florida's FTP exemption rate is less than 20 percent—much lower than Vermont's and Virginia's—and is explained by Florida's much more restrictive child care exemption limit (six months).[35] The data in table 2.2 can also be used to estimate the proportion of AFDC households who receive housing assistance who are still on welfare five years after program implementation. Nearly all assisted households under Michigan's TSMF and Vermont's WRP are on welfare in the fifth year of welfare reform. The analogous proportion under Florida's waiver is nearly 90 percent, of which four-fifths are nonexempt cases. Under Virginia's waiver, because of its two-year time limit, the proportion is somewhat more than half, of which about two-thirds are exempt cases.

Income of Assisted Households[36]

The simulated average monthly household incomes of assisted households are shown in table 2.3.[37] Under the Michigan and Vermont waivers, average incomes rise by 2 and 4 percent, respectively, presumably reflecting work incentives that are somewhat more enticing than those under AFDC and no time limits on assistance.[38] Under the Florida and Virginia waivers, they fall by 8 and 21 percent, respectively. These overall declines indicate that gains in income for those who obtain unsubsidized employment will be more than offset by the loss in income for those who do not find jobs and have their benefits either reduced (an option in Florida)[39] or eliminated (as in Virginia and Florida) as they hit the time limit. As shown earlier (table 2.2), 6 percent of Florida FTP participants (66,000 cases nationwide) hit the time limit and are not working; the comparable figures for Virginia are 33 percent (366,000 cases nationwide). Among those hitting the time limit and not working, incomes decline by about 62 percent in Florida (to $208) and 89 percent in Virginia (to $53).

Because of the work incentives of the Virginia and Florida waivers, cases can be expected to move off the rolls at lower income levels under the Virginia and Florida waivers than under the other two. As more cases go to work, those in states where payment standards are low will be disqualified from welfare receipt more quickly.[40] Thus, cases off welfare with lower earnings will tend to predominate. For the Virginia waiver, the family cap will exacerbate this effect.

For those with unsubsidized jobs on welfare, recipients under the Florida waiver have the lowest income and those under the Virginia waiver the highest. Those with unsubsidized jobs under all but the

Table 2.3 SIMULATED EFFECTS ON CASH INCOME OF ASSISTED HOUSEHOLDS

	Prewaiver	Florida FTP	Michigan TSMF	Vermont WRP	Virginia VIP
Unsubsidized job, on AFDC	$834	$709	$795	$810	$1,020
Unsubsidized job, off AFDC (before time limit)	$505	$858	$1,079	$1,087	$783
Unsubsidized job, hit time limit	$505	$375	—	—	$701
Subsidized job or work preparation, on AFDC	$466	$407	$481	$483	$437
Not employed, hit time limit	$505	$208	—	—	$53
Exempt	$486	$545	$521	$472	$477
Overall Average	$505	$442	$516	$523	$400

Source: Authors' simulations based on 1994 AFDC-QC data.
Notes: Appendix table 2B.3 shows food stamps, cash income, and total income, and divides assisted renters into public housing and other assistance.

Prewaiver cash income for "off AFDC" and "hit time limit" categories is the average income for all AFDC cases in assisted housing. These categories did not exist prewaiver.

Exempt category in Michigan limited to those younger than 16 years old. Other exemptions to be determined by Social Contract.

Neither impact evaluation data nor state data distinguish subsidized employment and employability program participation. Therefore these are combined.

For the category "subsidized job or work preparation, on AFDC" in Florida, the average income of those who had not reached the time limit was $439. The average income for those who hit the time limit but lost the parental portion of the benefit was $382.

Virginia waiver have lower average incomes than their counterparts under regular AFDC. This indicates that, although more households have some earnings under the waivers, these earnings are at a generally low level, pulling down the average. Virginia is an exception because, as noted, virtually all earnings are disregarded in the benefit calculation.

Those who hit the time limit under the Florida waiver and have unsubsidized jobs are worse off than prewaiver AFDC cases in assisted housing, while the comparable group under the Virginia waiver are better off. This occurs because of the strong impact on earnings under the Virginia waiver (recall that the simulation assumes that all those working while on welfare continue to work after they have hit the time limit). It is worth emphasizing, however, that this Virginia impact should be interpreted with caution because, unlike the earnings impact for the Florida waiver, it was derived from a comparison of data for two different years (1996 and 1994), not from a comparison between experimental (waiver) and control (regular AFDC) groups.

Those who hit the time limit and have no job, either unsubsidized or subsidized, are appreciably worse off under the Virginia waiver than they are under the Florida waiver, however, with average monthly incomes of $53 compared to $208, respectively. The more muted effect in Florida is attributable to the AFDC-extension provision under which at-risk children remain eligible for welfare even after the time limit has been reached (because there is no other income in the household). About 37 percent of cases under an FTP-type waiver fall into this category (412,000 households nationwide). But although they retain some welfare benefits, their incomes decline by 24 percent.[41]

The HUD Subsidized Housing Budget

Table 2.4 shows the impact of the simulated waiver on the HUD budget for assisted housing. Under the Michigan and Vermont waivers, tenant rent payments out-of-pocket increase, from $2.00 billion per year to $2.04 billion per year and $2.07 billion per year, respectively. These increases result in budget savings for HUD of between $39 and $69 million per year, less than one-half of one percent of HUD's annual budget. Under the Florida and Virginia waivers, tenant out-of-pocket payments decline to $1.83 billion per year and to $1.58 billion per year, respectively. These declines result in budget increases for HUD of $172 million and $424 million per year, respectively, about 1 percent to 2 percent of HUD's annual budget. On the intermediate assumption that the TANF impact is equivalent to half the states pursuing Michigan/Vermont type reforms and the other half Virginia/Florida reforms, there would be a net cost increase to HUD of one-half percent to one-and-one-half percent.

Table 2.4 SIMULATED EFFECTS ON THE HUD BUDGET AT YEAR FIVE
(Annual)

	Prewaiver	Florida FTP	Michigan TSMF	Vermont WRP	Virginia VIP
Total rent payments by AFDC households	$2.00 bil	$1.83 bil	$2.04 bil	$2.07 bil	$1.58 bil
Increase (decrease) in housing assistance budget	—	$172 mil	($39 mil)	($69 mil)	$424 mil

Housing Cost Burdens of Unassisted Households

The simulated housing cost burdens of unassisted renters and owners under each of the waivers are shown in table 2.5.[42] Panel I shows cost burdens on the assumption that all households remain in the current dwelling; Panel II shows cost burdens on the assumption that households whose incomes change also change their housing. (Both sets of data are derived from imputed housing costs, as outlined in the methodology section. The absolute costs are shown in appendix table 2B.4.)

As the "overall average" entries in the table indicate, the prewaiver average housing cost burdens of unassisted renters on welfare are

Table 2.5 SIMULATED EFFECTS ON HOUSING COST BURDEN FOR UNASSISTED RENTERS AND OWNERS[a]

	Prewaiver	Florida FTP	Michigan TSMF	Vermont WRP	Virginia VIP
I. Remain in Place					
A. Unassisted Renters					
Unsubsidized job, on AFDC	36%	39%	36%	35%	28%
Unsubsidized job, off AFDC (before time limit)	48%[b]	33%	34%	34%	40%
Unsubsidized job after time limit	—	71%	—	—	39%
Subsidized job or work preparation, on AFDC	50%	55%	49%	49%	52%
Not employed, hit time limit	—	91%	—	—	231%
Exempt	49%	44%	45%	49%	49%
Overall Average	48%	52%	47%	46%	52%
B. Owners					
Unsubsidized job, on AFDC	24%	24%	24%	22%	18%
Unsubsidized job, off AFDC (before time limit)	29%[b]	20%	19%	22%	19%
Unsubsidized job after time limit	—	41%	—	—	23%
Subsidized job or work preparation on AFDC	28%	37%	30%	31%	36%
Not employed, hit time limit	—	42%	—	—	122%
Exempt	30%	25%	15%	29%	29%
Overall Average	29%	31%	28%	28%	29%

Table 2.5 SIMULATED EFFECTS ON HOUSING COST BURDEN FOR UNASSISTED
RENTERS AND OWNERS[a] (continued)

	Prewaiver	Florida FTP	Michigan TSMF	Vermont WRP	Virginia VIP
II. Income-Induced Move					
A. Unassisted Renters					
Unsubsidized job, on AFDC	36%	40%	37%	37%	32%
Unsubsidized job, off AFDC (before time limit)	48%[b]	34%	33%	34%	42%
Unsubsidized job after time limit	—	64%	—	—	40%
Subsidized job or work preparation, on AFDC	50%	54%	49%	50%	53%
Not employed, hit time limit	—	74%	—	—	169%
Exempt	49%	45%	45%	50%	49%
Overall Average	48%	50%	47%	47%	51%
B. Owners					
Unsubsidized job, on AFDC	24%	24%	24%	23%	19%
Unsubsidized job, off AFDC (before time limit)	29%[b]	21%	19%	22%	19%
Unsubsidized job after time limit	—	38%	—	—	23%
Subsidized job or work preparation, on AFDC	28%	36%	30%	31%	36%
Not employed, hit time limit	—	38%	—	—	109%
Exempt	30%	25%	15%	29%	28%
Overall Average	29%	30%	28%	28%	29%

Source: Authors' simulations based on 1994 AFDC-QC data.
a. Appendix table 2B.4 provides further detail.
b. Figures are overall averages. These groups did not exist prewaiver.

almost 50 percent, about two-thirds higher than the 30 percent rule
of thumb for affordable housing under HUD programs. None of the
four waiver programs has a large effect on these burdens. For renters,
there is a 2 to 4 percentage point increase in the cost burden overall
under the Florida and Virginia waivers, and a 1 to 2 percentage point
decrease in rent burden under the Michigan and Vermont waivers.
The housing cost burdens after waiver implementation are of the same

order of magnitude for owners as for renters, though the prewaiver average cost burden for owners is lower (at about 29 percent).

Under all state waivers, the cost burden for the small fraction of recipients who move off the rolls without hitting the time limit is substantially less than that of their counterparts on welfare prewaiver. For renters in this subgroup, the average cost burden is roughly 33 percent to 40 percent of income, for owners about 19 percent to 22 percent. If they move, their housing expenditures in absolute terms are 10 percent to 30 percent higher (appendix table 2B.4)—suggesting that, along with spending a smaller fraction of their income on rent, they may also improve the quality of their housing.

For all other categories, the Michigan and Vermont waivers change housing cost burdens very little. This is consistent with the modest increase in income for those who obtain work with no loss of income due to being dropped from the rolls. The Florida and Virginia waivers, in contrast, lead to wide disparities depending on employment status and whether time limits have been hit. The average housing cost burdens for renters on welfare with unsubsidized jobs under the Florida waiver are 39 percent and for owners 24 percent of income. These percentages change little under an income-induced residence change, and are about equal to those of their counterparts with unsubsidized jobs before waiver. Under the Virginia waiver, they are lower—28 percent for renters and 18 percent for owners. A change in residence increases these rates slightly.

By contrast, for those with unsubsidized jobs after hitting the time limit, the housing cost burden under the Florida waiver is 71 percent for renters and 41 percent for owners, with no change in residence. With a residential move, these rates fall to 64 percent (more than double the 30 percent HUD standard for affordable housing) and 21 percent for renters and owners, respectively. Under the Virginia waiver, those who hit the time limit and are employed fare better. The renter housing cost burden of 40 percent is 20 percent lower than for the prewaiver group and almost identical to the burden experienced by their counterparts still on AFDC under the other waivers. As before, this result is due to the strong estimated earnings impact of the Virginia waiver.

Not surprisingly, those who hit the time limit and are not employed fare worst. Although the AFDC-extension provision under the Florida FTP mutes the effect relative to Virginia's VIP, severe distress results for this group under both policies. With no change in residence, renters under the Florida waiver have to spend nearly their entire cash income on rent, while renters under the Virginia waiver have rents more than twice their cash incomes. If they move, renters under the Florida policy still spend three-quarters of their incomes on rent, while those under the Virginia waiver still have rents above their incomes. For owners, the pattern is similar though less pronounced. Both those in subsidized work or work preparation and those who are exempt experience little change in housing consumption as a result of the waivers.

The major factors driving overall changes in housing cost burdens are the relative success of employment incentives in lowering cost burdens and the offsetting impact of time limits. Under waivers without time limits, there is a modest decrease in housing cost burdens across the board and a correspondingly slight change toward better living quarters. Under waivers with time limits and stronger work incentives, there are two very different impacts. Those who obtain unsubsidized jobs fare appreciably better and are able to afford better dwellings than prewaiver. Those who do not maintain employment experience severe housing affordability problems.

CONCLUSIONS

The results of this initial attempt to simulate the effects of welfare reform carry several implications. First, the substantial fraction of welfare housholds who are also housing assistance recipients are clearly vulnerable under TANF. Many are not working, have little outside income, and are on welfare for long periods. Their current average spell of welfare receipt bumps up against the TANF five-year time limit. And more than 75 percent of assisted households have accumulated more than the 24 months allowed by Florida's and Virginia's waiver programs.

Second, these simulations suggest very different scenarios for those on, and off, welfare, particularly under welfare policies with both time limits and financial incentives to work. The more liberal incentive policies elicit responses that are positive for both recipients and for housing budgets. Under the Virginia waiver, for example, with the most liberal disregard policy of the four, workforce participation doubles from the prewaiver period, and incomes of nonexempt cases who have not hit the time limit increase by 20 percent for all housing groups. These changes lead to improved living conditions and reduced rent burdens. Positive effects are also apparent but much less dramatic for the Michigan and Vermont waivers, with disregard policies only somewhat more liberal than those under AFDC.

But waiver policies with time limits put a substantial portion of the welfare population at risk. Virginia's VIP is the worst case. The roughly one-third of assisted renters hitting the time limit experience more than a 50 percent decline in income, triggering increased HUD expenditures of $424 million. The one-fifth of unassisted renters and owners experience housing cost burdens that rise by more than 50 percent, almost surely necessitating a move to lower quality dwellings. The ability of unassisted renters to maintain safe and healthy living conditions, with average monthly incomes of $53 to $208, is highly questionable.

One of the many questions unanswered by our research to date is whether those living in assisted housing will, in fact, experience the same effects of welfare reform as other welfare recipients. Will their low rates of work and outside earnings and their long spells on welfare lead to different effects for them? Harris (1996) and others show that the best predictor of future earnings is past earnings. Assisted households have particularly sparse past earnings. Will they be as responsive as unassisted households to the strong work incentives in a program such as VIP? Will they be as responsive to the strict time limits? We are now pursuing these important questions.

APPENDIX A: SIMULATION METHODS[43]

General Approach

Our general approach to the simulation was to ask: "What would be the characteristics of the AFDC caseload for a typical month in 1994 if the simulated state's waiver had been in effect nationwide for five years?" In doing so, we assumed that what the caseload actually looked like in 1994 was similar to what it would have looked like under the waiver, differing only in a few key aspects. First, the simulated caseload would differ in who was exempt from work requirements. Second, when the waiver included a time limit provision, a portion of those in the actual 1994 caseload would have hit the time limit and would not be receiving AFDC payments in the simulation. Third, the simulated caseload would differ from the actual caseload in the proportion of cases with earnings and their level of earnings.

Finally, when the waiver included a family cap on benefits, a certain portion of families would lose benefits because of this cap.

The underlying assumption is that, except for those whose benefits are terminated due to time limits, the five years of the waiver would not change the size or composition of the caseload. More explicitly, we assume that individuals do not change their patterns of welfare use under the waivers, except insofar as the waiver impact on earnings may be sufficiently large to disqualify some cases from benefit receipt. Therefore, waiver impacts can be applied to the 1994 data without adjusting for changes in caseload size or composition that have cumulated over time. Clearly, this assumption may be questioned. There are at least three ways in which requirements to participate in an employment and training program may affect caseloads: (1) the requirements may serve as a deterrent; (2) gains expected as a result of participation in an employment and training program may be an incentive (Moffitt 1996); and (3) as work experience cumulates under work requirements, the future tendency to resort to AFDC may be reduced.

While incorporating these aspects in a model would be highly desirable, available evidence does not permit us to do so with any confidence. As yet, welfare reform remains a black box, with many ill-understood and interacting components. The waiver evaluations we rely on in this study indicate little, if any, difference between the AFDC use by control and experimental groups.[44] Thus, deterrent and incentive effects do not appear to be shifting the composition of the caseload under the waivers studied, at least in the short term. With regard to the longer term (e.g., five years), research shows that change in welfare usage among participants in welfare-to-work initiatives has been slight (Friedlander and Burtless 1995). These observations support our assumption of caseload dynamics playing a minimal role.

Key Specifics

1. *Imputation of Cumulative Duration on AFDC.* The AFDC-QC database contains only the length of the current AFDC spell, not the total amount of time a case has been on the rolls. Because it is the latter that is relevant for time limits, we imputed the length of any prior spell by applying the "Watson equation" method used in the Urban Institute's AFDC-QC model. This method applies the results of a regression equation estimated using Survey of Income and Program Participation (SIPP) data. Independent variables are the age of the mother, the age of the youngest child, and the length of

the current spell. We assumed that the previous spell began at the birth of the eldest child. This will result in an underestimation of cases affected by time limits because any time on AFDC prior to the implementation of the waiver was not counted. However, we expect any resulting underestimation to be small.

2. *Imposition of Family Cap.* In Virginia, the only state with a family cap, we accounted for the fact that no additional assistance is provided for a child born to a family that has been on assistance for 10 months or more. However, we did not simulate the possibility that the family cap would occasion a decline in family size, which in turn might reduce housing expenditures (see discussion of *Housing Costs* below). Therefore, our results for Virginia may overstate the housing cost burden.

3. *Exemptions from Work Requirements.* By and large, exemptions in the waivers are similar to those for the JOBS program, so that data on exempt groups are readily available in the AFDC-QC. One problematic category is the child care exemption. Three of the four waivers in our sample lowered the age at which a child qualified the parent for this exemption, setting the qualifying age at some fraction of a year rather than in whole years.[45] Because the AFDC-QC data report only whole years, the fractional portion of the age of the youngest child was assigned a random number, subject to the provision that this age not exceed the length of time on welfare. The direction of any resulting bias is not known, but is expected to be small.

4. *Simulation of Employment and Earnings.* To simulate the portion of nonexempt cases with employment under the waiver if applied nationwide, we first derived from the evaluation or comparison data the relative increase in the percentage of AFDC cases with unsubsidized employment in the state being simulated.[46] Where data existed for subgroups, the relative increase for these subgroups was derived.[47] In cases of multiple or overlapping estimates for subgroup impacts, we averaged these effects. These relative increases were then applied to the percentages of nonexempt cases with employment in the 1994 AFDC-QC data for each subgroup in each state to obtain target percentages for unsubsidized employment. Cases without employment were then randomly assigned to employment until the target percentage was met for each subgroup and state.

A similar procedure was followed for simulating earnings under the waiver. From the evaluation or comparison data, we first derived a waiver effect on average monthly earnings for those cases with work. Next, we computed average monthly earnings for each subgroup and state from the 1994 AFDC-QC data and multiplied this by the waiver effect on earnings to obtain post-waiver average monthly earnings. For those cases with employment in the 1994 data, monthly earnings under the waiver were computed to be 1994 monthly earnings times the waiver effect. Those without earnings in the 1994 data but simulated as being employed under the waiver were assigned the post-waiver average monthly earnings for their subgroup and state. In deriving the waiver impact on earnings, we assumed that any gain in earnings reported in the evaluations was distributed evenly across all cases. This probably results in an overestimate of the earnings of AFDC cases because the evaluations report average earnings for the entire control group or experimental group, including those not currently receiving assistance. It is likely that those no longer receiving assistance have higher earnings, pushing up the average.

5. *Imposition of Time Limits.* Using the imputed cumulative duration and the duration of the current spell on AFDC, those cases that exceeded the time limit specified in the state waiver lost AFDC benefits.[48] Whatever earnings a case had when the time limit hit were assumed to continue after hitting the time limit.[49]

6. *Imputation of Housing Costs.* The AFDC-QC database does not contain information on housing costs. Because this information is required to estimate the effect of the waivers on the housing cost burdens of unassisted renters and owners, we imputed housing costs using the 1992 Panel Study of Income Dynamics (PSID). The PSID analysis sample includes cases receiving AFDC or food stamps, or who had incomes below the poverty level, and were not receiving housing assistance. We estimated separate OLS regressions for renters and owners. We defined the dependent variable as housing costs net of maintenance and utilities (rent for renters; mortgage, taxes, and insurance for owners). The independent variables were the number of persons in the household; the age, sex and race of the household head; household income; value of food stamps received; and whether the residence was located in a small town or rural area.[50] Household income was specified as a quadratic in the renter equations (this specification made no difference in the owner equation and therefore was unnecessary). The results of these regressions are shown in appendix table 2A.1.

One of the most powerful indicators of housing costs was small town or rural residence. Ownership expenses associated with such locations were $155 per month lower than in more urbanized areas,

Appendix Table 2A.1 OLS REGRESSION FOR IMPUTING HOUSING COSTS FOR
UNASSISTED RENTERS AND OWNERS

Variable	Ownership Costs		Renter Costs	
	Coef.	t-Stat	Coef.	t-Stat
Constant	3,284.31	1.96	2,129.53	3.46
# persons in household	180.04	0.85	219.74	2.60
Age of household head	−25.00	−1.28	−13.13	−1.95
Annual food stamps/10,000	−291.92	−0.12	−845.51	−0.91
Female headed household	−51.57	−0.07	275.69	0.99
Minority household head	−759.38	−0.91	−190.03	−0.58
Annual income/10,000	487.14	2.45	1,884.60	4.98
(Annual income/10,000)^2			−280.06	−3.20
Small town/rural	−1,854.69	−2.77	−1,108.38	−4.37
R^2	0.23		0.32	
Number of observations	70		200	

Source: 1992 Panel Study of Income Dynamics.
Note: Small town/rural status was defined as residence in either the fringe county of a metropolitan area, an urban population of less than 20,000, or a completely rural area.

while renter costs were $92 per month lower. Because the AFDC-QC data do not contain any locational information, we specified a logit model to estimate the probability of residing in a small town or rural area. The independent variables were the same as the OLS on costs. The results of this model are shown in appendix table 2A.2. For owner-occupied households, larger families, the value of food stamps received, and a minority household head all increase the probability of urban residence, while for renters, older, female, and/or minority household heads are associated with an urban location. We used the logit results to impute small town or rural area of residence for cases in the AFDC-QC database.

Appendix Table 2A.2 LOGIT REGRESSION RESULTS FOR IMPUTING RURAL
RESIDENCE
Depvar = Logistic transformed measure of probability of rural
residence

Variable	Owners		Renters	
	Coef.	Std. error	Coef.	Std. error
Constant	2.12	1.28	0.85	0.86
# persons in household	−0.29	0.18	−0.01	0.13
Age of household head	0.00	0.02	−0.02	0.01
Annual food stamps/10,000	−1.96	2.03	0.40	1.45
Female headed household	0.17	0.56	−0.73	0.40
Minority household head	0.49	0.67	−1.04	0.44
Annual income/10,000	−0.13	0.18	0.29	0.63
(Annual income/10,000)^2			−0.12	0.16
−2 log likelihood	88.65		227.80	
Number of observations	70		200	

Source: 1992 Panel Study of Income Dynamics.
Note: Small town/rural status was defined as residence in either the fringe county of a
metropolitan area, an urban population of less than 20,000, or a completely rural area.

Appendix Table 2B.1 SIMULATED EFFECTS ON EMPLOYMENT STATUS OF ASSISTED HOUSEHOLDS
(Number of Households Affected)

	Prewaiver	Florida FTP	Michigan TSMF	Vermont WRP	Virginia VIP
A. Assisted Renters					
Employed					
Unsubsidized job, on AFDC	89,642	87,195	112,657	141,063	75,916
Unsubsidized job, off AFDC (before time limit)	(366)	8,698	4,736	5,581	8,076
Unsubsidized job after time limit	—	60,655	—	—	143,192
Subsidized job or work preparation, on AFDC	493,823	725,461	993,230	562,090	148,336
Not employed, hit time limit	—	65,837	—	—	365,859
Exempt	542,152	178,137	15,360	417,249	384,604
TOTAL	1,125,983	1,125,983	1,125,983	1,125,983	1,125,983
A1. Public Housing					
Employed					
Unsubsidized job, on AFDC	26,223	30,986	33,871	43,202	24,660
Unsubsidized job, off AFDC (before time limit)	(84)	2,748	2,746	2,005	2,305
Unsubsidized job after time limit	—	19,226	—	—	46,909
Subsidized job or work preparation, on AFDC	172,638	272,509	376,176	207,954	56,101
Not employed, hit time limit	—	23,237	—	—	133,236
Exempt	220,650	70,889	6,802	166,434	156,384
TOTAL	419,595	419,595	419,595	419,595	419,595

A2. Other Assisted Housing

Employed					
Unsubsidized job, on AFDC	63,419	56,209	78,786	97,861	51,256
Unsubsidized job, off AFDC (before time limit)	(282)	5,950	1,990	3,576	5,771
Unsubsidized job after time limit	—	41,429	—	—	96,283
Subsidized job or work preparation, on AFDC	321,185	452,952	617,054	354,136	92,235
Not employed, hit time limit	—	42,600	—	—	232,623
Exempt	321,502	107,248	8,558	250,815	228,220
TOTAL	706,388	706,388	706,388	706,388	706,388

Source: 1994 AFDC-QC data.

Notes: Numbers may not add to 100 percent due to rounding. Prewaiver "unsubsidized job off AFDC" not interpretable. Prewaiver estimate of unsubsidized employment based on QC respondents reporting some earnings. This item yields a slightly higher employment rate than the question of whether the respondent is employed.

Exemptions in Michigan are limited to those younger than 16 years old. Other exemptions to be determined by Social Contract. Neither impact evaluation data nor state data distinguish subsidized employment and employability program participation. Therefore these are combined.

A sizable proportion of those categorized as "subsidized job. . ." in Florida are those whose AFDC was extended because termination would put a child at risk. As a fraction of all cases, the proportion of assisted renters in this category is 36.6 percent.

Appendix Table 2B.2 SIMULATED EFFECTS ON EMPLOYMENT STATUS OF UNASSISTED HOUSEHOLDS

	Prewaiver Households	%	Florida FTP %	Michigan TSMF %	Vermont WRP %	Virginia VIP %
A. Unassisted Renters						
Employed	295,112	9.1	17.4	11.9	13.6	22.2
Unsubsidized job, on AFDC	295,112	9.1	11.0	11.2	12.9	9.8
Unsubsidized job, off AFDC (before time limit)	(1,205)	—	1.0	<1.0	<1.0	1.0
Unsubsidized job after time limit	—	—	5.4	—	—	11.4
Subsidized job or work preparation, on AFDC	1,275,563	39.4	60.8	86.6	36.5	16.1
Not employed, hit time limit	—	—	4.1	—	—	20.7
Exempt	1,668,166	51.5	17.9	1.7	49.8	40.9
TOTAL	3,240,046	100.0%	100.0%	100.0%	100.0%	100.0%

B. Unassisted Owners						
Employed	24,596	11.7	18.1	13.7	15.6	21.9
Unsubsidized job, on AFDC	24,596	11.7	11.5	13.0	14.9	10.7
Unsubsidized job, off AFDC (before time limit)	(223)	—	<1.0	<1.0	<1.0	<1.0
Unsubsidized job after time limit	—	—	5.9	—	—	10.5
Subsidized job or work preparation, on AFDC	89,654	42.8	46.4	82.0	28.0	15.0
Not employed, hit time limit	—	—	4.3	—	—	16.6
Exempt	95,141	45.4	31.1	4.2	56.0	46.3
TOTAL	209,614	100.0%	100.0%	100.0%	100.0%	100.0%

Source: 1994 AFDC-QC data.

Notes: Numbers may not add to 100 percent due to rounding. Prewaiver "unsubsidized job off AFDC" not interpretable.

Prewaiver estimate of unsubsidized employment based on QC respondents reporting some earnings. This item yields a slightly higher employment rate than the question of whether the respondent is employed.

Exemptions in Michigan are limited to those younger than 16 years old. Other exemptions to be determined by Social Contract.

Neither impact evaluation data nor state data distinguish subsidized employment and employability program participation. Therefore these are combined.

A sizable proportion of those categorized as "subsidized job. . ." in Florida are those whose AFDC was extended because termination would put a child at risk. As a fraction of all cases, the proportions in this category are 24.7 percent and 19.8 percent of unassisted renters and owners, respectively.

Appendix Table 2B.3   SIMULATED EFFECTS ON FOOD STAMPS, CASH INCOME, AND TOTAL INCOME

		Prewaiver	Florida FTP	Michigan TSMF	Vermont WRP	Virginia VIP
Public housing						
Unsubsidized job, on AFDC	Food stamps	$208	$215	$204	$204	$136
	Cash income	$830	$699	$755	$786	$1,034
	Total	$1,038	$914	$959	$990	$1,170
Unsubsidized job, off AFDC (before time limit)	Food stamps	$288	$136	$117	$124	$97
	Cash income		$879	$1,141	$1,029	$909
	Total	$288	$1,015	$1,258	$1,153	$1,006
Unsubsidized job after time limit	Food stamps		$225			$203
	Cash income		$378			$731
	Total		$603			$934
Subsidized job or work preparation, on AFDC	Food stamps	$256	$266	$253	$253	$252
	Cash income	$464	$414	$488	$490	$474
	Total	$720	$680	$741	$743	$726
Not employed, hit time limit	Food stamps		$217			$261
	Cash income		$271			$60
	Total		$488			$321
Exempt	Food stamps	$270	$242	$222	$250	$257
	Cash income	$498	$536	$525	$485	$465
	Total	$768	$778	$747	$735	$722
Overall averages	Food stamps	$260	$253	$248	$246	$244
	Cash income	$505	$449	$515	$521	$404
	Total	$765	$702	$763	$767	$648

Other assisted housing					
Unsubsidized job, on AFDC					
Food stamps	$196	$195	$191	$197	$130
Cash income	$835	$715	$812	$821	$1,013
Total	$1,031	$910	$1,003	$1,018	$1,143
Unsubsidized job, off AFDC (before time limit)					
Food stamps	$279	$133	$126	$129	$131
Cash income	$75	$848	$993	$1,119	$714
Total	$354	$981	$1,119	$1,248	$845
Unsubsidized job after time limit					
Food stamps		$225			$194
Cash income		$374			$685
Total		$599			$879
Subsidized job or work preparation, on AFDC					
Food stamps	$250	$254	$241	$238	$241
Cash income	$467	$402	$477	$478	$442
Total	$717	$656	$718	$716	$683
Not employed, hit time limit					
Food stamps		$221			$253
Cash income		$174			$49
Total		$395			$302
Exempt					
Food stamps	$254	$220	$153	$241	$240
Cash income	$477	$552	$517	$464	$472
Total	$731	$772	$670	$705	$712
Overall averages					
Food stamps	$247	$239	$234	$233	$230
Cash income	$505	$438	$516	$524	$398
Total	$752	$677	$750	$757	$628

Appendix Table 2B.3 SIMULATED EFFECTS ON FOOD STAMPS, CASH INCOME, AND TOTAL INCOME (continued)

		Prewaiver	Florida FTP	Michigan TSMF	Vermont WRP	Virginia VIP
All assisted renters						
Unsubsidized job, on AFDC	Food stamps	$200	$202	$195	$200	$132
	Cash income	$834	$709	$795	$810	$1,020
	Total	$1,034	$911	$990	$1,010	$1,152
Unsubsidized job, off AFDC (before time limit)	Food stamps	$281	$133	$121	$127	$174
	Cash income	$58	$858	$1,079	$1,087	$638
	Total	$339	$991	$1,200	$1,213	$812
Unsubsidized job after time limit	Food stamps		$225			$197
	Cash income		$375			$701
	Total		$600			$898
Subsidized job or work preparation, on AFDC	Food stamps	$252	$258	$246	$243	$249
	Cash income	$466	$407	$481	$483	$437
	Total	$718	$665	$727	$726	$686
Not employed, hit time limit	Food stamps		$220			$256
	Cash income		$208			$53
	Total		$428			$309
Exempt	Food stamps	$261	$229	$184	$244	$245
	Cash income	$486	$545	$521	$472	$477
	Total	$747	$774	$705	$717	$722
Overall averages	Food stamps	$252	$244	$239	$238	$235
	Cash income	$505	$442	$516	$523	$400
	Total	$757	$686	$755	$760	$635

Unassisted renters					
Unsubsidized job, on AFDC					
Food stamps	$201	$212	$197	$191	$137
Cash income	$977	$836	$927	$948	$1,168
Total	$1,178	$1,048	$1,124	$1,139	$1,305
Unsubsidized job, off AFDC (before time limit)					
Food stamps	$224	$142	$138	$141	$147
Cash income	$438	$1,060	$1,175	$1,090	$922
Total	$662	$1,202	$1,313	$1,230	$1,069
Unsubsidized job after time limit					
Food stamps		$221			$193
Cash income		$423			$816
Total		$644			$1,009
Subsidized job or work preparation, on AFDC					
Food stamps	$253	$255	$243	$247	$240
Cash income	$568	$527	$595	$604	$556
Total	$821	$782	$838	$851	$796
Not employed, hit time limit					
Food stamps		$223			$263
Cash income		$333			$128
Total		$556			$391
Exempt					
Food stamps	$253	$218	$188	$239	$241
Cash income	$605	$652	$602	$583	$582
Total	$858	$870	$790	$821	$823
Overall averages					
Food stamps	$248	$240	$236	$235	$229
Cash income	$624	$574	$636	$641	$572
Total	$872	$814	$872	$876	$801

Appendix Table 2B.3   SIMULATED EFFECTS ON FOOD STAMPS, CASH INCOME, AND TOTAL INCOME (continued)

		Prewaiver	Florida FTP	Michigan TSMF	Vermont WRP	Virginia VIP
Owners						
Unsubsidized job, on AFDC	Food stamps	$241	$239	$234	$232	$178
	Cash income	$834	$783	$780	$848	$1,052
	Total	$1,075	$1,022	$1,014	$1,080	$1,230
Unsubsidized job, off AFDC (before time limit)	Food stamps	$238	$172	$96	$146	$124
	Cash income	$484	$1,001	$1,350	$1,143	$1,006
	Total	$722	$1,173	$1,446	$1,289	$1,130
Unsubsidized job after time limit	Food stamps		$234			$216
	Cash income		$412			$755
	Total		$646			$971
Subsidized job or work preparation, on AFDC	Food stamps	$283	$294	$273	$275	$278
	Cash income	$502	$423	$513	$488	$444
	Total	$785	$717	$786	$763	$722
Not employed, hit time limit	Food stamps		$242			$295
	Cash income		$353			$126
	Total		$595			$421
Exempt	Food stamps	$278	$243	$166	$263	$261
	Cash income	$521	$583	$651	$522	$536
	Total	$799	$826	$817	$785	$797
Overall averages	Food stamps	$276	$264	$262	$260	$255
	Cash income	$550	$536	$560	$568	$537
	Total	$826	$800	$822	$828	$792

Breakdown for Florida cases on AFDC, subsidized job, or work prep.

	Owners	Assisted Renters	Public Housing	Other Assisted	Unassisted Renters
Not hit time limit					
Food stamps	$292	$247	$254	$242	$246
Cash income	$434	$439	$435	$430	$559
Total	$726	$686	$709	$672	$805
Hit time limit, AFDC extended					
Food stamps	$296	$267	$275	$263	$268
Cash income	$407	$382	$382	$383	$479
Total	$703	$649	$657	$646	$747

Appendix Table 2B.4 HOUSING COSTS AND HOUSING COST-TO-INCOME RATIOS FOR UNASSISTED RENTERS AND OWNERS

		Prewaiver	Florida FTP	Michigan TSMF	Vermont WRP	Virginia VIP
Unassisted renters						
Unsubsidized job, on AFDC	Ave. cost (post-waiver)	$350	$333	$345	$349	$376
	Cost burden (after move)	36%	40%	37%	37%	32%
	Cost burden (no move)	36%	39%	36%	35%	28%
Unsubsidized job, off AFDC (before time limit)	Ave. cost (post-waiver)	$248	$357	$386	$369	$327
	Cost burden (after move)	57%	34%	33%	34%	42%
	Cost burden (no move)	57%	33%	34%	34%	40%
Unsubsidized job after time limit	Ave. cost (post-waiver)		$334			$331
	Cost burden (after move)		64%			40%
	Cost burden (no move)		71%			39%
Subsidized job or work preparation, on AFDC	Ave. cost (post-waiver)	$284	$286	$294	$300	$283
	Cost burden (after move)	50%	54%	49%	50%	53%
	Cost burden (no move)	50%	55%	49%	49%	52%
Not employed, hit time limit	Ave. cost (post-waiver)		$248			$216
	Cost burden (after move)		74%			169%
	Cost burden (no move)		91%			231%
Exempt	Ave. cost (post-waiver)	$298	$291	$272	$288	$292
	Cost burden (after move)	49%	45%	45%	50%	49%
	Cost burden (no move)	49%	44%	45%	49%	49%
Overall averages	Ave. cost (post-waiver)	$297	$293	$300	$301	$288
	Cost burden (after move)	48%	50%	47%	47%	51%
	Cost burden (no more)	48%	52%	47%	46%	52%

Breakdown for Florida cases on AFDC, subsidized job, or work prep.

Not hit time limit	Ave. cost (post-waiver)	$290				
	Cost burden (after move)	52%				
	Cost burden (no move)	51%				
Hit time limit, AFDC extended	Ave. cost (post-waiver)	$279				
	Cost burden (after move)	58%				
	Cost burden (no move)	62%				
Owners						
Unsubsidized job, on AFDC	Ave. cost (post-waiver)	$198	$191	$187	$194	$204
	Cost burden (after move)	24%	24%	24%	23%	19%
	Cost burden (no move)	24%	24%	24%	22%	18%
Unsubsidized job, off AFDC (before time limit)	Ave. cost (post-waiver)	$146	$209	$253	$251	$142
	Cost burden (after move)	30%	21%	19%	22%	19%
	Cost burden (no move)	30%	20%	19%	22%	19%
Unsubsidized job after time limit	Ave. cost (post-waiver)		$173			$179
	Cost burden (after move)		38%			23%
	Cost burden (no move)		41%			23%
Subsidized job or work preparation, on AFDC	Ave. cost (post-waiver)	$159	$154	$156	$151	$151
	Cost burden (after move)	28%	36%	30%	31%	36%
	Cost burden (no move)	28%	37%	30%	31%	36%
Not employed, hit time limit	Ave. cost (post-waiver)		$135			$137
	Cost burden (after move)		38%			109%
	Cost burden (no move)		42%			122%
Exempt	Ave. cost (post-waiver)	$155	$147	$97	$151	$151
	Cost burden (after move)	30%	25%	15%	29%	28%
	Cost burden (no move)	30%	25%	15%	29%	27%

Appendix Table 2B.4 HOUSING COSTS AND HOUSING COST-TO-INCOME RATIOS FOR UNASSISTED RENTERS AND OWNERS
(continued)

	Prewaiver	Florida FTP	Michigan TSMF	Vermont WRP	Virginia VIP
Overall averages					
Ave. cost (post-waiver)	$157	$157	$158	$159	$157
Cost burden (after move)	29%	30%	28%	28%	29%
Cost burden (no more)	29%	31%	28%	28%	29%
Breakdown for Florida cases on AFDC, subsidized job, or work prep.					
Not hit time limit					
Ave. cost (post-waiver)	$156				
Cost burden (after move)	36%				
Cost burden (no move)	36%				
Hit time limit, AFDC extended					
Ave. cost (post-waiver)	$151				
Cost burden (after move)	37%				
Cost burden (no move)	38%				

Notes

This chapter is part of a larger project examining the interactions between welfare reform and actual and proposed changes in housing policy, and assessing alternative policy scenarios for reconfiguring government housing assistance. The authors gratefully acknowledge the support of The Ford Foundation and supplementary support from the Fannie Mae Foundation. They also are grateful to Paul Cullinan, Sheila Dacey, Linda Giannarelli, Pam Holcomb, Ruth Katz, Ed Lezear, Pam Loprest, Lydia Millington, Demetra Nightingale, Carla Pedone, Sharon Parrot, LaDonna Pavetti, and Steve Savner for their advice; to Paul Leonard for his comments on a preliminary draft presented at the midyear meeting of the American Real Estate and Urban Economics Association; and to David Kantor and Sally Katz for their research assistance.

1. A state must spend at least 80 percent of its pre-TANF expenditures.

2. About four percent of AFDC households receiving housing assistance also include at least one child receiving SSI, and an even smaller proportion include at least one immigrant receiving SSI. Available data do not allow us to calculate what proportion of these children have the types of disabilities that will now be excluded.

3. For example, children dropped from SSI will be added to the AFDC household, thereby increasing the AFDC payment.

4. When this chapter was written, the administration and both houses of Congress were contemplating changes in housing policy that would alter the automatic increases in housing subsidies to compensate for losses in income from welfare. Such a change was subsequently passed.

5. Although 1115 waiver authority has been available since the 1970s, states only began to define the direction of welfare reform during the Reagan years (Nightingale 1997).

6. Of the remaining states, three applications were approved but not implemented and four were pending. Thus, for the purposes of this analysis, we assume that the state waiver programs are the best representation of what the state is likely to do under TANF. There is currently no information on whether states with AFDC 1115 waivers will pursue welfare reform that corresponds to their waivers, in part because there is relatively little information required in the state plans and in part because many states were relatively vague about whether they would maintain their waivers (Savner 1997).

7. The third criterion required that we examine programs that had been operating for a sufficient period of time so that impacts could be observed. However, because welfare reform was very much in flux during the early 1990s, two of the waivers we have examined (Florida's FTP and Michigan's TSMF) were subsequently modified.

8. We recognize that these six states constitute a judgment sample, at best, and not a systematic or even a quota sample.

9. We cannot identify precisely which children will be dropped from SSI. However, we know that the majority will be those who qualified for SSI under the Individualized Functional Assessment (IFA) procedure. Therefore, for each state, we randomly dropped the appropriate proportion of children who had qualified through IFA.

10. We were unable to account for the exclusion of a subgroup of legal immigrants from SSI and food stamps. Excluded from this restriction are refugees who have been in the U.S. for less than five years and aliens with 40 quarters of work history in the U.S. (CBO 1996).

11. We expect the effects of these PRWORA provisions on housing will be modest. Food stamps are not counted as income by housing programs, so changes in food stamp benefits will not change the housing subsidy calculations for assisted households. Furthermore, many states have indicated that they plan to pick up the costs of AFDC, food stamps, and SSI for legal immigrants who, in any event, are present in a very small

proportion of AFDC households. Children on SSI also constitute a small proportion, and the roughly one-quarter that are expected to be dropped (CBO 1996) reduce this proportion even further.

12. EITC is not counted as income for housing assistance programs.

13. These liberalizations, which have received much less public attention than newly imposed restrictions on welfare receipt, should result in increases in the welfare rolls as additional households previously ineligible for AFDC now qualify for assistance. According to the Urban Institute TRIM microsimulation model, to change these features alone reduces HUD housing subsidies by a maximum of 0.7 percent (Giannarelli 1997). We will also make any necessary adjustments for the seven states that currently count some portion of housing assistance as income. Preliminary indications are that HUD will recertify income of assisted households in these states, resulting in an increased housing subsidy. Congressional proposals to liberalize the income eligibility rules of public housing, if passed into law, could increase these impacts significantly by increasing the number of two-parent families in public housing.

14. Reported sanction rates vary widely in the evaluation literature from one-third for Florida's FTP (Bloom et al. 1997) to 2.6 percent for Michigan's TSMF (Werner and Kornfeld 1996). As more precise data become available, we will incorporate them in future work, along with possible deterrent and incentive effects on caseload size. According to a report by the General Accounting Office (GAO), less than one percent of the monthly AFDC caseload experience full family sanctions on benefits in states reporting the highest number of such sanctions. Of these, approximately one-third later returned to AFDC (GAO 1997).

15. There is at least some reason to expect that these responses will be different, though there are plausible arguments for expecting both more positive, and more negative, effects. For impacts on working, for example, more positive effects would occur if housing acts as a "springboard" or "platform" for recipients, while more negative effects are consistent with both the more disadvantaged profile of housing assistance residents and with housing assistance acting to "cushion" the blows of time limits and work requirements.

16. Therefore, while the economic climate may influence the absolute magnitude of the numbers we present, it may not be a significant factor in determining the size of the relative change.

17. Because unassisted renter households constitute such a large majority of all AFDC households, their profile is roughly equivalent to that for all AFDC households.

18. The education variable has a great deal of missing data and should be interpreted particularly cautiously.

19. The employment hours variable should also be interpreted carefully because of substantial missing data.

20. Because of substantial missing data in the work hours variable, we are reluctant to interpret the resulting distributions. If we assume that the cases with missing data are distributed the same as cases with full data, there is little difference in the percentage of heads of owner households and assisted households who are working 30 hours or more per week.

21. Missing data on the work hours variable also hinders interpretation of differences in average outside earnings.

22. States comprising the lowest quintile of monthly AFDC payments in 1994 were: Mississippi, Alabama, Tennessee, South Carolina, Arkansas, Texas, Louisiana, Kentucky, and Indiana (also Puerto Rico).

23. WAGES, the statewide waiver program that superseded FTP in all but the two original pilot counties, has a family cap and full family sanction.

24. At the time of this writing, there was no information available on the implementation of this extension provision. Therefore, we assumed that welfare benefits would continue for the children in an AFDC unit if that unit received no other income. Subsequent findings from some welfare reform evaluation studies suggest that our interpretation of this provision may have been too liberal.

25. The waivers do not vary substantially in their approach to asset limits or exemptions. Florida, Vermont, and Virginia converge in asset limits and are quite generous, while Michigan is least so. Although Vermont's rule allowing recipients to retain all savings from earnings has the potential of being the most generous, it is unlikely that savings would exceed the $5,000 level allowed by Florida and Virginia in many cases. Florida's child care exemption is the most restrictive, while Michigan leaves most decisions regarding exemptions to negotiation as part of the Social Contract.

26. This alternative ordering of the states is borne out by some rough calculations (not shown) comparing earnings under the disregard to the prewaiver AFDC payment standard. Virginia offers the greatest financial incentive for work, followed by Florida, Michigan, and Vermont. The calculation assumes a full-time job at the minimum wage. The result for Virginia occurs both because its AFDC payment is the lowest of the four states ($291 for a family of three) and because its earned income disregard is most liberal.

27. Even under TANF, states may provide their own funds to support recipients after the federal time limit is reached.

28. Because this is a somewhat different subgroup than that reported in table 2.1 because it excludes the exempt, it has a somewhat higher rate of housing assistance receipt (25.7 percent compared to 24.6 percent).

29. The relatively large increase under Vermont's waiver is presumably due to a larger proportion of households in assisted housing who (a) have children younger than 18 months old and (b) have received AFDC for nearly three years—two features unique to Vermont.

30. Appendix table 2B.1 provides the number of households in each category and includes a breakdown of assisted households into public housing and other assisted housing groups. (Appendix table 2B.2 provides the proportions for unassisted renters and owners.)

31. In interpreting the figures for the proportion of households with unsubsidized employment, it is important to bear in mind that the data do not permit the explicit simulation of what happens to cases after they hit the time limit. We assumed that the same waiver effect for employment applied to those cases reaching the time limit as to those who did not. Thus, in our simulations all cases in unsubsidized work *after* hitting the time limit were also in unsubsidized work at an earlier time *before* hitting the time limit. And the waiver effect on employment for the two states with time limits is the sum of those with unsubsidized jobs, whether their benefits have been terminated by the time limits or not. When this is taken into account, it seems clear that the more generous income disregards of Florida and Virginia are successful in inducing more unsubsidized employment, though whether these disregards would act as such an incentive in states where benefit levels were more ample remains a question.

32. This large proportion is also likely to occur because of the lack of information about exempt groups.

33. As noted earlier, research just being released on welfare reform suggests that this assumption may have been too liberal.

34. In Vermont, this applied only to those on AFDC for 30 months if a single parent and 15 months if a two-parent family.

35. The very low exemption rate for Michigan shown in the table reflects the only category that is stipulated in the program, namely, minors age 16 or younger. The actual rate would presumably be higher, but there is no way to estimate it with available information.

36. All simulations assume housing policies in effect through August 1997. Proposed changes, especially the elimination of subsidy adjustments if incomes decrease because of sanctions or noncompliance with welfare reform, would undoubtedly affect these results. Some of these changes have now been adopted.

37. Earnings and income were deflated to 1994 because we are using the 1994 AFDC-QC for the simulations. Only average cash income is shown. The complete results showing the value of food stamps and the total of cash income plus food stamps are shown in appendix table 2B.3.

38. In particular, the more liberal earnings disregards compared to the "30 and 1/3" rule that prevailed in the prewaiver period and the emphasis on engagement in some work-related activity.

39. Benefit reduction refers to child-only cases where AFDC is extended to avoid risk to the child(ren).

40. Florida and Virginia have the lowest payment standards of the four states.

41. There is little change in income for those in subsidized work or work preparation or for the exempt group. These changes are driven entirely by exemption rules. Florida's case is somewhat different because the AFDC extension cases received AFDC for the child only.

42. Housing costs were deflated to 1994 dollars. The housing cost burden of renters is the percentage of total household income that is spent on rent, while for owners it is the percentage of income spent on mortgage payments, taxes, and insurance. Neither renter nor owner costs include utilities, and owner costs do not include maintenance and repair.

43. In addition to the elements listed here, we also incorporated changes in the food stamp provision of PRWORA, the removal of a proportion of SSI children from the rolls, and did not increase food stamps if the case reached the time limit and we experienced a decline in income.

44. The potential deterrent effect of work requirements is most troubling. There is anecdotal evidence that this effect is responsible for the reduction in caseload in several sites (Pavetti 1997). However, no studies provide an accurate assessment of this effect under different programs, nor what the economic circumstances of those who fail to "show up" may be.

45. In Michigan, this may be negotiated as part of the Social Contract.

46. For example, if the percent of cases with unsubsidized employment were 10 percent in the control group and 15 percent in the experimental group, the relative increase would be 50 percent.

47. Examples of such subgroups include those defined by the number of parents in the unit, the duration of AFDC receipt, and the type of time limit faced.

48. It is possible that time limits might invoke a behavioral response of early withdrawal from AFDC to conserve benefits. This does not confound our simulation, however, because it is irrelevant whether a case withdrew voluntarily or not. Either way, it would not be receiving benefits.

49. It might be argued that earnings would increase after hitting the time limit because the loss of AFDC benefits would be such a strong incentive to work, particularly for those cases without any earnings. However, it might also be argued that earnings would

fall after hitting the time limit, because AFDC may be combined with certain work-enabling features, such as child care and transportation assistance.

50. Defined on the basis of the Beale code in the PSID as either the fringe county of a metropolitan area, an urban area with population less than 20,000, or a completely rural area.

References

Bloom, Daniel, et al. 1997. *The Family Transition Program: Implementation and Early Impacts of Florida's Initial Time-Limited Welfare Program.* New York: Manpower Demonstration Research Corporation.

Congressional Budget Office (CBO). 1996. "Federal Budgetary Implications of the Personal Responsibility and Work Opportunity Reconciliation Act of 1996." *CBO Memorandum.* Washington, D.C.: Author.

Friedlander, Daniel, and Gary Burtless. 1995. *Five Years After: The Long-Term Effects of Welfare-to-Work Programs.* New York: Russell Sage Foundation.

General Accounting Office (GAO). 1997. *Welfare Reform: States' Early Experiences with Benefit Termination.* GAO-HEHS-97-74. Washington, D.C.: Author.

Giannarelli, Linda. 1997. Unpublished tabulations from TRIM, July 17.

Harris, Kathleen. 1996. "Life after Welfare: Women, Work, and Repeat Dependency," *American Sociological Review* 61: 407–426.

Moffitt, Robert. 1996. "The Effect of Employment and Training Programs on Entry and Exit from Welfare Caseload." *Journal of Policy Analysis and Management* 15(1, Winter): 32–50.

Nightingale, Demetra. 1997. Personal communication.

Pavetti, LaDonna. 1997. Personal communication.

Savner, Steven. 1997. Personal communication.

U.S. Department of Health and Human Services. 1994. *AFDC.–Quality Control (QC) Database.* Washington, D.C.: U.S. Government Printing Office.

Vermont Department of Social Welfare. 1997. *Third Annual Report to the General Assembly on Vermont's Welfare Restructuring Project.* Waterbury, Vt. January.

Virginia Department of Health and Human Resources (VA-DHR). 1996. *Making Welfare Work: Virginia's Transformation from Dependency to Opportunity.* Richmond, Va.: Author.

Virginia Department of Social Services (VA-DSS). 1997. *Virginia Independence Program: Monthly Report.* March.

Wallace, John, and James Riccio. 1997. "The Structure and Implementation of Housing-Related Self-Sufficiency Programs: Lessons from Work-to-

Welfare." In *The Implications of Welfare Reform for Housing*. Baltimore, Md.: Evergreen House. July 22.

Werner, Alan, and Robert Kornfeld. 1994. *The Evaluation of To Strengthen Michigan Families: Second Annual Report: First-Year Impacts*. Cambridge, Mass.: Abt Associates. November.

_____. 1995. *The Evaluation of To Strengthen Michigan Families: Third Annual Report: Second-Year Impacts*. Cambridge, Mass.: Abt Associates. November.

_____. 1996. *The Evaluation of To Strengthen Michigan Families: Fourth Annual Report: Third-Year Impacts*. Cambridge, Mass.: Abt Associates. June.

Chapter Three

HOUSING AND WELFARE REFORM: GEOGRAPHY MATTERS

G. Thomas Kingsley and Peter Tatian

About one-fifth of all households that received Aid to Families with Dependent Children (AFDC) income in 1995 also received housing assistance through public housing and other Department of Housing and Urban Development (HUD) programs. Furthermore, those receiving HUD assistance account for a much larger share of long-term welfare recipients—those likely to have the most difficulty finding and retaining employment—than welfare families that do not receive federal housing assistance. Among AFDC beneficiaries in 1994, for example, the median cumulative period of welfare recipiency for those who also received HUD assistance was 57 months; for those not receiving HUD assistance, the comparable period was 37 months (Newman and Harkness 1998).

As benefits are reduced under the new welfare reform law, outcomes and opportunities for welfare households receiving housing assistance will be quite different from those for welfare recipients who do not receive housing subsidies. First, the housing assistance formula will provide an important cushion. Families receiving HUD assistance will be assured a place to live. If their welfare payments are reduced and they do not find a job or other replacement income, by law, their housing subsidy will go up as their welfare payment goes down. Second, where sizable numbers of assisted families live together in one project, special opportunities for providing welfare-to-work and other supportive services exist that are not possible where recipients are spread through the private housing stock. Housing assistance could thus be a platform for making welfare-to-work programs more effective. Research by Newman and Schnare (1988, 1992) on the relationships between welfare and housing assistance, and on the potential of using assisted housing as a context for initiatives to help the poor move toward self-sufficiency, laid a strong foundation for this idea several years ago. And it now appears that HUD is begining to give more emphasis to this theme in its programs (HUD 1996a).

There are good reasons, therefore, for designers of welfare reform response strategies to pay attention to the relationship between welfare and housing assistance. But more information is needed before they can devise workable approaches. Of first importance is finding out whether the nature and extent of HUD assistance, and the overlap between HUD assistance and welfare, are relatively uniform in different urban areas or whether these characteristics vary substantially from place to place. If the latter is the case, no single "one size fits all" approach is likely to make sense.

Until recently, data have not been available even to characterize differences in the patterns of housing assistance across cities, let alone to look at variations in the overlap between housing benefits and other forms of public assistance. In the last few years, however, HUD has made important progress in improving its internal data systems. One of its new data sets, A Picture of Subsidized Households (APSH) permits analysis of these relationships. It contains detailed data on HUD-assisted housing and its beneficiaries by location as of 1995–96 for each of HUD's three major types of assistance: public housing (low-rent projects owned and operated by local public housing authorities, or PHAs); publicly assisted housing (privately owned projects with subsidies to assure reduction in tenant rents); and tenant-based assistance (where beneficiaries do not live in projects but receive subsidies to help pay the rent in units of their own choosing in the private housing market). This paper uses data from the APSH to measure variations in patterns of HUD assistance, and the overlap between welfare and housing assistance, across the nation's 100 largest metropolitan areas.

THE APSH DATA FILE

Before low-income households can receive HUD assistance, their income and other characteristics must be certified to determine their eligibility and the subsidy amount they are entitled to receive. After they begin to receive assistance, their incomes are regularly recertified, normally on an annual cycle. The certification/recertification forms that document the results contain a wealth of information about each household, including data on demographic characteristics and household composition as well as income, by source.[1]

Certifications are performed locally, but over the past few years HUD has made a major effort to enforce the requirement that the data for each household be submitted to its central office as well. HUD assembles the information in two large machine-readable data files: the MTCS file for public housing tenants and households receiving tenant-based assistance and the TRACS file for those living in publicly assisted housing. These files have already been used for valuable research (see, for example, Goering, Kamely, and Richardson 1994; and Khadduri and Martin 1997).

To make information about its assistance programs available to a broader range of audiences, HUD compiled the APSH file from these and other internal records for release on the Internet.[2] APSH contains summary demographic and income characteristics for the tenants of each individual public and publicly assisted housing project in the country, and for households receiving tenant-based assistance under the jurisdiction of each local PHA. An important contribution of APSH is that it also records the residential location of most assisted households (by census tract), so that varying spatial patterns of HUD assistance can be examined within urban areas.

For this analysis, we group the data into three main program categories as follows (dates in parenthesis are the status dates for information in the file):[3]

1. *Public Housing* (9/96).
2. *Publicly Assisted Housing,* which includes: (a) Section 8 Moderate Rehabilitation (9/96); (b) Section 8 New Construction and Substantial Rehabilitation (10/95); (c) Section 236 (10/95); and (d) other subsidized projects insured by the Federal Housing Administration (FHA) (10/95).
3. *Tenant-Based Assistance* (9/96), which includes the Section 8 Certificate and Voucher programs.

We then create a subset of the file containing data for the 100 largest metropolitan areas (Metropolitan Statistical Areas [MSAs] and Primary Metropolitan Statistical Areas [PMSAs], as defined by the U.S. Bureau of the Census, ranked by 1990 population).[4] We focus on variations in housing assistance across large metropolitan areas because we judge that metropolitan-wide labor market and housing market conditions are ultimately the context in which responses to welfare reform, and devolution more generally, need to be worked out. The central city is too small a unit for analysis and service planning, and both metropolitan housing and labor market conditions can vary dramatically within states.

TOTAL ASSISTED HOUSEHOLDS

Table 3.1 summarizes the dimensions of the APSH. Altogether, APSH registers a total of 4.21 million households that receive housing assistance in the United States (50 states and the District of Columbia), plus 6,000 in various territories (including Guam and the Virgin Islands). Of the U.S. total, 28 percent are in public housing, 40 percent are in publicly assisted housing, and 32 percent receive tenant-based assistance.

Over half of the U.S. total (58 percent) live in the 100 largest metropolitan areas, which together account for 60 percent of all assisted households in public housing and publicly assisted housing, and 53 percent of those receiving tenant-based assistance. Of the 1.69 million households in publicly assisted housing, 52 percent are in Section 8 New Construction and Substantial Rehabilitation projects, 25 percent are in Section 236 projects, 6 percent are in Section 8 Moderate Rehabilitation units, and the remaining 17 percent are in other subsidized FHA-insured projects.

REPORTING RATES AND GEOCODING

The limitations of this database need to be emphasized. HUD data files contain accurate counts of the total number of assisted households in each project, but they do not have certification records for all of these households. In creating the APSH record for a project, HUD summarized the characteristics of those for which they had certification data and blew them up proportionately to yield project totals. If

Table 3.1 ASSISTED HOUSEHOLDS (IN THOUSANDS), BY PROGRAM

| | | United States (50 States + D.C.) | | |
	Total	Total	100 Largest Metros	Rest of U.S.	Territories
Public Housing	1,188	1,184	709	475	4
Publicly Assisted Housing					
Sec. 8 Mod. Rehab.	105	105	53	52	0
Sec. 8 New Const. & Sub. Rehab.	879	879	496	383	0
Sec. 236	429	429	297	132	0
Other FHA with Subsidies	280	280	176	105	0
Subtotal	1,694	1,694	1,021	672	0
Tenant-Based Assistance	1,333	1,331	708	623	2
Total	4,214	4,208	2,438	1,770	6

30 percent of the available certification records were for elderly house-holds, for example, the file indicates 30 percent of all project house-holds as being elderly.

Table 3.2 summarizes information on the completeness of data in APSH for the largest 100 metropolitan areas. In the median case, data on household characteristics are based on completed certification re-ports for 80 percent of all assisted households, with reporting rates ranging from a low of 36 percent (Anaheim, CA) to a high of 96 percent (Tucson, AZ). Median reporting rates are 83 percent for public hous-ing, 77 percent for publicly assisted housing, and 88 percent for tenant-based assistance.

The completeness of APSH geocoding reaches even higher percent-ages, but also varies widely. In the median case overall, census tract identifiers are on the file for the residences of 87 percent of all assisted households. By program, the medians are 85 percent for public hous-ing, 93 percent for publicly assisted housing, and 96 percent for tenant-based assistance. In the publicly assisted housing category, HUD considered information provided on locations of Section 8 Mod-erate Rehabilitation projects to be both fragmented and suspect and did not include any census tract codes for that program in APSH. Implicitly, therefore, average geocoding rates for the other components of publicly assisted housing are higher than those shown on the table.

In most areas, then, household reporting and geocoding rates are quite high. However, to ensure that we are not relying on estimates from housing authorities with large amounts of missing data, in this

Table 3.2 HOUSEHOLD REPORTING AND GEOCODING RATES FOR
100 LARGEST METROPOLITAN AREAS

	Median	Mean	Minimum	Maximum	Std. Dev.	Coef. Var.
Percent of Assisted Households **with Certification Records**						
Public Housing	83	76	0	99	20	0.26
Publicly Assisted Housing	77	75	18	96	12	0.16
Tenant-Based Assistance	88	81	31	99	19	0.23
Total	80	77	36	96	12	0.16
Percent of Assisted Households, **Census Tract Codes on File**						
Public Housing	85	76	0	100	25	0.33
Publicly Assisted Housing	93	90	0	100	14	0.16
Tenant-Based Assistance	96	83	0	100	24	0.29
Total	87	83	0	99	16	0.19

paper: (1) when we report on household characteristics for programs within metropolitan areas, we include only areas where reporting rates are 60 percent or higher; (2) when we report on spatial patterns for any program within metropolitan areas, we include only those areas where geocoding success rates are 60 percent or higher.

Unfortunately, some of the largest and most important metropolitan areas are missing sufficient data and are excluded from parts of our analysis. Appendixes A and B show which specific metropolitan areas do not meet the minimal reporting or geocoding criteria. These excluded areas include: Chicago (for all programs); Atlanta and Philadelphia (for public housing and tenant-based assistance); Boston (for both public and publicly assisted housing); Washington, D.C. (for tenant-based assistance and publicly assisted housing); Los Angeles (for tenant-based assistance); Pittsburgh (for public housing); and Minneapolis (for publicly assisted housing). Taken together, the metropolitan areas excluded from our analyses of household characteristics account for about one-quarter of all the households receiving housing assistance.

The absence of reliable data for these metropolitan areas prevents us from fully describing the distribution of welfare recipients among a large portion of housing-assisted households. Nevertheless, our main conclusion, that there is enormous variation in the extent to which these two types of assistance overlap, seems to be well supported by the data from the remaining three-quarters of the population.

THE PATTERN OF FEDERAL HOUSING ASSISTANCE

This section looks at the overall extent of housing assistance provided, program mix, types of households served (by age and race), project size, and spatial concentration in poverty areas.

How Much Housing Assistance Is Provided?

The amount of housing assistance now provided in America's metropolises varies greatly. As might be expected, larger areas generally have substantial assistance programs. The four largest are the metropolitan areas of New York (264,100 assisted households), Chicago (119,900), Los Angeles (117,000) and Boston (78,100). Together, these account for 14 percent of the U.S. total, 23 percent of the total in the 100 largest metropolitan areas. We examine the distribution in relation to comparative needs, relating the number of households receiving HUD assistance to the total number of low-income renter households in each area (from the 1990 census).[5]

We would not expect the distribution to be uniform. Over the years, HUD has allocated assistance to localities based on a mix of measures of need and administrative readiness to use additional funds. As noted earlier, some localities have been much more aggressive in seeking HUD assistance than others. In the past, when one city has been unable to take advantage of its initial allocation (often because it did not have a sufficient number of projects in the pipeline ready for construction), HUD has reallocated assistance to other areas that were prepared to proceed. Nonetheless, the actual variations (tables 3.3 and 3.4) are even more substantial than could have been expected. Overall, the number of HUD-assisted households as a share of all low-income renters ranges from 8 percent (Anaheim–Santa Ana) to a high of 50 percent (Providence). The median share across the top 100 metropolises is 22 percent.

Among the five metropolitan areas ranking highest by this measure, three are in the northeast (Providence, Hartford, and Pittsburgh) and two are in the South (Mobile and Knoxville). Of the five lowest, three are in California (Anaheim–Santa Ana, Riverside–San Bernardino, and San Diego) and two are in Texas (Houston and Austin).

PROGRAM MIX

There are also marked variations in the particular HUD programs different areas have chosen to emphasize. Across the 100 metropolitan areas, the share of all assisted households in public housing ranges from 0 to 60 percent. For publicly assisted housing, the range is from 0 to 74 percent, and the tenant-based assistance shares range from 8 percent to 97 percent. Among programs operated by PHAs, older cities generally have a higher share in public housing, since they demonstrated the greatest needs in the 1950s, 1960s, and early 1970s, when that program was growing rapidly. Cities that have experienced rapidly growing poverty populations in the more recent period, when tenant-based assistance has been dominant, have larger shares in that program. The characteristics of the local developer community and housing market conditions are, of course, also important.

THE PATTERN OF HUD ASSISTANCE INTENSITY

In general, however, metropolitan areas do not specialize primarily in only one form of housing assistance. Some metropolitan areas rank quite highly in assistance intensity (assisted households as a share of low-income renters) for all three types of HUD programs, while others

Table 3.3 SELECTED HOUSING ASSISTANCE INDICATORS FOR 100 LARGEST METROPOLITAN AREAS

Indicators	N	Median	Mean	High	Low	Std. Dev.	Coef. Var.
Pct. HUD-Asst. Hshlds. of Low-Income Renters (1990)							
Public Housing	100	5.9	6.0	14.9	0.0	3.6	0.60
Publicly Assisted Housing	100	9.0	9.1	25.1	0.0	4.1	0.45
Tenant-Based Assistance	100	6.3	6.8	22.8	1.7	3.1	0.46
Total	100	22.1	21.9	50.1	7.8	7.6	0.35
Pct. of HUD-Assisted Households by Program							
Public Housing	100	26.2	25.8	59.9	0.0	11.2	0.43
Publicly Assisted Housing	100	41.1	41.4	74.1	0.2	12.3	0.30
Tenant-Based Assistance	100	30.6	32.8	96.8	7.8	14.7	0.45
Total	100	100.0	100.0	100.0	100.0	0.0	0.00
Pct. Elderly Household Head							
Public Housing	79	28.4	31.0	83.5	12.5	11.5	0.37
Publicly Assisted Housing	89	42.1	44.4	73.7	22.9	11.5	0.26
Tenant-Based Assistance	85	14.9	16.0	39.6	5.0	6.7	0.42
Total	90	30.7	32.0	57.3	17.6	8.2	0.26
Pct. African-American Household Head							
Public Housing	79	55.2	51.5	96.9	1.1	30.1	0.58
Publicly Assisted Housing	89	33.4	33.5	72.5	1.6	19.1	0.57
Tenant-Based Assistance	85	46.6	46.7	97.0	1.9	25.3	0.55
Total	90	40.9	41.0	84.5	0.0	23.0	0.00

Pct. Hispanic Household Head							
Public Housing	79	5.5	15.6	96.9	0.1	21.6	1.38
Publicly Assisted Housing	89	4.0	11.8	83.9	0.3	16.1	1.16
Tenant-Based Assistance	85	5.6	14.5	94.7	0.1	19.4	1.33
Total	90	4.9	13.2	93.7	0.4	17.7	1.34
Pct. in Large Projects (250+ Units)							
Public Housing	99	32.4	32.0	89.1	0.0	23.7	0.74
Publicly Assisted Housing	100	10.4	12.9	74.2	0.0	11.4	0.88
Total	100	13.0	14.8	61.8	0.0	11.4	0.77
Pct. in High-Poverty Tracts (30% + Poverty)							
Public Housing	82	45.9	47.9	88.6	0.0	20.1	0.42
Publicly Assisted Housing	98	20.9	23.5	62.2	0.0	12.2	0.52
Tenant-Based Assistance	83	15.1	17.0	58.3	0.1	11.5	0.68
Total	95	23.7	26.6	66.4	0.0	13.1	0.49

Table 3.4 HIGHEST AND LOWEST METROPOLITAN AREAS FOR KEY INDICATORS

Indicators	Highest 5		Lowest 5	
Pct. HUD-Asst. Households of Low-Income Renters	Providence, RI	50	Anaheim–Santa Ana, CA	8
	Hartford, CT	44	Riverside–San Bernardino, CA	9
	Knoxville, TN	36	Houston, TX	9
	Mobile, AL	35	San Diego, CA	9
	Pittsburgh, PA	35	Austin, TX	10
Pct. Elderly Household Head	Miami-Hialeah, FL	57	Charleston, SC	18
	New Haven–Meriden, CT	55	Albuquerque, NM	20
	Providence, RI	53	Bakersfield, CA	21
	Bergen-Passaic, NJ	51	Tucson, AZ	22
	Worcester, MA	50	Columbia, SC	22
Pct. African-American Household Head	Norfolk–Virginia Beach, VA	84	El Paso, TX	2
	Charleston, SC	82	Honolulu, HI	2
	Gary-Hammond, IN	82	Scranton/Wilkes-Barre, PA	3
	Richmond-Petersburg, VA	82	Salt Lake City–Ogden, UT	4
	Raleigh-Durham, NC	81	Worcester, MA	5
Pct. Hispanic Household Head	El Paso, TX	94	Akron, OH	0
	San Antonio, TX	69	Memphis, TN-AR-MS	0
	Albuquerque, NM	63	Johnson City–Kingsport, TN-VA	0
	Miami-Hialeah, FL	59	Mobile, AL	1
	Tucson, AZ	48	Birmingham, AL	1

Pct. in Large Projects (250+ Units)

City	Pct.	City	Pct.
New York, NY	62	Bakersfield, CA	0
New Orleans, LA	40	Baton Rouge, LA	0
Richmond-Petersburg, VA	39	Charleston, SC	0
Birmingham, AL	38	Fresno, CA	0
Chicago, IL	34	Grand Rapids, MI	0
		Johnson City–Kingsport, TN-VA	0
		Lansing–East Lansing, MI	0
		Oxnard-Ventura, CA	0
		Vallejo-Fairfield-Napa, CA	0
		Wichita, KS	0

Pct. in High-Poverty Tracts (30%+ Poverty)

City	Pct.	City	Pct.
New York, NY	66	Vallejo-Fairfield, CA	0
Mobile, AL	61	San Jose, CA	2
Flint, MI	52	Honolulu, HI	3
Gary-Hammond, IN	52	Bergen-Passaic, NJ	6
El Paso, TX	50	Scranton/Wilkes-Barre, PA	10

Figure 3.1 METROPOLITAN VARIATIONS IN HOUSING ASSISTANCE INTENSITY:
PUBLICLY ASSISTED HOUSING VS. PUBLIC HOUSING

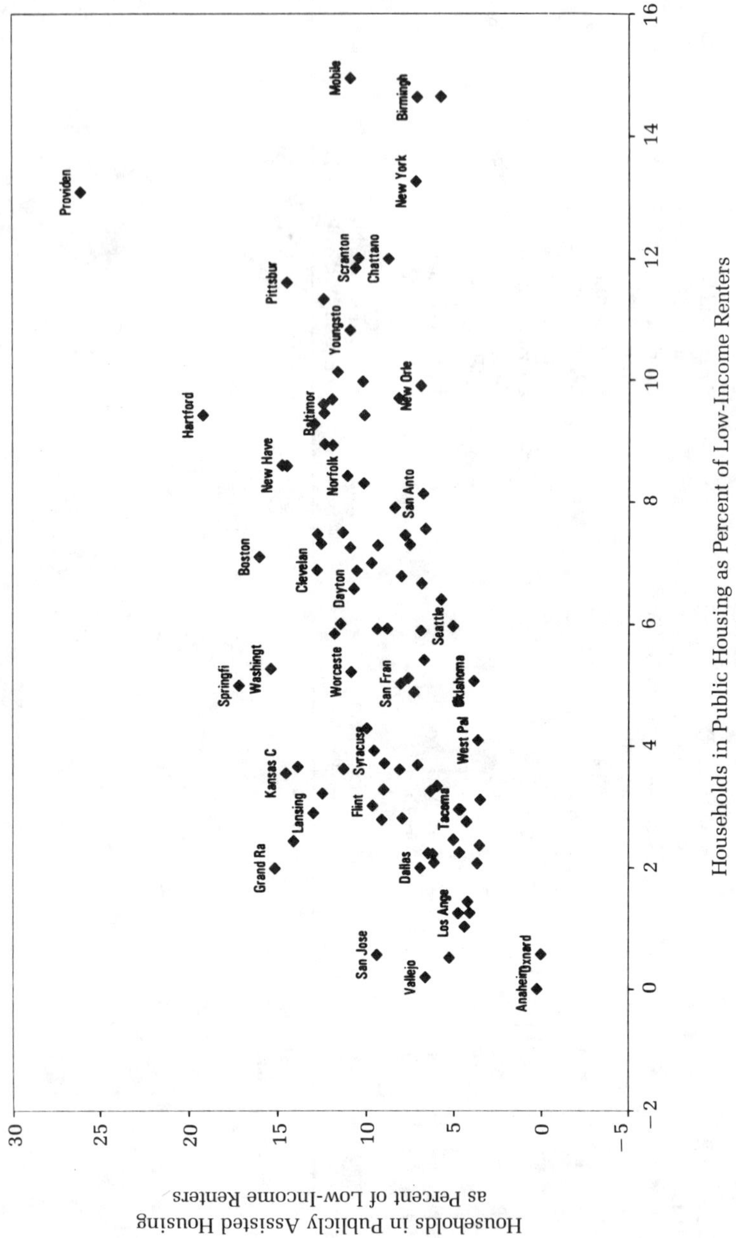

Households in Public Housing as Percent of Low-Income Renters

Households in Publicly Assisted Housing
as Percent of Low-Income Renters

rank close to the bottom in all categories. Intensity scores for public housing and publicly assisted housing are highly correlated with overall HUD assistance intensity (correlation coefficients of 0.76 and 0.79, respectively) and for tenant-based assistance somewhat less so (0.52).

Still, there are notable variations around these tendencies, as illustrated in the scatter diagrams in figures 3.1 and 3.2. Figure 3.1 plots the assistance intensity for publicly assisted housing compared with that for public housing. Those ranking highest for publicly assisted housing are generally in the midwest and northeast, and those for public housing in these same regions and in the southeast. Southwestern metropolises are typically on the low side in both categories. Some of those ranking highest for publicly assisted housing, however (e.g., Grand Rapids; Kansas City; Springfield, MA), have comparatively low intensities for public housing, and others (e.g., Birmingham, New York, and New Orleans) have comparatively high intensities. Figure 3.2 plots the intensity for tenant-based assistance compared with that for public housing. Here, western and southwestern metropolises are clearly in a stronger position. Oakland; Vallejo, CA; San Jose; and Albuquerque, for example, have high intensities for tenant-based assistance. But some eastern metropolises (e.g., Hartford; Bridgeport, CT; Knoxville; Providence) are on the high side in this category as well. Metropolitan areas with the lowest intensities for tenant-based assistance are spread across the spectrum with respect to public housing intensity (e.g., Lansing, Detroit, Memphis, New York).

To search for possible explanations of the pattern of variation in HUD assistance across metropolitan areas, we ran correlation analyses relating HUD assistance intensities (total and by program type) to a series of other 1990 census variables used to characterize metropolitan conditions. These include total population size, unemployment rate, poverty rate, education levels (shares of adults who had not graduated from high school), shares of households in different racial/ethnic groups, shares of population that were foreign born or had moved from a different house over the preceding five years, the ratio of central city to metropolitan median incomes, and indexes of segregation/concentration (dissimilarity indexes) with respect to the internal census tract distributions of poverty and African-American residence.

This analysis does not identify any strong patterns or relationships, with none of the correlation coefficients exceeding 0.50. For total HUD assistance intensity, the highest coefficients relate to the percentage of the population that had moved over the preceding five years (−0.47), the dissimilarity index for African Americans (+0.33), and

Figure 3.2 METROPOLITAN VARIATIONS IN HOUSING ASSISTANCE INTENSITY:
TENANT-BASED ASSISTANCE VS. PUBLIC HOUSING

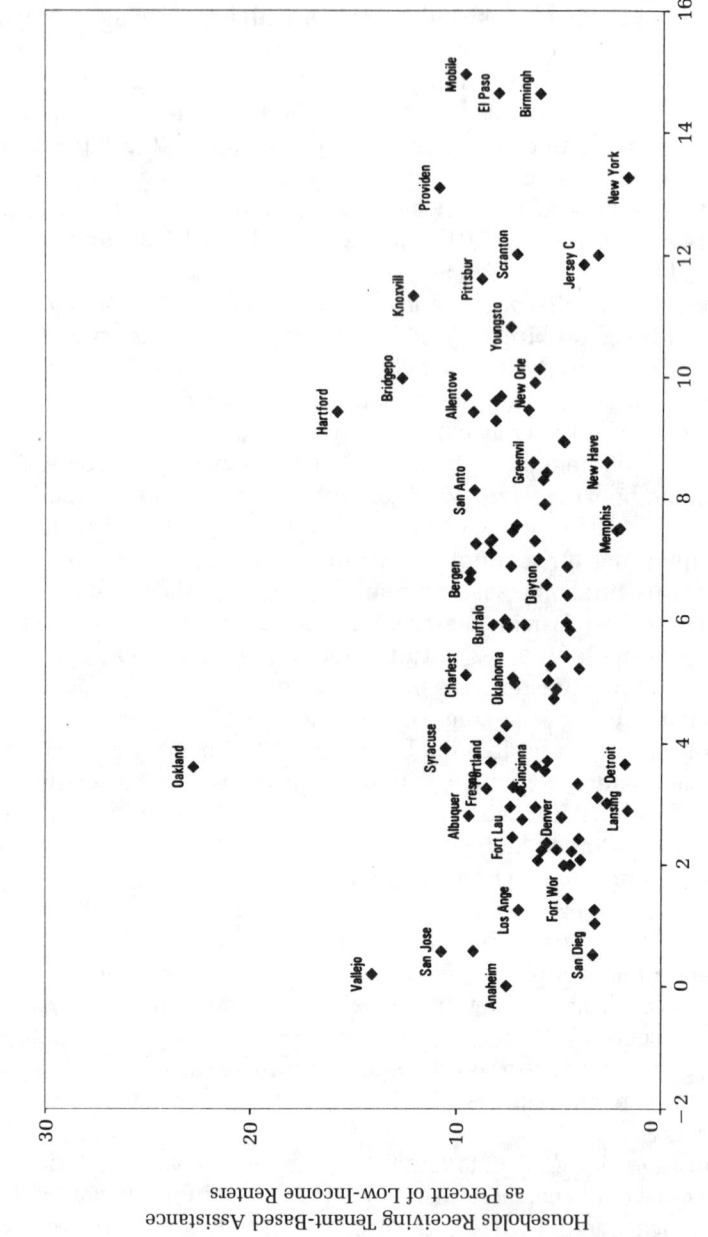

Households in Public Housing as Percent of Low-Income Renters

Households Receiving Tenant-Based Assistance
as Percent of Low-Income Renters

the ratio of central city to metropolitan median incomes (− 0.32). The highest for public housing relate to percentages of the population that had not graduated from high school (+ 0.49) or had moved over the preceding five years (− 0.48) and the household poverty rate (+ 0.33). For publicly assisted housing, the top coefficients relate to the dissimilarity index for African Americans (+ 0.43), the ratio of central city to metropolitan median incomes (− 0.40), the percentage of the population that had moved over the preceding five years (− 0.37), and the dissimilarity index for poverty (+ 0.35). None of the correlation coefficients relating to the intensity of tenant-based assistance are above 0.30.

All of this reinforces our earlier supposition that the spatial distribution of HUD assistance has been strongly influenced by metropolitan-specific institutional factors. Over time, local officials and developers in some metropolitan areas have taken advantage of HUD programs much more aggressively than in others, and HUD's allocation procedures have not forced an even distribution.

AGE AND RACE OF HOUSEHOLD HEAD[6]

Metropolitan variations with respect to these topics are also sizable. For all programs together, households headed by persons 62 years of age or higher account for from 18 to 57 percent of all assisted households across metropolitan areas. It is clear that some local housing programs have concentrated their assistance much more predominantly on the elderly. The highest metropolitan elderly shares are 84 percent in public housing and 74 percent in publicly assisted housing, although only 40 percent in tenant-based assistance. Metropolitan areas with the highest shares by this measure overall include Miami-Hialeah; New Haven–Meriden; Providence; Bergen-Passaic, NJ; and Worcester, MA.

The racial composition of housing program beneficiaries is, of course, influenced considerably by the racial composition of the metropolitan population as a whole, and there is more variation here than in the age spectrum. Households headed by African Americans account for 41 percent of all HUD-assisted households in these metro areas, on average, with shares ranging from a low of 2 percent to a high of 85 percent. Again, there are differences among programs. Metropolitan African-American shares reach highs of 97 percent in public housing and tenant-based assistance, and 72 percent in publicly assisted housing. Except for Gary-Hammond, IN, the metropolitan areas ranking highest by this measure are all in the southeastern region.

Assisted households headed by Hispanics represent 11 percent of the total, on average, but their shares are quite high in some metropolitan areas where Hispanics make up a large share of the overall population (El Paso, San Antonio, Albuquerque, Miami-Hialeah, and Tucson). The highest metropolitan scores are 97 percent in public housing, 95 percent in tenant-based assistance, 84 percent in publicly assisted housing, and 94 percent overall.

SHARE IN LARGE PROJECTS

The media image of public housing has focused on towering center-city projects in which the poorest of the poor, and a host of accompanying social problems, have been concentrated. Actually, such projects do not dominate the inventory. Nonetheless, they are important because they represent a particularly difficult policy challenge that becomes even more urgent in the context of welfare reform.

Among our metropolitan areas, 32 percent of the households in public housing, on average, live in large projects (250 or more housing units). Only 13 percent of those in publicly assisted housing live in such projects. The ranges by this measure, as before, are substantial. At the low end, 10 metropolitan areas have no assisted households in large projects. At the other extreme, 62 percent of the assisted households in New York, 40 percent in New Orleans, and 34 percent or more in Richmond-Petersburg, Birmingham, and Chicago, are large-project residents.

CONCENTRATION IN HIGH-POVERTY NEIGHBORHOODS[7]

The stereotype of housing assistance in the United States also includes the vision of concentration in distressed inner-city neighborhoods. The data show this image is correct for some programs and places but not for all. Public housing best fits this image. Across metropolitan areas, the average share of assisted households living in high-poverty census tracts (30 percent or more of all households poor in 1989) is 48 percent for public housing, but only 24 percent for publicly assisted housing and 17 percent for tenant-based assistance. The high metropolitan scores reach 89 percent for public housing, 62 percent for publicly assisted housing, and 58 percent for tenant-based assistance.

Taking all programs together, metropolitan areas with the largest share of their housing assistance recipients in high-poverty areas are a mixed lot: New York (66 percent), Mobile (61 percent), Flint (52 percent), Gary-Hammond (52 percent), and El Paso (50 percent). At the other extreme, five metropolitan areas have fewer than 10 percent of their recipients in high-poverty tracts (Vallejo, San Jose, Honolulu, Bergen-Passaic, and Scranton/Wilkes-Barre).

THE WELFARE/HOUSING ASSISTANCE OVERLAP

It would, of course, be valuable if we could analyze the shares of housing assistance beneficiaries that are dependent on welfare income. The APSH file, however, has only one variable that pertains to this issue, which lumps AFDC and General Assistance together and identifies the number of households for whom that combination of benefits constitutes more than half their income.

Table 3.5 shows that 876,000 households in the United States (50 states plus D.C.) meet this definition, 21 percent of all HUD-assisted households on the APSH file.[8] These welfare/housing overlap households account for 20 percent of all households in public housing and 28 percent of those receiving tenant-based assistance, but only 16 percent of those in publicly assisted housing. Almost two-thirds (60 percent) reside in the 100 largest metropolitan areas.

Metropolitan Variations

Table 3.6 presents data on variations in the extent of overlap. In the lowest metropolis for public housing, only 1 percent of all public housing residents have welfare as their dominant income source. In

Table 3.5 HUD-ASSISTED HOUSEHOLDS WITH MAJORITY OF INCOME FROM WELFARE

		United States (50 States + D.C.)			
	Total	Total	100 Large Metros	Rest of U.S.	Territories
Households (thousands)					
Public Housing	233	232	143	89	1
Publicly Assisted Housing	269	269	170	99	0
Tenant-Based Assistance	374	373	209	164	1
Total	876	874	522	352	2
Percent of All HUD-Assisted					
Public Housing	19.6	19.6	20.2	18.7	25.0
Publicly Assisted Housing	15.9	15.9	16.6	14.7	10.0
Tenant-Based Assistance	28.1	28.0	29.5	26.3	50.0
Total	20.8	20.8	21.4	19.8	33.3

Table 3.6 INDICATORS OF WELFARE HOUSING ASSISTANCE OVERLAP FOR 100 LARGEST METROPOLITAN AREAS

Indicators	N	Median	Mean	High	Low	Std. Dev.	Coef. Var.
Share of HUD-Assisted Households with Majority Welfare Income							
Public Housing	79	25.6	25.6	49.5	0.8	9.1	0.36
Publicly Assisted Housing	89	16.3	16.7	33.5	4.4	5.8	0.34
Tenant-Based Assistance	85	27.9	27.7	43.7	11.9	7.3	0.26
Total	90	22.2	22.4	35.9	11.0	5.5	0.25
HUD-Assisted Households with Majority Welfare Income as Pct. of All Households with Public Assistance Income in 1989							
Public Housing	79	3.8	4.6	13.4	0.0	2.9	0.62
Publicly Assisted Housing	89	3.9	4.4	12.3	0.0	2.3	0.52
Tenant-Based Assistance	85	5.4	5.8	17.6	1.0	3.0	0.51
Total	90	14.3	14.9	29.0	4.6	5.5	0.37
Dissimilarity Index for Welfare Households							
Public Housing	79	0.40	0.42	0.79	0.00	0.14	0.33
Publicly Assisted Housing	88	0.59	0.58	0.81	0.34	0.09	0.16
Tenant-Based Assistance	85	0.24	0.25	0.50	0.14	0.07	0.28

the highest, welfare is the dominant income source for 50 percent of all public housing beneficiaries. The overlap ranges from 12 percent to 44 percent for tenant-based assistance, and from 4 percent to 34 percent for publicly assisted housing—variations that strongly suggest that welfare reform will have much more powerful housing implications in some metropolitan areas than in others.

Of the five metropolitan areas where the overlaps are highest (table 3.7), two are in California's economically troubled Central Valley (Fresno and Bakersfield). The others are Riverside–San Bernardino, Tacoma, and Youngstown-Warren, OH. In these areas, 31 percent to 36 percent of all HUD beneficiaries have welfare as their dominant income source. The lowest overlaps are in a mixed group of areas (Little Rock, Bergen-Passaic, Grand Rapids, New York, and Albany-Schenectady).

Correlation analyses relating the size of the welfare overlap group as a share of all HUD-assisted households to the series of descriptive variables used earlier in analyzing patterns of housing assistance intensity give no clues to explain the variations. The first indicator, the HUD-assisted proportions in metropolitan areas with welfare income dominant, bears a very weak (and negative) relationship to housing-assistance intensity in those areas (correlation coefficient of -0.12). In other words, those metropolises that have been successful in securing high levels of HUD assistance do not tend to have high shares dependent on welfare income. Of all the other variables examined, the highest correlation was between the welfare share of HUD-assisted households and 1995 metropolitan unemployment rates ($+0.32$). The second indicator, the welfare/housing assistance overlap group in relation to the metropolitan area's public assistance population, is no more illuminating. HUD overlap households account for between 5 percent and 29 percent of 1989 households receiving public assistance income across the 100 metropolitan areas, figures that are certainly biased downwards by the use of 1989 public assistance income data.[9] The highest scores (all above 24 percent) are for Hartford, Bridgeport-Milford, Greensboro/Winston-Salem, Richmond-Petersburg, and Omaha. The lowest scores (all below 7 percent) are for San Diego; Detroit; Riverside–San Bernardino; Flint; and Stockton, CA.

CONCENTRATION WITHIN METROPOLITAN AREAS

The design of service programs to assist welfare-overlap households weather the transition of welfare reform should clearly be influenced by the degree to which these households are concentrated in the as-

Table 3.7 HIGHEST AND LOWEST METROPOLITAN AREAS FOR KEY INDICATORS

Indicators	Highest 5		Lowest 5	
Pct. HUD-Assisted Households with Majority Welfare Income	Fresno, CA	36	Little Rock, AR	11
	Riverside–San Bernardino, CA	34	Bergen-Passaic, NJ	12
	Bakersfield, CA	34	Grand Rapids, MI	13
	Tacoma, WA	32	New York, NY	13
	Youngstown-Warren, OH	31	Albany-Schenectady, NY	14
HUD-Assisted Households with Majority Welfare Income as Pct. of All Households with Public Assistance Income in 1989	Hartford, CT	290	San Diego, CA	46
	Bridgeport-Milford, CT	279	Detroit, MI	53
	Greensboro/Winston-Salem, NC	274	Riverside–San Bernardino, CA	59
	Richmond-Petersburg, VA	252	Flint, MI	61
	Omaha, NE-IA	248	Stockton, CA	65
Public Housing Dissimilarity Index—Households with Majority Welfare Income (Projects)	Providence, RI	0.79	Vallejo-Fairfield, CA	0.00
	Omaha, NE-IA	0.75	San Jose, CA	0.15
	Worcester, MA	0.74	Stockton, CA	0.17
	Miami-Hialeah, FL	0.66	Los Angeles–Long Beach, CA	0.20
	Kansas City, MO-KS	0.62	Richmond-Petersburg, VA	0.22
Publicly Assisted Housing Dissimilarity Index—Households with Majority Welfare Income (Projects)	Allentown-Bethlehem-Easton, PA	0.81	Charleston, SC	0.34
	New Haven–Meriden, CT	0.77	Bakersfield, CA	0.35
	Cleveland, OH	0.74	Greenville-Spartanburg, SC	0.40
	Albany-Schenectady, NY	0.74	San Antonio, TX	0.41
	Tampa–St. Petersburg, FL	0.72	Austin, TX	0.43
Tenant-Based Assistance Dissimilarity Index—Households with Majority Welfare Income (Census Tracts)	New Haven–Meriden, CT	0.50	San Antonio, TX	0.14
	Hartford, CT	0.48	Richmond-Petersburg, VA	0.16
	Miami-Hialeah, FL	0.44	Dayton-Springfield, OH	0.16
	Stockton, CA	0.40	Albuquerque, NM	0.16
	New York, NY	0.40	Wichita, KS	0.16

sisted stock. The aggregate metropolitan distributions of the overlap for public and publicly assisted housing are displayed in table 3.8. There are very few projects in which welfare recipients dominate the tenantry and many that have few to no welfare tenants. Projects in which more than half of the tenants receive the majority of their income from welfare account for only 11 percent of all units in public housing and 7 percent in publicly assisted housing. Those with less than 10 percent of such tenants account for 48 percent of all units in public housing and 53 percent in publicly assisted housing.

What about the welfare income dissimilarity index, which identifies the share of all HUD-assisted welfare households that would have to move to create a perfectly even distribution across assisted projects (or tracts)?[10] If all of the welfare households resided exclusively in one project, the value of the index would be 1.00. If they were already evenly spread, the value would be 0.00. The bottom panel of table 3.6 displays the values of this index for HUD programs across metropolitan areas. The metropolitan median is highest for publicly assisted housing (0.59), followed by public housing (0.40), and, considerably below that, tenant-based assistance (0.24). Once again, the variation across metropolises is substantial.

For public housing projects, values range from 0.00 to 0.79. Three metropolitan areas have index values in excess of 0.70 (Providence, Omaha, and Worcester) followed fairly closely by Miami-Hialeah (0.66) and Kansas City (0.62) (see table 3.7). The five lowest by this measure have values of less than 0.25 (four of which are in California).

Table 3.8 HOUSEHOLDS WITH MAJORITY OF INCOME FROM WELFARE AS PERCENT OF ALL PROJECT OCCUPANTS: 100 LARGEST METROPOLITAN AREAS

	Public Housing			Publicly Assisted Housing		
	Pct. Projects	Households		Pct. Projects	Households	
		Pct.	Cum. Pct.		Pct.	Cum. Pct.
80–100%	0.2	0.2	0.2	0.2	0.0	0.0
70–80	0.4	0.5	0.7	0.6	0.5	0.5
60–70	2.4	2.3	3.0	1.7	1.7	2.2
50–60	7.5	7.5	10.5	4.6	4.8	7.0
40–50	11.6	11.1	21.6	8.1	8.1	15.1
30–40	13.2	11.8	33.4	9.5	9.8	24.9
20–30	12.5	9.3	42.7	10.5	11.1	36.0
10–20	12.7	9.5	52.2	10.9	10.9	46.9
0–10	39.5	47.8	100.0	53.8	53.1	100.0
Total	100.0	100.0	100.0	100.0	100.0	100.0

Welfare recipients are generally more segregated in publicly assisted housing projects. Here the index values range from 0.34 to 0.81. The five highest all have values above 0.70. All of them except one (Tampa–St. Petersburg) are in the northeast or midwest regions (Allentown-Bethlehem, PA; New Haven–Meriden; Cleveland; and Albany-Schenectady). Those with the five lowest scores are all located in the south and southwest.

Dissimilarity index values for tenant-based assistance (based on census tracts) are all considerably lower than those found in the other two programs. The five highest all fall in the range from 0.40 to 0.50 (New Haven–Meriden, Hartford, Miami-Hialeah, Stockton, and New York). The five lowest all fall below 0.16 (San Antonio, Richmond-Petersburg, Dayton-Springfield, Albuquerque, and Wichita).

IMPLICATIONS FOR LOCAL POLICIES

There are marked differences across metropolitan areas in the level of HUD assistance and the overlap between housing assistance and welfare. In general, levels of housing assistance are somewhat lower, and relative reliance on tenant-based (as opposed to project-based) assistance higher, in the southwest than in the east and midwest. But beyond that, metropolitan patterns of housing assistance exhibit major differences within regions.

The clear implication is that strategies to respond to welfare reform from the perspective of housing need to address every metropolis on its own terms. The most sensible approaches to furthering self-sufficiency (and patterns of emphasis within those approaches) are certain to differ in different places. HUD itself faces a daunting challenge. It needs to adopt policies that incorporate both strong incentives and support but to recognize that a "one-size-fits-all" approach will not be effective. HUD's policies need not only to allow but to encourage local managers to devise differing strategies that will work effectively in quite different sets of local circumstances.

How should variations in the characteristics reviewed here influence local policies? The strength and character of other local service institutions (e.g., employment-linkage and training programs, day care) and other features of the local political and institutional environment may play important roles. Nonetheless, certain broad conclusions can be made. Fundamentally, differences in the basic features of HUD's three types of assistance programs suggest the need for

differences in approach—with relative priority for a given metropolitan area depending on the pattern of HUD assistance in that area.
What we say next about public housing is applicable in all cities, in
other words, but the emphasis these ideas receive should depend on
how large the number of public housing beneficiaries is compared to
the numbers in tenant-based assistance and publicly assisted housing,
and how large a share of public housing units is occupied by welfare
recipients.

PUBLIC HOUSING

The public housing projects that include high proportions of welfare
households offer a difficult challenge but also a special opportunity.
Because such households live together in the same complex, it should
be possible to design an efficient service package to help move them
toward self-sufficiency. All projects need to consider job preparation
and job referral services (see, for example, Gueron and Pauly 1991;
and Brown 1997) plus the related services needed to permit tenants
to accept jobs once they find them, such as day care and transportation. In public housing projects where serious social problems are
concentrated, additional services are likely to be required (e.g., family
counseling, drug treatment, and rehabilitation).

Project- or neighborhood-based services are winning favor in social
policy more broadly in the 1990s because they encourage the effi-
ciency and responsiveness of a more holistic approach. Families in
need can go to one nearby location to get help with the particular mix
of problems they face, rather than having to travel to a large number
of different service offices, each of which offers only one type of
assistance. In other words, project-based services can diminish the
fragmentation that has been blamed for much of the ineffectiveness of
social service provision over the past decade.

A project-based approach also facilitates the mounting of *community building* initiatives, where the tenants organize themselves and,
as a group, work on activities to strengthen their own individual and
collective capacities. Such initiatives are already underway in public
housing in a number of cities (Naparstek, Dooley, and Smith, 1997).
The argument here is that, by taking responsibility for their own
futures, tenants are much more likely to build social capital (group
capacities and support networks) and overcome attitudes of dependency—things that outside service professionals cannot provide but
which may well be essential to surmounting current barriers. Community building does not do away with the need for services provided
by outside professionals but, rather, can set the stage for making such

services more effective. For example, professionals will still be needed to provide job training and to operate citywide networks to link people to jobs, but community building strategies can help instill and reinforce the basic values, motivations, and skills needed for tenants to take advantage of these services.

Welfare recipients are not always spatially concentrated within the public housing stock, however. What approach is best in a project where, say, only 20 percent of the tenants are welfare recipients? The answer is likely to vary depending on project-specific circumstances. In some projects the same things—mix of community building and outside services—may well be appropriate. It should be remembered in this connection that, as welfare reform is implemented locally, prospects for today's low-wage workers could shift substantially and the "working poor" are likely to need the same service supports. Whatever the circumstances, project-by-project data on tenant composition and location in the APSH file should be very helpful to PHA managers as they design self-sufficiency strategies for their tenants overall.

Project size, no doubt, also makes a difference. A support program that works well in a 2,000-unit project is unlikely to be possible or even appropriate in a 20-unit project. Where the PHA has several small projects in a distressed neighborhood, it might make more sense to partner with other agencies (governmental and nongovernmental) on a community building/service provision strategy for the neighborhood as a whole, rather than trying to accomplish it solely within its own projects. In fact, it generally should be more appropriate for PHAs to partner actively with local welfare agencies and other social service providers in a coordinated local response to welfare reform. It is extremely important for PHAs to communicate to these other agencies the special opportunities that exist for providing services in the assisted housing context. In metropolitan areas where the welfare/housing assistance overlap is particularly high, this could assume substantial priority in the overall program, but it is likely to warrant some attention in all cities. PHAs should undertake serious analysis of the strategies and capacities of other relevant local agencies, work to influence the agendas of those agencies in support of public housing tenants—and probably only then, depending on the result, mount their own special assistance programs to address gaps and deficiencies.[11]

Publicly Assisted Housing

Welfare recipients make up a substantially smaller share of the tenants of publicly assisted housing nationally than they do of public housing.

Nonetheless, the publicly assisted stock is larger, and the absolute number of welfare recipients in these programs is also larger, than in public housing (269,000 vs. 232,000—see table 3.5).

The circumstances in the publicly assisted housing stock are in many ways similar to those in public housing. Here too are project-based programs with varying mixes of project sizes and tenant composition in various types of neighborhoods. Theoretically, basic opportunities and methods of adaptation as discussed above for welfare-to-work and other self-sufficiency oriented programs in housing projects ought to be applicable here as well. There is a major difference, however. In publicly assisted housing, there is no PHA— no overall controlling authority with the power to design and implement strategies, like those we have discussed in relation to public housing, for the publicly assisted stock as a whole. Any such strategy would have to have the active support of a large number of individual project owners in the metropolitan area. And it is by no means clear that these owners generally have either the capacity or the incentives to implement approaches like these.

What can be done? At the national level, HUD can certainly use the "bully pulpit," informing owners and managers of publicly assisted projects about the implications of welfare reform law and means of addressing them. Other relevant national organizations can do the same. The National Affordable Housing Management Association (NAHMA) has already done so, making the topic a key agenda item at its national conference in June 1997. And HUD can go further. It is already in the process of designing reforms of publicly assisted housing to respond to serious financial and other difficulties in many projects. As it works with owners to design viable futures for projects where sizable numbers of welfare and working-poor households are concentrated, it should certainly give welfare reform implications considerable attention. When moving tenants toward self-sufficiency is seen as a prominent objective, rather than simply housing finance and management, project work-out strategies are likely to look quite different.

Local groups who are planning initiatives to respond to welfare reform ought to be able to influence the owners of publicly assisted projects as well. They might begin by notifying all such owners in their areas of welfare-to-work and related services programs that are available locally, and by offering to develop project-based support packages for interested owners. A next step might be to use APSH to identify projects with large numbers of welfare recipients and working-poor tenants, and to set up meetings with the owners of those projects where interventions are likely to have the highest payoffs.

They could then (perhaps in collaboration with local HUD offices) use a mix of carrots and sticks to induce those owners to participate.

TENANT-BASED ASSISTANCE

This is the most important component of HUD assistance as it pertains to welfare reform, because of the high proportion of welfare/housing overlap households. APSH shows a total of 373,000 welfare households receiving tenant-based assistance—61 percent more than in public housing and 39 percent more than in publicly assisted housing. While some private projects house relatively high concentrations of voucher and certificate holders, the bulk of this population is spread through the private rental stock in small numbers. Thus, the project-based approaches to helping families move toward self-sufficiency (community building and intensive services) as discussed above for public housing are generally not applicable.

At the same time, opportunities for moving households receiving tenant-based assistance toward self-sufficiency may be more promising. Since program beneficiaries are less concentrated, they are less likely to be held back by negative social conditions that may exist in their immediate environment. Tenant-based assistance also offers the option for physical mobility that does not exist in project-based programs. Moving from one residence to another may well be important in accessing a suitable range of employment opportunities. In addition, although HUD and the local PHAs have very little control over the buildings in which the tenants live, the PHAs that administer tenant-based assistance do have opportunities to influence the behavior of program beneficiaries. All voucher and certificate holders are obligated to meet with the PHAs for recurrent income recertifications and lease renewals, for example, and when they want to move. At these times, the PHAs can offer self-sufficiency–oriented counseling and linkages to welfare-to-work and related service programs. Counseling and services related to mobility opportunities can also be part of this package.

A more forceful approach might be appropriate for welfare households that are accepted for tenant-based assistance in the future. A willingness to develop and act on a personal plan to move toward self-sufficiency, taking advantage of relevant counseling and other services, could be made a requirement for gaining and retaining housing assistance. Activities embracing these themes are already underway. HUD's Family Self-Sufficiency program, now being implemented by many PHAs, is built around them, and HUD is now begining a Regional Opportunity Counseling Initiative for tenant-based programs in 16 metropolitan regions, which will take them a step further with regard to physical mobility options.

IMPLICATIONS OF VARYING METROPOLITAN CONTEXTS

We have outlined general approaches to addressing the objective of moving HUD beneficiaries to self-sufficiency in the context of each of HUD's three major types of programs, and we have noted that the emphasis to be placed on each would, of course, vary depending on the composition of HUD assistance in each area. We have also noted but not yet discussed other local conditions likely to affect how those concerned with housing think about local welfare-reform response strategies. In this section, we discuss implications of two of them: the overall level of HUD assistance in the area and local labor market conditions.

VARIATIONS IN HOUSING ASSISTANCE INTENSITY

In areas where HUD beneficiaries represent a high share of all low-income renters and welfare recipients represent a high share of HUD-assisted households, all of what is discussed above ought to assume high priority in local welfare reform responses. From the perspective of managing the currently assisted stock, these places also warrant priority attention from HUD.

As shown in this chapter, there is considerable variation across metropolitan areas in this regard, and this variation is not closely related to the distribution of total population or even poverty. HUD and related national interest groups ought to use data such as that in APSH as a basis for setting their own priorities in furthering movement to self-sufficiency among assisted families. Allocations of support for these activities can be expected to make a bigger difference in some metropolitan areas than in others.

There is another side to the coin, however. It seems obvious that the areas with *low* housing assistance intensity—where the smallest share of HUD eligibles is served—face the most formidable housing-related problems as welfare reform is implemented. Congress has exacerbated these problems by recently curtailing further growth in the number of households HUD can assist (Kingsley 1997). For current welfare recipients not now receiving housing assistance, this means a substantially reduced chance of receiving such assistance in the future even if they are clearly eligible for it (new slots will open up only as current beneficiaries move off of the rolls). And the costs of shelter will play a critical role in the pressures that will be put on those who lose AFDC income.

In a recent report, HUD (1996b) estimates that nationwide there are 5.3 million renter households *not* receiving housing assistance (2.4 million of whom are welfare or SSI beneficiaries) that have "worst case housing needs," that is, they either live in seriously substandard housing or pay more than 50 percent of their monthly income for rent. The vast majority do not have seriously substandard housing quality. The only housing problem for 89 percent of them is excessive rent burden. Clearly, families with such excessive rent burdens are particularly vulnerable when their income is reduced for any reason. Those whose welfare and other benefits are reduced in the reform process will need to find not just a job, but a job that keeps their income at least at its previous level, so they are able to continue to make their rent payments and avoid eviction.

The metropolitan areas that have both low current housing assistance intensity and high-rent housing markets are the areas that need to be watched particularly closely in this regard over the next few years.

VARIATIONS IN LOCAL LABOR MARKET CONDITIONS

As of this writing, the U.S. economy is doing a remarkable job of creating new employment opportunities, and unemployment is being reduced almost everywhere. But here also, there are dramatic variations across metropolitan areas. Figure 3.3 illustrates this variation by plotting 1995 unemployment rates against housing assistance intensity for the 100 largest metropolises.

Two things stand out. First, the unemployment pattern does not reflect the simple "snowbelt vs. sunbelt" dichotomy that dominated thinking about economic development patterns in the 1980s. Among the strongest local economies, some are in the southwest (e.g., Austin, Phoenix), but others are in the southeast (e.g., Charlotte, Raleigh) and even the midwest (e.g., Minneapolis, Cincinnati, Indianapolis). Of the six with extremely high levels of unemployment (rates in excess of 8 percent), four were in California (Fresno, Bakersfield, Stockton, and Riverside), the other two being El Paso and Jersey City. Those with medium high unemployment (6 to 8 percent) include areas from virtually all U.S. regions.

Second, the correlation between unemployment and housing assistance intensity (0.07) is very low, indicating that the metropolitan areas in which the smallest shares of low-income renters actually

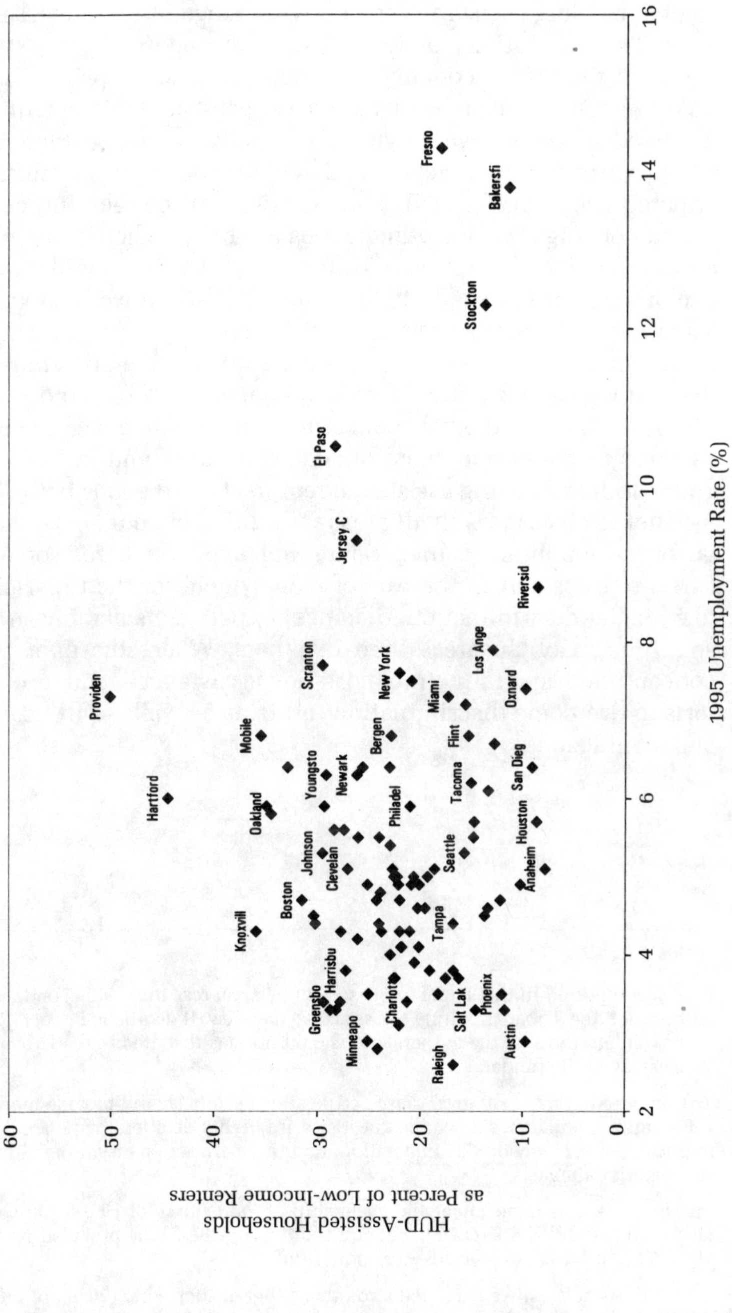

Figure 3.3 METROPOLITAN VARIATIONS: UNEMPLOYMENT RATES AND HOUSING ASSISTANCE INTENSITY

receive housing assistance span a wide range of labor market conditions. These variations too will affect local welfare-to-work strategies.

Where the local economy is strong, the task is primarily one of linking people to the jobs that are being generated, along with providing needed supportive services (job training, transportation, child care). All of the approaches we have discussed for self-sufficiency–oriented programs for HUD beneficiaries will be relevant, especially where housing assistance intensities are high. Where unemployment rates remain high, however, different mechanisms will have to be explored. Aggressive efforts to further welfare-to-work linkages may lead mostly to frustration if the private economy is not creating nearly enough new employment opportunities to meet the potential need. In these areas, publicly supported employment of some kind may prove essential. PHAs and others concerned with housing ought to be active partners in the development of such initiatives and in devising programs to link housing assistance recipients to the jobs being created.

Patterns of services in all areas will differ, of course, depending on other metropolitan characteristics not explored here. For example, barriers that stand in the way of employment for the inner-city poor (e.g., racial discrimination, distance) appear considerably stronger in some metropolitan areas than in others. Where the poor are most concentrated spatially, transportation assistance—and probably efforts to overcome discrimination in hiring as well—will take on special significance.

Notes

Findings reported in this paper are based, in part, on research being conducted by the authors for the Urban Institute's *Assessing the New Federalism* Project. The views expressed are those of the authors and should not be attributed to the Urban Institute, its trustees, or its funders.

1. Compared to most surveys, these certification results should provide more accurate information on incomes since the questions are highly detailed (by person by source), applicants must provide documentation, and there are serious legal penalties for misrepresenting the facts.

2. The work was done under the leadership of Paul Burke of HUD's Office of Policy Development and Research. Full documentation on the file is provided on the World Wide Web at *http://www.huduser.org/data.html*.

3. For this analysis, we excluded two other programs for which data are presented in APSH: Indian Housing Projects (mostly located outside of metropolitan areas), and

Low-Income Housing Tax Credit (LIHTC) projects (no data on characteristics of beneficiaries).

4. In almost all cases, records contained PMSA/MSA codes directly. In some, however, it was necessary to identify the metropolitan area in which projects were located by using other codes (e.g., for counties or PHAs) and then to link to metropolitan area locations from those. The Census classifies our largest metropolitan agglomerations as Consolidated Metropolitan Statistical Areas (CMSAs). These are aggregates of geographically proximate Primary Metropolitan Statistical Areas (PMSAs). Metropolitan Statistical Areas (MSAs) are separate, freestanding metropolitan areas. Since we ranked PMSAs and MSAs by size, some smaller PMSAs within CMSAs are not included. We also excluded suburban PMSAs that did not have large central cities within their own boundaries. Thus the data set used for this analysis does not contain information on all HUD-assisted households in all CMSAs.

5. Low-income households are those whose incomes are below 80 percent of the median income in their localities. This measure is the upper bound for HUD assistance programs eligibility.

6. As noted earlier, analysis of these factors relies on household certification data and, for them, we report on variations across only the metropolitan areas for which the data exceed our 60 percent reporting threshold: 79 metropolitan areas for public housing, 89 for publicly assisted housing, 85 for tenant-based assistance, and 90 for total housing assistance.

7. In this section we report data only on those metropolitan areas where census-tract identifiers are on file for 60 percent or more of all assisted households: 82 metropolitan areas meet this standard for public housing, 83 for tenant-based assistance, 98 for publicly assisted housing, and 95 overall.

8. How does this 876,000 overlap number in the APSH file stack up in relation to other data sources that pertain to this topic? We have been able to identify only two other sources that are even generally relevant, and these do not use the same definitions. However, after reviewing them, we conclude that the APSH appears to be in the right "ballpark" and should be adequate for our purposes.

The first such source should be the most comparable: data from the quality control statistics maintained by the AFDC program. According to this source, there were 4.82 million households receiving AFDC income in 1995, and 973,000 of them (20 percent) were also HUD assisted. That number is fairly close to the 876,000 total recorded in APSH, and definitional differences could well account for the gap. On one hand, the AFDC number might be expected to be higher because (1) it includes AFDC recipient households that receive less than half their income from AFDC, and (2) there have been AFDC caseload reductions since 1995 (a substantial share of the units in the APSH file have September 1996 status dates). On the other hand, this excess should at least be somewhat offset by the fact that the APSH number covers General Assistance as well as AFDC income. Also, some potential for error exists in both files: in the AFDC file due to sampling error and the potential of respondents to improperly identify their housing status, and in the APSH file due to the lack of 100 percent coverage of certification records.

The second source defines the overlap in a way that should yield a less close match. It is a recent HUD analysis (1997) based on the 1993 American Housing Survey, indicating that 1.54 million HUD-assisted households then received *any* income from AFDC, General Assistance, and/or SSI. In addition to the more inclusive income definition, one would expect the 1993 number to be higher because welfare rolls declined substantially in many states between 1993 and the 1995/96 status dates of APSH.

9. This is because (1) the denominator we had to use includes groups not represented in the numerator and includes persons with any SSI income in addition to any AFDC

or General Assistance income, and (2) welfare caseloads in many metropolitan areas have declined since 1990.

10. For public and publicly assisted housing, the index relates to the distribution of welfare households in all projects in the area; for tenant-based assistance, it relates to the distribution across census tracts.

11. HUD is now working to develop new information and other forms of assistance to help PHAs address the challenges of the welfare reform environment. Of special interest is its Jobs-Plus demonstration—an effort being started in a number of cities to test ways of implementing intensive welfare-to-work programs along with relevant supportive services in the context of public housing (see detailed discussion in chapter 6).

References

Brown, Amy. 1997. *Work First: How to Implement an Employment Focused Approach to Welfare Reform*. New York: Manpower Demonstration Research Corporation.

Goering, John, Ali Kamely, and Todd Richardson. 1994. *The Location and Racial Composition of Public Housing in the United States*. Washington, D.C.: U.S. Department of Housing and Urban Development.

Gueron, Judith M., and Edward Pauly. 1991. *From Welfare to Work*. New York: Russell Sage Foundation.

HUD. *See* U.S. Department of Housing and Urban Development.

Hughes, Mark Alan. 1997. "The Administrative Geography of Devolving Social Welfare Programs." Joint Occasional Paper 97-1 of the Center for Public Management and the Center on Urban and Metropolitan Policy. Washington, D.C.: The Brookings Institution.

Khadduri, Jill, and Marge Martin. 1997. "Mixed-Income Housing in the HUD Multi-Family Stock." *Cityscape* 3(2).

Kingsley, G. Thomas. 1997. "Federal Housing Assistance and Welfare Reform: Uncharted Territory." Policy Brief A-19 in the series *New Federalism: Issues and Options for States*. Washington, D.C.: The Urban Institute, December.

Naparstek, Arthur J., Dennis Dooley, and Robin Smith. 1997. *Community Building in Public Housing: Ties That Bind People and Their Communities*. Washington, D.C.: U.S. Department of Housing and Urban Development.

Newman, Sandra J., and Joseph Harkness. 1998. "The Effects of Welfare Reform on Housing: A National Analysis." (This volume.)

Newman, Sandra J., and Ann B. Schnare. 1992. *Beyond Bricks and Mortar: Reexamining the Purpose and Effects of Housing Assistance*. Washington, D.C.: The Urban Institute Press.

_____. 1988. *Subsidizing Shelter: The Relationship between Welfare and Housing Assistance.* Washington, D.C.: The Urban Institute Press.

U.S. Department of Housing and Urban Development. 1997. *Characteristics of HUD-Assisted Renters and Their Units in 1993.* Washington, D.C.: U.S. Department of Housing and Urban Development.

_____. 1996a. *Public Housing that Works: The Transformation of America's Public Housing.* Washington, D.C.: U.S. Department of Housing and Urban Development.

_____. 1996b. *Rental Housing Assistance at a Crossroads: A Report to Congress on Worst Case Housing Needs.* Washington, D.C.: U.S. Department of Housing and Urban Development.

Appendix 3.A NUMBER OF ASSISTED HOUSEHOLDS AND HOUSEHOLD REPORTING AND GEOCODING RATES FOR 100 LARGEST METROPOLITAN AREAS

	Number of Assisted Households				Percent of Households with Certification Records				Percent of Households with Census Tract Codes on File			
	Total	Public Housing	Tenant-Based Assist.	Publicly Assisted Housing	Total	Public Housing	Tenant-Based Assist.	Publicly Assisted Housing	Total	Public Housing	Tenant-Based Assist.	Publicly Assisted Housing
Akron, OH PMSA	15,108	4,613	4,072	6,424	90	96	93	84	64	5	100	91
Albany-Schenectady-Troy, NY MSA	15,704	5,176	5,114	5,413	83	86	92	71	72	42	100	77
Albuquerque, NM MSA	8,623	1,198	4,030	3,395	69	43	65	82	64	81	35	92
Allentown-Bethlehem-Easton, PA-NJ MSA	11,763	4,154	4,118	3,490	87	85	90	85	75	77	75	74
Anaheim–Santa Ana, CA PMSA	11,239	0	10,880	359	36	0	37	18	0	0	0	0
Atlanta, GA MSA	49,405	17,698	12,976	18,731	51	33	43	73	77	74	53	98
Austin, TX MSA	9,129	2,907	2,965	3,257	83	76	86	86	74	40	83	96
Bakersfield, CA MSA	4,841	992	2,366	1,483	90	94	93	82	91	93	86	96
Baltimore, MD MSA	52,679	17,523	12,208	22,948	80	89	68	78	92	99	79	93
Baton Rouge, LA MSA	5,420	1,347	1,668	2,406	82	68	92	83	87	86	82	91
Bergen-Passaic, NJ PMSA	17,370	5,051	7,141	5,178	83	76	93	75	83	50	100	93
Birmingham, AL MSA	17,420	9,186	3,791	4,444	86	85	94	81	79	69	100	84
Boston, MA PMSA	78,143	17,596	20,811	39,736	59	55	89	45	80	26	100	96
Bridgeport-Milford, CT PMSA	9,574	2,903	3,707	2,965	72	81	81	53	90	92	92	86
Buffalo, NY PMSA	19,984	5,155	7,188	7,641	86	98	99	67	95	86	100	97
Charleston, SC MSA	7,739	1,773	3,327	2,639	84	75	98	73	92	83	100	87
Charlotte-Gastonia-Rock Hill, NC-SC MSA	17,418	6,173	5,841	5,404	84	91	90	70	83	85	74	91
Chattanooga, TN-GA MSA	7,273	3,648	974	2,651	82	80	97	79	82	72	100	91
Chicago, IL PMSA	119,852	36,869	31,926	51,058	42	41	44	42	82	92	46	95
Cincinnati, OH-KY-IN PMSA	26,801	4,601	7,851	14,349	87	92	80	89	84	33	97	95

Cleveland, OH PMSA	40,880	10,384	11,193	19,302	67	77	32	83	76	96	17	95
Columbia, SC MSA	8,983	2,330	2,655	3,998	90	97	99	80	81	62	100	80
Columbus, OH MSA	27,281	8,485	5,802	12,993	86	79	89	89	82	55	97	94
Dallas, TX PMSA	31,825	4,732	10,657	16,436	80	93	97	65	95	88	100	96
Dayton-Springfield, OH MSA	17,368	4,976	4,304	8,088	87	88	83	88	90	97	85	86
Denver, CO PMSA	25,811	4,273	7,546	13,993	77	71	77	79	78	79	65	85
Detroit, MI PMSA	58,965	11,145	5,518	42,301	71	83	86	66	78	11	100	98
El Paso, TX MSA	11,686	6,018	3,310	2,358	82	87	81	72	88	98	64	96
Flint, MI MSA	4,757	933	838	2,986	80	91	68	80	91	64	94	100
Fort Lauderdale–Hollywood–Pompano Beach, FL PMSA	12,480	2,069	6,176	4,235	72	89	68	69	61	75	41	83
Fort Worth–Arlington, TX PMSA	11,223	1,572	5,049	4,602	72	83	69	71	84	96	78	86
Fresno, CA MSA	11,111	1,989	5,249	3,873	88	83	96	79	92	81	96	93
Gary–Hammond, IN PMSA	10,283	3,578	1,939	4,766	67	86	64	54	88	72	100	96
Grand Rapids, MI MSA	8,698	787	1,903	6,008	61	33	31	74	80	64	31	97
Greensboro/Winston-Salem–High Point, NC MSA	20,329	6,657	6,542	7,131	88	94	92	78	88	87	87	90
Greenville-Spartanburg, SC MSA	12,753	3,725	2,750	6,277	88	91	93	85	84	71	100	85
Harrisburg-Lebanon-Carlisle, PA MSA	10,599	2,817	3,545	4,237	88	92	90	83	77	90	57	84
Hartford, CT PMSA	25,553	5,412	9,108	11,032	63	62	65	62	83	80	70	94
Honolulu, HI MSA	13,671	3,970	5,070	4,632	86	88	99	69	95	88	100	95
Houston, TX PMSA	25,737	3,036	9,718	12,982	74	25	87	76	94	100	92	93
Indianapolis, IN MSA	20,836	2,457	4,110	14,268	63	69	32	71	87	100	45	97
Jacksonville, FL MSA	15,028	2,132	4,595	8,301	72	0	79	87	97	93	100	98
Jersey City, NJ PMSA	19,762	8,885	2,926	7,950	54	48	51	60	78	63	72	96
Johnson City–Kingsport-Bristol, TN-VA MSA	7,986	2,617	2,145	3,224	90	87	96	89	84	68	95	92
Kansas City, MO-KS MSA	28,907	4,301	6,961	17,645	75	80	78	73	88	72	81	95
Knoxville, TN MSA	16,054	5,060	5,452	5,542	63	45	57	85	73	73	54	91
Lansing–East Lansing, MI MSA	6,093	1,003	576	4,514	74	75	98	71	83	0	98	100
Las Vegas, NV MSA	10,384	3,313	3,721	3,349	70	39	93	76	94	94	100	88

Appendix 3.A NUMBER OF ASSISTED HOUSEHOLDS AND HOUSEHOLD REPORTING AND GEOCODING RATES FOR 100 LARGEST METROPOLITAN AREAS (continued)

	Number of Assisted Households				Percent of Households with Certification Records				Percent of Households with Census Tract Codes on File			
	Total	Public Housing	Tenant-Based Assist.	Publicly Assisted Housing	Total	Public Housing	Tenant-Based Assist.	Publicly Assisted Housing	Total	Public Housing	Tenant-Based Assist.	Publicly Assisted Housing
Little Rock–North Little Rock, AR MSA	9,890	2,877	3,329	3,684	73	69	73	77	87	87	75	96
Los Angeles–Long Beach, CA PMSA	116,969	11,221	63,040	42,708	55	71	40	73	72	87	53	96
Louisville, KY-IN MSA	22,233	7,066	6,024	9,143	85	86	91	81	93	90	97	93
Memphis, TN-AR-MS MSA	17,243	6,183	1,731	9,330	81	88	73	79	96	91	100	99
Miami-Hialeah, FL PMSA	34,812	9,784	10,438	14,591	77	81	90	65	59	8	100	71
Milwaukee, WI PMSA	24,110	4,897	7,399	11,814	75	94	91	58	98	95	100	98
Minneapolis–St. Paul, MN-WI MSA	45,902	10,951	14,063	20,888	75	93	87	57	82	39	100	93
Mobile, AL MSA	11,681	4,920	3,177	3,584	92	98	98	79	88	85	100	80
Nashville, TN MSA	22,219	8,088	4,848	9,283	88	88	99	82	93	89	100	92
New Haven–Meriden, CT MSA	10,930	3,605	1,143	6,182	66	51	93	69	96	88	100	100
New Orleans, LA MSA	25,821	11,082	7,034	7,705	63	60	52	77	68	67	41	95
New York, NY PMSA	264,050	158,176	20,636	85,238	79	83	82	72	98	99	100	95
Newark, NJ PMSA	36,194	12,356	6,773	17,066	58	37	75	67	92	86	100	96
Norfolk–Va. Beach–Newport News, VA MSA	29,342	9,816	6,639	12,886	68	61	77	69	94	98	83	96
Oakland, CA PMSA	57,127	5,969	37,760	13,399	68	70	65	75	54	88	39	82
Oklahoma City, OK MSA	12,686	3,952	5,721	3,013	80	51	95	91	90	75	100	90
Omaha, NE-IA MSA	12,099	3,396	4,697	4,006	93	90	98	91	89	83	99	84
Orlando, FL MSA	10,629	2,280	4,783	3,566	74	85	64	82	79	72	68	99
Oxnard-Ventura, CA PMSA	3,506	204	3,294	8	54	54	54	62	0	0	0	0
Philadelphia, PA-NJ PMSA	64,723	22,416	19,220	23,087	57	36	57	77	48	18	48	84
Phoenix, AZ MSA	20,368	3,789	8,688	7,891	89	85	92	88	85	33	100	95
Pittsburgh, PA PMSA	53,880	17,885	13,654	22,341	74	53	72	91	79	78	62	90

Area												
Portland, OR PMSA	20,592	3,965	9,011	7,616	82	92	76	85	91	89	94	89
Providence, RI PMSA	31,077	8,122	6,781	16,174	69	69	89	61	90	77	91	96
Raleigh-Durham, NC MSA	11,857	4,522	3,297	4,038	87	98	99	64	94	95	100	87
Richmond-Petersburg, VA MSA	16,006	5,317	1,599	9,091	81	88	98	75	91	91	100	88
Riverside–San Bernardino, CA PMSA	14,787	2,143	5,646	6,998	72	59	63	84	97	94	100	96
Rochester, NY MSA	15,260	2,554	5,681	7,026	83	89	98	70	94	94	100	90
Sacramento, CA MSA	17,107	2,957	5,890	8,261	88	91	99	79	97	86	100	100
St. Louis, MO-IL MSA	39,262	10,547	12,037	16,678	83	84	91	77	78	46	98	88
Salt Lake City–Ogden, UT MSA	9,975	1,525	4,024	4,425	95	93	95	96	88	89	98	79
San Antonio, TX MSA	24,214	8,181	9,249	6,785	88	94	99	66	94	97	100	83
San Diego, CA MSA	20,517	1,147	7,591	11,779	73	33	55	88	98	92	100	97
San Francisco, CA PMSA	27,407	7,377	8,218	11,812	79	77	78	80	81	68	75	93
San Jose, CA PMSA	17,671	480	9,185	8,006	92	99	99	85	99	100	100	97
Scranton/Wilkes-Barre, PA MSA	14,930	6,063	3,609	5,258	86	76	96	91	80	66	100	83
Seattle, WA PMSA	27,348	10,376	8,201	8,771	82	87	83	75	98	100	100	95
Springfield, MA MSA	14,625	2,482	3,596	8,548	71	87	92	57	93	81	97	96
Stockton, CA MSA	5,352	1,062	2,641	1,649	95	99	99	85	97	95	95	100
Syracuse, NY MSA	12,247	1,995	5,388	4,865	89	97	99	74	96	96	100	92
Tacoma, WA PMSA	7,288	1,426	3,589	2,273	88	95	90	80	97	100	97	96
Tampa–St. Petersburg–Clearwater, FL MSA	22,740	7,314	6,391	9,035	83	80	97	75	89	73	100	95
Toledo, OH MSA	10,775	2,838	2,205	5,732	81	89	73	79	77	68	47	94
Tucson, AZ MSA	7,119	1,250	3,660	2,209	96	86	99	96	95	100	100	85
Tulsa, OK MSA	12,201	2,392	4,255	5,555	91	91	99	84	89	83	100	85
Vallejo-Fairfield-Napa, CA PMSA	6,609	60	4,457	2,092	75	97	71	83	79	100	71	94
Washington, DC-MD-VA MSA	65,291	13,148	13,697	38,446	57	70	42	58	81	92	41	90
West Palm Beach–Boca Raton–Delray Beach, FL MSA	8,195	2,137	4,170	1,889	70	76	75	52	62	29	78	66

Appendix 3.A NUMBER OF ASSISTED HOUSEHOLDS AND HOUSEHOLD REPORTING AND GEOCODING RATES FOR 100 LARGEST METROPOLITAN AREAS (continued)

| | Number of Assisted Households | | | Percent of Households with Certification Records | | | | Percent of Households with Census Tract Codes on File | | | |
	Total	Public Housing	Tenant-Based Assist.	Publicly Assisted Housing	Total	Public Housing	Tenant-Based Assist.	Publicly Assisted Housing	Total	Public Housing	Tenant-Based Assist.	Publicly Assisted Housing
Wichita, KS MSA	4,752	809	1,555	2,387	73	65	63	83	74	53	60	91
Wilmington, DE-NJ-MD PMSA	8,589	2,936	2,074	3,579	66	29	97	80	85	73	94	91
Worcester, MA MSA	8,314	2,150	1,685	4,478	71	83	97	55	96	87	100	99
Youngstown-Warren, OH MSA	9,453	3,504	2,415	3,534	81	95	56	84	93	100	78	95

Appendix 3.B METRO AREAS WITH HOUSEHOLD REPORTING RATES BELOW 60
PERCENT

Program Type	Metro Area
Public Housing	Albuquerque, NM MSA
	Anaheim–Santa Ana, CA PMSA
	Atlanta, GA MSA
	Boston, MA PMSA
	Chicago, IL PMSA
	Grand Rapids, MI MSA
	Houston, TX PMSA
	Jacksonville, FL MSA
	Jersey City, NJ PMSA
	Knoxville, TN MSA
	Las Vegas, NV MSA
	New Haven–Meriden, CT MSA
	New Orleans, LA MSA
	Newark, NJ PMSA
	Oklahoma City, OK MSA
	Oxnard-Ventura, CA PMSA
	Philadelphia, PA-NJ PMSA
	Pittsburgh, PA PMSA
	Riverside–San Bernardino, CA PMSA
	San Diego, CA MSA
	Wilmington, DE-NJ PMSA
Tenant-Based Assistance	Anaheim–Santa Ana, CA PMSA
	Atlanta, GA MSA
	Chicago, IL PMSA
	Cleveland, OH PMSA
	Grand Rapids, MI MSA
	Indianapolis, IN MSA
	Jersey City, NJ PMSA
	Knoxville, TN MSA
	Los Angeles–Long Beach, CA PMSA
	New Orleans, LA MSA
	Oxnard-Ventura, CA PMSA
	Philadelphia, PA-NJ PMSA
	San Diego, CA MSA
	Washington, DC-MD-VA MSA
	Youngstown-Warren, OH MSA
Publicly Assisted Housing	Anaheim–Santa Ana, CA PMSA
	Boston, MA PMSA
	Bridgeport-Milford, CT PMSA
	Chicago, IL PMSA
	Gary-Hammond, IN PMSA
	Milwaukee, WI PMSA
	Minneapolis–St. Paul, MN-WI MSA
	Springfield, MA MSA
	Washington, DC-MD-VA MSA

Appendix 3.B METRO AREAS WITH HOUSEHOLD REPORTING RATES BELOW 60
PERCENT (continued)

Program Type	Metro Area
	West Palm Beach–Boca Raton–Delray Beach, FL MSA Worcester, MA MSA
Total (All Programs)	Anaheim–Santa Ana, CA PMSA Atlanta, GA MSA Boston, MA PMSA Chicago, IL PMSA Jersey City, NJ PMSA Los Angeles–Long Beach, CA PMSA Newark, NJ PMSA Oxnard-Ventura, CA PMSA Philadelphia, PA-NJ PMSA Washington, DC-MD-VA MSA

Metro Areas with Geocoding Rates below 60 Percent

Public Housing	Akron, OH PMSA Albany-Schenectady-Troy, NY MSA Anaheim–Santa Ana, CA PMSA Austin, TX MSA Bergen-Passaic, NJ PMSA Boston, MA PMSA Cincinnati, OH-KY-IN PMSA Columbus, OH MSA Detroit, MI PMSA Lansing–East Lansing, MI MSA Miami-Hialeah, FL PMSA Minneapolis–St. Paul, MN-WI MSA Oxnard-Ventura, CA PMSA Philadelphia, PA-NJ PMSA Phoenix, AZ MSA St. Louis, MO-IL MSA West Palm Beach–Boca Raton–Delray Beach, FL MSA Wichita, KS MSA
Tenant-Based Assistance	Albuquerque, NM MSA Anaheim–Santa Ana, CA PMSA Atlanta, GA MSA Chicago, IL PMSA Cleveland, OH PMSA Fort Lauderdale–Hollywood–Pompano Beach, FL PMSA Grand Rapids, MI MSA Harrisburg-Lebanon-Carlisle, PA MSA Indianapolis, IN MSA Knoxville, TN MSA Los Angeles–Long Beach, CA PMSA New Orleans, LA MSA

Appendix 3.B METRO AREAS WITH HOUSEHOLD REPORTING RATES BELOW 60
PERCENT (continued)

Program Type	Metro Area
	Oakland, CA PMSA
	Oxnard-Ventura, CA PMSA
	Philadelphia, PA-NJ PMSA
	Toledo, OH MSA
	Washington, DC-MD-VA MSA
Publicly Assisted Housing	Anaheim–Santa Ana, CA PMSA
	Oxnard-Ventura, CA PMSA
Total (All Programs)	Anaheim–Santa Ana, CA PMSA
	Miami-Hialeah, FL PMSA
	Oakland, CA PMSA
	Oxnard-Ventura, CA PMSA
	Philadelphia, PA-NJ PMSA

Metro Areas with either Household Reporting or Geocoding Rates below 60 Percent

Public Housing	Akron, OH PMSA
	Albany-Schenectady-Troy, NY MSA
	Albuquerque, NM MSA
	Anaheim–Santa Ana, CA PMSA
	Atlanta, GA MSA
	Austin, TX MSA
	Bergen-Passaic, NJ PMSA
	Boston, MA PMSA
	Cincinnati, OH-KY-IN PMSA
	Columbus, OH MSA
	Detroit, MI PMSA
	Grand Rapids, MI MSA
	Houston, TX PMSA
	Jacksonville, FL MSA
	Jersey City, NJ PMSA
	Knoxville, TN MSA
	Lansing–East Lansing, MI MSA
	Las Vegas, NV MSA
	Miami-Hialeah, FL PMSA
	Minneapolis–St. Paul, MN-WI MSA
	New Haven–Meriden, CT MSA
	New Orleans, LA MSA
	Newark, NJ PMSA
	Oklahoma City, OK MSA
	Oxnard-Ventura, CA PMSA
	Philadelphia, PA-NJ PMSA
	Phoenix, AZ MSA
	Pittsburgh, PA PMSA
	Riverside–San Bernardino, CA PMSA
	St. Louis, MO-IL MSA
	San Diego, CA MSA
	West Palm Beach–Boca Raton–Delray Beach, FL MSA
	Wichita, KS MSA
	Wilmington, DE-NJ-MD PMSA

Appendix 3.B METRO AREAS WITH HOUSEHOLD REPORTING RATES BELOW 60
PERCENT (continued)

Program Type	Metro Area
Tenant-Based Assistance	Albuquerque, MN MSA
	Anaheim–Santa Ana, CA PMSA
	Atlanta, GA MSA
	Chicago, IL PMSA
	Cleveland, OH PMSA
	Fort Lauderdale–Hollywood–Pompano Beach, FL PMSA
	Grand Rapids, MI MSA
	Harrisburg-Lebanon-Carlisle, PA MSA
	Indianapolis, IN MSA
	Jersey City, NJ PMSA
	Knoxville, TN MSA
	Los Angeles–Long Beach, CA PMSA
	New Orleans, LA MSA
	Oakland, CA PMSA
	Oxnard-Ventura, CA PMSA
	Philadelphia, PA-NJ PMSA
	San Diego, CA MSA
	Toledo, OH MSA
	Washington, DC-MD-VA MSA
	Youngstown-Warren, OH MSA
Publicly Assisted Housing	Anaheim–Santa Ana, CA PMSA
	Boston, MA PMSA
	Bridgeport-Milford, CT PMSA
	Chicago, IL PMSA
	Gary-Hammond, IN PMSA
	Milwaukee, WI PMSA
	Minneapolis–St. Paul, MN-WI MSA
	Oxnard-Ventura, CA PMSA
	Springfield, MA MSA
	Washington, DC-MD-VA MSA
	West Palm Beach–Boca Raton–Delray Beach, FL MSA
	Worcester, MA MSA
Total (All Programs)	Anaheim–Santa Ana, CA PMSA
	Atlanta, GA MSA
	Boston, MA PMSA
	Chicago, IL PMSA
	Jersey City, NY PMSA
	Los Angeles–Long Beach, CA PMSA
	Miami-Hialeah, FL PMSA
	Newark, NJ PMSA
	Oakland, CA PMSA
	Oxnard-Ventura, CA PMSA
	Philadelphia, PA-NJ PMSA
	Washington, DC-MD-VA MSA

HOUSING, TRANSPORTATION, AND ACCESS TO SUBURBAN JOBS BY WELFARE RECIPIENTS IN THE CLEVELAND AREA

Claudia Coulton, Laura Leete, and Neil Bania

The implementation of work requirements and time limits under welfare reform will push more low-skill workers into local labor markets. Ohio's Temporary Assistance for Needy Families (TANF) legislation (Ohio House Bill 408, 1997), for example, calls for adult recipients to participate in 30 hours of work activity and for welfare cash benefits to be terminated after three years of receipt. The Cleveland area represents one-fourth of Ohio's welfare caseload and has one of the highest rates of welfare participation in the country. As such, it is an important example of the labor market challenges posed by the welfare system's new emphasis on work.

In this chapter we use Cleveland as a case study to examine one much discussed barrier to the employment of welfare recipients—the spatial mismatch between where welfare families live and the job openings for which they are most likely to be qualified. We also explore the extent to which the mismatch might be overcome by transportation or residential relocation.

BACKGROUND

A fundamental question raised by welfare reform's emphasis on rapid progress through the public assistance system into regular employment is how quickly former welfare recipients can be absorbed into local labor markets without displacing current workers. The Cleveland–Akron labor market is projected to need to double its entry-level jobs just to absorb recipients who have been on welfare for five years (Leete and Bania 1997). Although regional welfare caseloads and job markets vary considerably, there is evidence that Cleveland is not alone in anticipating a major influx into the labor market. A study of metropolitan Chicago, for example, estimates that there would be about six job seekers for every entry-level job if all adult welfare recipients in the area were to seek work (Carlson and Theodore 1995). This sudden influx of low-skill workers into local labor markets is expected, in turn, to depress the wages of both new and existing workers competing for these types of jobs (Mishel and Schmitt 1995).

Though local labor markets should eventually adjust to the increased labor supply, whether welfare recipients can effectively reach widely disbursed employment locations is a major question. Nearly three-quarters of the poor live in urban areas (U.S. Bureau of the Census 1993) where deindustrialization and the shift of low-skill jobs to outlying areas have moved the jobs further from where the poor live (Galster and Mincy 1993; Kasarda 1993). Central city residents have less access to employment than have suburban residents as measured by the ratio of jobs to people within neighborhoods and by average travel times (Holzer 1991). Youth who tend to work closer to home and African-American men and women have been particularly disadvantaged by this suburbanization of jobs (Ellwood 1986; Ihlanfeldt and Sjoquist 1989, 1990).

Overcoming these distances through long commutes is particularly difficult for low-wage workers. The poor rely on public transportation to a greater degree than other workers and welfare recipients in particular have very poor access to automobiles (Ong 1997). Yet public transportation is not well suited to reaching jobs in suburban locations, the areas of greatest growth in low-skill employment (Hughes 1991, 1995; Ihlanfeldt 1994).

The residential locations of welfare recipients may also affect their chances of working over and above the commuting barriers. In addition to obviously different commute times, overall employment levels in suburban neighborhoods are much higher than most central city neighborhoods where welfare recipients are concentrated. Living around neighbors who work may enable welfare recipients to work through better information flow about jobs, and changed norms and expectations regarding work or improved community resources (Coulton 1996). Further, employers may have a more favorable attitude toward applicants who live in neighborhoods they perceive as better (Kirschenman and Neckerman 1991) or closer in both a geographical and social sense.

The relative effect on wages of distance from jobs as compared to social characteristics of the neighborhood of residence was examined for full-time male workers in Los Angeles (Pastor and Adams 1996). The poverty rate of the neighborhood was found to have a greater effect on residents' wages than did the average travel time to work, suggesting that social influences within the neighborhood of residence may be more important than its spatial location. Furthermore, commuting long distances to jobs in more affluent areas was found to very substantially raise the wages of residents of poor neighborhoods—an effect that held for persons commuting by automobile but not for those using public transit. Although the study was not able to control for the possible endogeneity of wages and type of transportation used, it does suggests that efficient methods of commuting out of poor neighborhoods to concentrations of job openings in the suburbs can contribute to poverty reduction. It also supports the contention that living in a neighborhood that both is close to jobs and has high levels of employment can reduce poverty.

Given these apparent advantages, how feasible is it to expect that welfare recipients can move closer to suburban job concentrations within a region? One problem is that the overall supply of affordable housing has declined in recent years (Apgar 1993). Although estimates vary, there may be as many as two low-income households for each affordable rental unit (Lazere 1995). Moreover, affordable housing tends to be spatially clustered in declining neighborhoods. For example, Bogdon and Can (1997) found that low-cost rental units were highly concentrated within the City of Syracuse and quite sparse in the suburbs, where job growth is increasingly located.

Programs to reduce the spatial barriers to employment for inner-city residents have, most often, involved support for commuting. The widely known Bridges to Work program recognizes that, in addition to transportation, it is necessary to strengthen employer and neighborhood networks. An alternative strategy to better linking inner-city residents to suburban jobs is to enable the urban poor to relocate their residences to areas with better job opportunities. Two well-known programs support such relocation. The Gautreaux program in Chicago has been able to demonstrate significant increases in employment and earnings among a group of former public housing residents selected by lottery for suburban relocation (Popkin, Rosenbaum and Meaden 1993). The Moving to Opportunity program (see chapter 5 of this volume) is testing a similar strategy in several other cities.

Despite these innovations, the effort to move large numbers of welfare recipients into the lower-skill tier of the labor market rapidly must rely in the short run on existing patterns of job locations, transportation, and housing. This chapter examines those patterns for the Cleveland area in order to provide a baseline for formulating interventions and policy options.

METHODOLOGY

For this study we need geographically specific estimates of adult welfare recipients, job openings for which they can qualify, and the availability of rental housing that they can afford on the earnings of an entry-level job. In addition, we need estimates of public transit commute times between residential areas and employment areas, and geographically specific definitions of reasonable commuting distances from employment centers. In each case, the geographic area for the analysis is the Cleveland–Akron metropolitan area labor market.

Location of Welfare Recipients

A cross-section of the Aid to Families with Dependent Children (AFDC) June 1995 caseload extracted from the computerized benefit files of the County agency that administers entitlement programs provides our location. All active recipients ages 18 or over are included. An active recipient is defined as one who received cash benefits in that month. The study includes 37,688 adult recipients. Additionally, a five-year welfare history—created for a random sample of 2,000 recipients by extracting and linking benefit information from the preceding 60 months of files—is used to identify long-term recipients, the group most likely to be affected by welfare time limits.

The home addresses of the total caseload and of the random sample are geocoded and maps generated to display the neighborhood locations of recipients. Ratios of long-term to short-term recipients are calculated for each neighborhood and suburban municipality to examine the concentration of recipients who had been out of the labor force for an extended period.

Number and Location of Available Jobs

Estimating the number and locations of forecasted job openings takes three steps (Leete and Bania 1995). First, we need to determine the occupations for which the majority of welfare recipients are likely to be qualified. The second step is to estimate the expected number of job openings within these occupations. Third, we allocate these open-ings to the geographic locations of the industries in which they are expected to occur.

LOW-SKILL OCCUPATIONS

As a starting point, we identify those occupations that could be con-sidered to represent job opportunities for current welfare recipients. In order to reduce the list of 407 occupational classifications reported in the U.S. Census to a more manageable set, we identify three cate-gories of low-skill occupations with relatively homogeneous skill and educational requirements: entry level occupations, requiring 11 or 12 years of education and less than six months of job-specific training; short-term training occupations, requiring high school graduation and 6 to 12 months of additional education or training; and long-term training occupations, requiring from 1 to 3 years of post-secondary education and/or training (possibly corresponding to community col-lege or vocational education).

We assign occupations to these categories on the basis of occupa-tional skill content, for which we use two types of measures. First, we measure occupational requirements via the general educational development (GED) and specific vocational preparation (SVP) scores developed by the U.S. Department of Labor in *The Dictionary of Oc-cupational Titles* (U.S. Department of Labor 1977).[1] These measures are an idealized version of the training and skills an employer would like to see in an employee. Second, we measure actual worker char-acteristics in each occupation using data from the Public Use Micro-data Sample (PUMS) of the 1990 Census on the education levels of workers in an occupation in the Cleveland–Akron metropolitan area. To measure minimum acceptable education levels for workers in a given occupation, we compute the first quartile of education in each occupation. This is a measure of the characteristics of workers ac-tually hired into an occupation under current conditions in the local labor market.

We look at both types of measures for each of the 407 occupational categories. Using factor analysis on GED, SVP, and the first quartile level of education, we construct a "skill content" index that rises with each of these variables.[2] Occupations are ranked by this index and cut-points are selected to create each group of occupations. Seventy occupations are designated as entry level, 36 require short-term train-ing, and 142 require long-term training. Starting hourly wages in 1990 (defined as the first quartile of the hourly wage) in these occupation groups in the Cleveland–Akron metropolitan area were $5.05, $6.37, and $6.77, respectively.[3]

PROJECTIONS OF JOB OPENINGS BY OCCUPATION

Projections of the expected number of annual openings by occupation for the years 1991–2000 were taken from the Ohio Bureau of Employment Services (OBES 1993). Annual job openings come from two sources: the annual growth projections for each occupation and the expected number of net annual replacement openings. These projections are full-employment forecasts; they forecast changes in equilibrium employment, under normal labor force growth.[4]

GEOGRAPHIC LOCATIONS OF INDUSTRIES AND JOB OPENINGS

Ohio's ES202 data for the third quarter of 1994, geocoded to the zip code level, are used to estimate actual employment by industry in each location.[5] Employment by industry is then converted to employment by occupation using an industry-occupation matrix for northeast Ohio derived from the 1990 Census. Anticipated job openings at each skill level are then estimated for each zip code by allocating job openings in a specific occupation in proportion to the existing geographic distribution of employment in that occupation.

Commute Times

We also estimate average public transit commute times from key inner-city neighborhoods with concentrations of welfare recipients to the largest employment centers in the metro area. We use published bus schedules from public transit providers to compute average rush hour travel times between major intersections within each of the neighborhoods or job centers of interest.[6]

Location of Affordable Housing

We also want to determine the degree to which affordable rental housing is available near the region's entry-level job openings. The contract value for rent in the 1990 Census is used to calculate the supply of affordable housing units throughout the Cleveland–Akron labor market, using the U.S. Department of Housing and Urban Development's 30 percent of income measure to define affordable (Bogdon and Can 1997).[7] We followed this rule of thumb in identifying the supply of housing units that could be affordable to an entry-level job holder with no other wage earner present in the household (the most common situation for families leaving welfare for work). Thus, we counted as affordable all units whose contract rent was under $300 per month in 1990. We count only affordable rental units that have at least one bedroom. Efficiency units are rare and would not be suitable for a parent and one or two children—the typical welfare family unit.

In setting the top rental price for an affordable unit, we assume that the former welfare family would be paying the total rent themselves without the assistance of a housing subsidy. While Newman (1995) found that 23 percent of welfare recipients nationally also receive housing subsidies, most are unit-based subsidies (such as publicly owned estates or Section 8 supported buildings), rather than tenant-based vouchers. It is true that tenants with vouchers may well be able to afford market rents over the $300 threshold that we have established. However, tenant-based assistance represents only about one-quarter of assisted housing units in Cleveland, a level that is much lower than in many other cities (see chapter 3). Thus, we suspect that relatively few welfare recipients taking entry-level jobs in Cleveland will be able to afford housing above our $300 cut-off. For buildings that are subsidized, we believe that the contract rents reported in the Census (the rent required by the landlord, which may, or may not, include utilities) do reflect the rent paid by the tenant. Therefore, these units will tend to show up in our counts as affordable whenever tenants of these buildings were paying less than $300 at the time of the Census.

One additional methodological issue of concern stems from the fact that the Census provides the contract rent value for occupied units only. The question arises as to how to assess the value of unoccupied units. Some studies (e.g., Turner and Edwards 1993) impute the rent for unoccupied units using housing characteristics and the rental prices of occupied units. We have chosen to assume that the vacant units represent the normal churning in the rental market rather than a potential unused supply, and do not count them in our analysis. We believe this choice is justified based on our knowledge of the geographic distribution of rental vacancy rates.[8]

Defining Commute Zones

A final component of our methodology is to define commute zones around employment areas. To this end, we analyze data from the Census Transportation Planning Package (CTPP), a special tabulation of the 1990 Census that enumerates the number of persons commuting and average commute times, by transportation mode and departure times (rush hour/non-rush hour), between each possible pair of transportation analysis zones (TAZs) in the metropolitan area.[9] First (as described below), we identify four geographic areas that constitute areas of suburban job growth concentration. We then identify the TAZs included in each of these geographic areas. Second, using the CTPP data we identify the TAZs from which residents commuting alone by automobile to the job cluster TAZs (during rush hour) do so in an average of 20 minutes or less.[10, 11] We then identify a commute zone as a circle drawn from the centroid of the job cluster area. This is the circle that encompasses as many of these residence TAZs as possible while minimizing the inclusion of other TAZs from which commutes are longer. The exact construction of these commute zones is necessarily ad hoc, because the TAZs from which commute times are above and below 20 minutes are not perfectly contiguous areas. Nevertheless, in each case the commute zone captures the preponderance of the areas from which the average commute to the job cluster is 20 minutes or less.

RESULTS

By comparing the geographic distribution of potential job seekers under welfare reform, job openings for which they might qualify, existing public transit routes, and housing that they can afford, we are able to provide a case study of the factors affecting job accessibility in northeast Ohio. It should be noted that the spatial patterns described here are undoubtedly more similar to those in other northern industrial cities than to those in younger cities in the South or West. In addition, the Cleveland region is among the most segregated of U.S. metropolitan areas, both economically (Coulton, Chow, Wang and Su 1996) and racially (Massey and Denton 1993), and these forces tend to influence the locations of welfare recipients, housing, and jobs. Nevertheless, we believe the resulting patterns are instructive of some of the spatial challenges presented by welfare reform.

Where AFDC Recipients Live

In the Cuyahoga County caseload in June 1995, the average adult AFDC recipient had 2.2 children. The majority of these individuals (58 percent) had received cash benefits for at least 36 of the 60 months studied, and had spent extended periods of time out of the labor force

(Coulton, Verma, and Guo 1996). The geographic distribution of the residences of all these adult recipients is presented in figure 4.1. The larger concentration of welfare recipients within the City of Cleveland, primarily in east side neighborhoods, is apparent. In contrast, the presence of welfare recipients in the suburbs is scant, with the exception of east side suburbs sharing boundaries with the City of Cleveland.

The number and percentage of welfare recipients living in the City of Cleveland, its suburbs, and in neighboring counties appear in table 4.1. A full 72 percent of area recipients live in Cuyahoga County, 55 percent of these within the City of Cleveland. Another 20 percent live in the City of Akron and the county in which it is situated. The

Figure 4.1 RESIDENCES OF ADULT (AGES 18 AND OVER) AFDC RECIPIENTS IN CUYAHOGA COUNTY, JUNE 1995

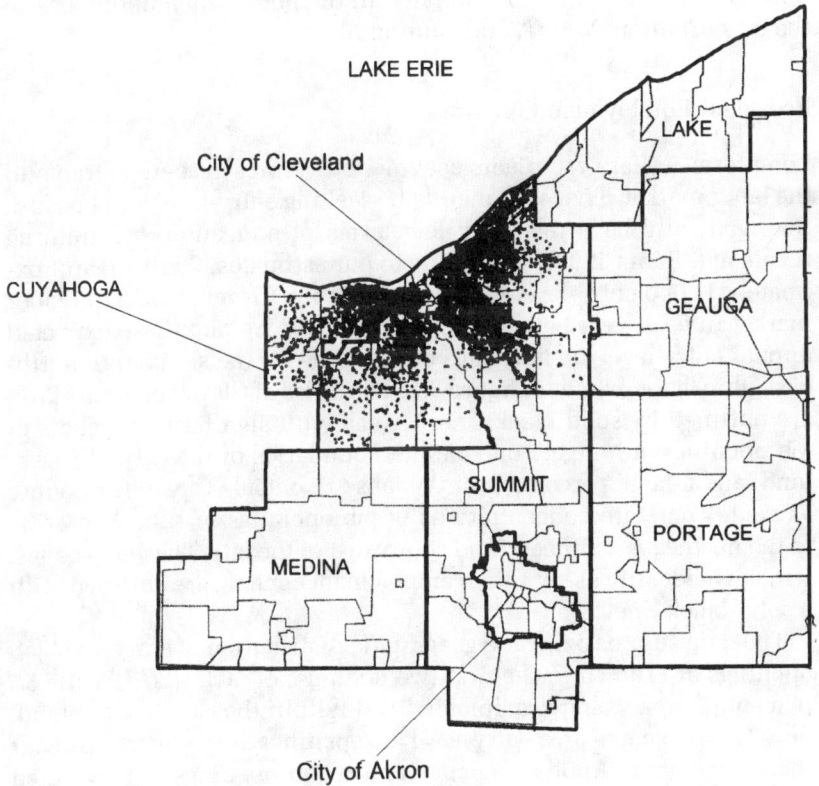

Source: Coulton, Verma, and Guo (1995).

Table 4.1 AFDC RECIPIENTS AGES 18 YEARS AND OVER BY RESIDENCE,
CLEVELAND–AKRON METROPOLITAN AREA, JUNE 1995

	Number	Percent
City of Cleveland (Cuyahoga County)	28,091	55.0%
Cuyahoga County Suburbs	8,684	17.0%
Geauga County	290	0.6%
Lake County	1,378	2.7%
Medina County	676	1.3%
Portage County	1,689	3.3%
Summit County	10,275	20.1%
TOTAL	51,083	100.0%

remaining 8 percent live in the outlying suburban counties. Long-term recipients are more spatially concentrated than the caseload as a whole, and tend to be concentrated in the poorest neighborhoods of the city (Coulton, Verma, and Guo 1996).

Projected Employment Openings

Long-term welfare recipients seeking jobs represent new entrants to the labor market. They will mainly be seeking entry-level jobs because they generally have relatively low levels of education and training (Leete and Bania 1997). According to our estimates, there are approximately 11,000 entry-level job openings in the Cleveland–Akron labor market in each year between 1995 and 2000. We plot these expected annual entry-level job openings by zip code for the six-county northeast Ohio labor market in figure 4.2. The cities of Cleveland and Akron are outlined by solid black lines. Areas with significant numbers of job openings are largely outside the boundaries of the City of Cleveland, and a large percentage of the jobs are outside Cuyahoga County as well. There are concentrations of job openings in suburban areas to the northeast, southeast, and southwest of the city. These zip codes, which we identify as suburban employment centers, are outlined with a solid black line.

The data summarizing the geographic distribution of entry-level job openings are shown in the first two columns of table 4.2.[12] While 55 percent of area welfare recipients lived within the City of Cleveland, only 11.8 percent of area entry-level job openings are expected to occur there each year. Another 5.6 percent of job openings are expected within the City of Akron. The remaining 82.6 percent of job openings are expected to occur in suburban areas. As discussed later, nearly

Figure 4.2 PROJECTED ANNUAL JOB OPENINGS IN ENTRY-LEVEL
OCCUPATIONS, 1995–2000, CLEVELAND–AKRON METROPOLITAN
AREA BY ZIP CODE

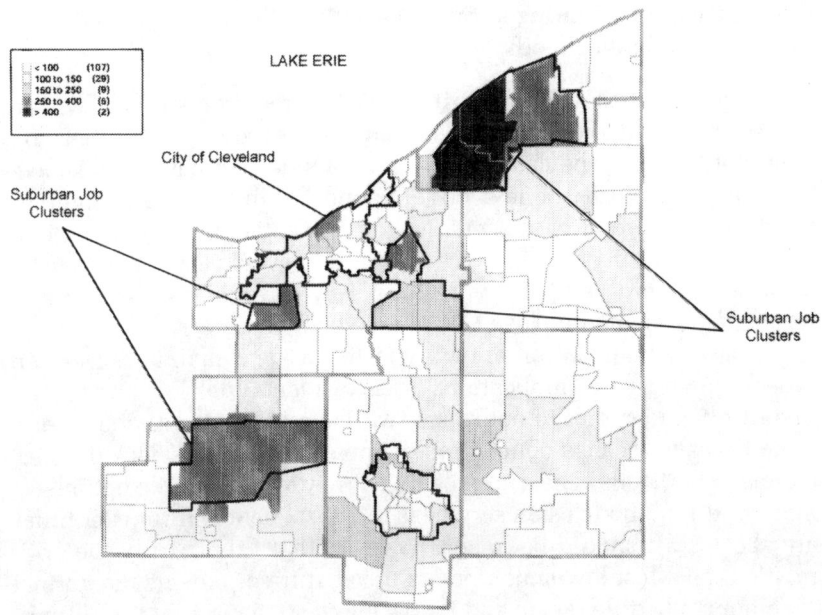

Source: Leete and Bania (1995).

Table 4.2 AFFORDABLE RENTAL UNITS AND JOB OPENINGS BY LOCATION

	Entry-Level Job Openings		Affordable Units	
Location	Number	Percent	Number	Percent
City of Cleveland (Cuyahoga County)	1,232	11.8	43,425	56.3
Cuyahoga County Suburbs	3,712	35.6	10,927	14.2
Geauga County	487	4.7	543	0.7
Lake County	1,545	14.8	1,769	2.3
Medina County	726	7.0	1,189	1.5
Portage County	475	4.6	2,882	3.7
City of Akron (Summit County)	579	5.6	12,325	16.0
Summit County Suburbs	1,657	15.9	4,070	5.3
TOTAL	10,413	100.0	77,130	100.0

25 percent of these are located in four areas of outlying suburban employment concentration, which we highlighted above.

Feasibility of Commuting to Entry-Level Jobs from Inner-City Neighborhoods

We have shown that the majority of AFDC recipients reside within the perimeter of the City of Cleveland, primarily in the inner-city neighborhoods of the east and near west side. We have also shown that the vast majority of new jobs are expected in suburban neighborhoods. In the worst case scenario, the AFDC recipient seeking employment following reform lives in the inner city, does not have access to an automobile, and therefore must rely on public transit. If and when they become employed, they are likely to be earning relatively low wages, which do not allow them to buy and maintain a car. In order to quantify the implications of the residential/job location spatial mismatch under these conditions, we have estimated average commute times to areas of concentrated employment from selected inner-city neighborhoods. The commute times we used were quite optimistic, figured at rush hour when service is most frequent and transfer times are shortest. It should be noted, however, that this is truly the optimistic case. Most low-skill workers travel at times outside the normal rush hour schedule (Leete and Bania 1997), so that actual travel times by bus could be considerably longer. In addition, employment in the suburbs is quite dispersed even within zip codes, so it is likely that commuters will have a significant walk from the bus stop to their ultimate employment destination.

An example of this analysis is presented in figure 4.3. This shows the number of jobs accessible, by public transit commute times, to the population that resides in the neighborhood of East 116th and Kinsman Avenues. Only 929 entry-level job openings are expected to be available each year within a 30-minute bus commute from this location. Naturally, these numbers increase as commute time increases. Seventeen percent of the region's jobs were completely inaccessible from this area of the city via public transportation.

Similarly, table 4.3 presents the share of the region's entry-level jobs that can be reached from five neighborhoods in the City of Cleveland within commutes of various lengths. The neighborhoods represented in this table are among those most likely to be affected by welfare reform. The specified commute times are based on the census data for the region, and represent how long it takes for the average resident of the region to get to work by public transportation (50th percentile

Figure 4.3 PUBLIC TRANSPORTATION COMMUTE TIMES FOR RESIDENTS IN
THE VICINITY OF EAST 116TH ST. AND KINSMAN RD.,
CLEVELAND, OH

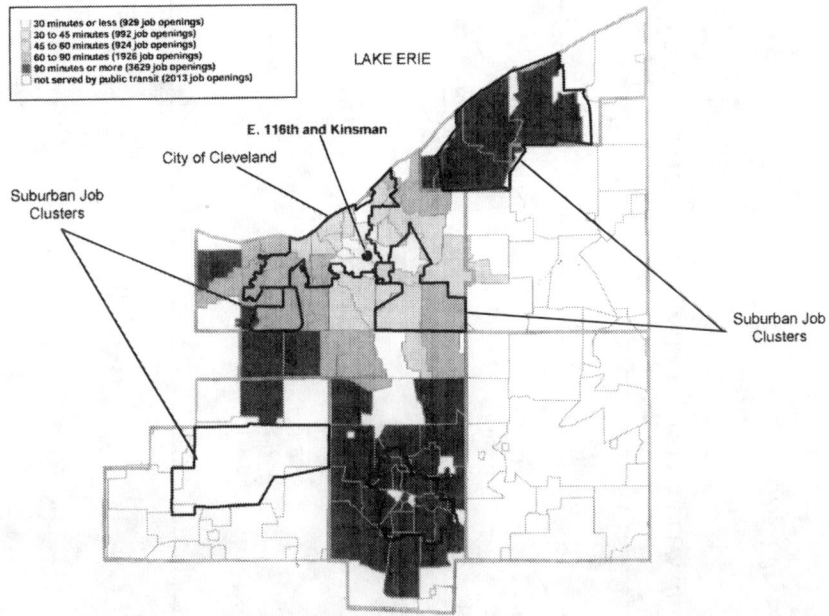

Source: Authors' calculations from published public transit schedules.

commute). The 75th and 95th percentile commute times are also
listed. Automobile commute times are included for comparison. In
an average length commute, inner-city residents with automobiles can
reach about one-third of all area job openings; if the auto commute
time is doubled, three-quarters of the jobs can be reached. Public
transit commutes limit job accessibility. Inner-city residents can reach
only 8 percent to 15 percent of the job openings with an average length
commute on public transit. That amounts to little more than 1,000
positions.

As a final illustration of the feasibility of suburban employment for
city residents, we examine the total existing commute flows from the
City of Cleveland to four suburban job clusters. This analysis enumerates individuals commuting between each residence TAZ and each
workplace TAZ in 1990. These figures are shown in table 4.4, by public
transit and by private automobile, together with their shares of total
suburban area employment. The suburban areas chosen are just ex-

Table 4.3 PERCENT OF ENTRY-LEVEL JOBS ACCESSIBLE WITHIN VARIOUS COMMUTE TIMES FROM SELECTED NEIGHBORHOODS, CLEVELAND–AKRON METROPOLITAN AREA

Neighborhood (Point of Origin)	Average Commute (50th Percentile)		75th Percentile Commute		95th Percentile Commute	
	20 minutes Auto	37 minutes Public Transit	25 minutes Auto	45 minutes Public Transit	40 minutes Auto	80 minutes Public Transit
Cleveland West Side (W. 45 and Bridge)	33.9%	11.5%	44.3%	16.6%	70.3%	43.4%
Cleveland Near East Side (E. 66 and Scoville)	35.4	12.7	48.9	16.5	73.6	43.3
Cleveland East Side (E. 89 and Cedar)	27.8	8.3	48.5	11.1	70.7	39.5
Cleveland Mt. Pleasant (E. 116 and Kinsman)	38.3	9.2	50.9	17.0	73.3	40.9
Cleveland Empowerment Zone (E. 105 and Euclid)	35.0	15.0	51.0	21.0	75.0	44.0

Source: Leete, L., and Bania, N. (1997).

Table 4.4 COMMUTE FLOWS FROM CITY OF CLEVELAND TO SUBURBAN JOB CLUSTER BY COMMUTE MODE, 1990

Job Cluster	Total Employment in Cluster	Car Commuters from City of Cleveland		Bus Commuters from City of Cleveland	
		Number	Percent of Cluster Employment	Number	Percent of Cluster Employment
Southeast Cuyahoga County (Zip codes 44122, 44128, 44146, 44139)	37,619	3,055	8.1	148	0.4
Southwest Cuyahoga County (Zip code 44130)	25,677	1,131	4.4	56	0.2
Lake County (Zip codes 44060, 44077, 44094)	43,542	387	0.9	5	0.0
Medina County (Zip code 44256)	13,614	28	0.2	0	0.0
TOTAL	120,452	4,601	3.8	209	0.2

amples of major employment centers. It should be noted that these data represent a best case scenario for inner-city welfare recipients. It includes all employed individuals, not just those commuting to entry-level jobs, and includes residents from all areas of the City regardless of proximity to public transit, freeways, and so on. Also, non-welfare recipients, whites, and individuals with higher levels of education and training face fewer social, information, and racial discrimination barriers when seeking employment in the suburbs. Even on this measure, less than 4 percent of employment in the suburban areas is held by individuals commuting by car from Cleveland. Only 0.2 percent of total employment (209 individuals out of a total of 120,405) is accounted for by individuals commuting by bus from Cleveland.

These commute flow data are open to more than one interpretation. They could reflect barriers to city-to-suburb employment searches and commuting, but they could be a result of individuals moving to the suburbs after they gain employment there. The latter interpretation implies that the suburban housing stock to date has been sufficient to accommodate these flows. The next question we pose is in this spirit. If the city-to-suburb commute is either impossible (particularly for those requiring public transit) or undesirable, how adequate is the stock of housing in the suburbs that is affordable for low-income families?

Location of Affordable Housing

An alternative to our "worst case" scenario (inner-city residents seeking suburban employment while using public transit) is for individuals entering the labor market to relocate to suburban housing in closer proximity to areas of employment concentration. Due to the inconsistency of public transit availability in suburban areas, under this scenario we must assume that former welfare recipients do have access to automobile transportation. To examine the feasibility of this scenario, we look at the distribution of affordable rental housing in the area, in conjunction with the location of job openings. The spatial distribution of rental units with a contract rental price of $300 or less is represented by census tract in figure 4.4. The greatest concentrations of affordable housing are in neighborhoods within the City of Cleveland, largely in the same neighborhoods that currently house most welfare recipients. The closest area with a significant number of job openings is the downtown, where we estimate there are approximately 877 entry-level job openings each year. Other areas of concentrated job openings have fewer affordable housing units.

Figure 4.4 NUMBER OF HOUSING UNITS WITH MONTHLY RENT LESS THAN
$300 BY CENSUS TRACT, CLEVELAND–AKRON METROPOLITAN
AREA, 1990, WITH SUBURBAN JOB CLUSTER AND COMMUTE RINGS

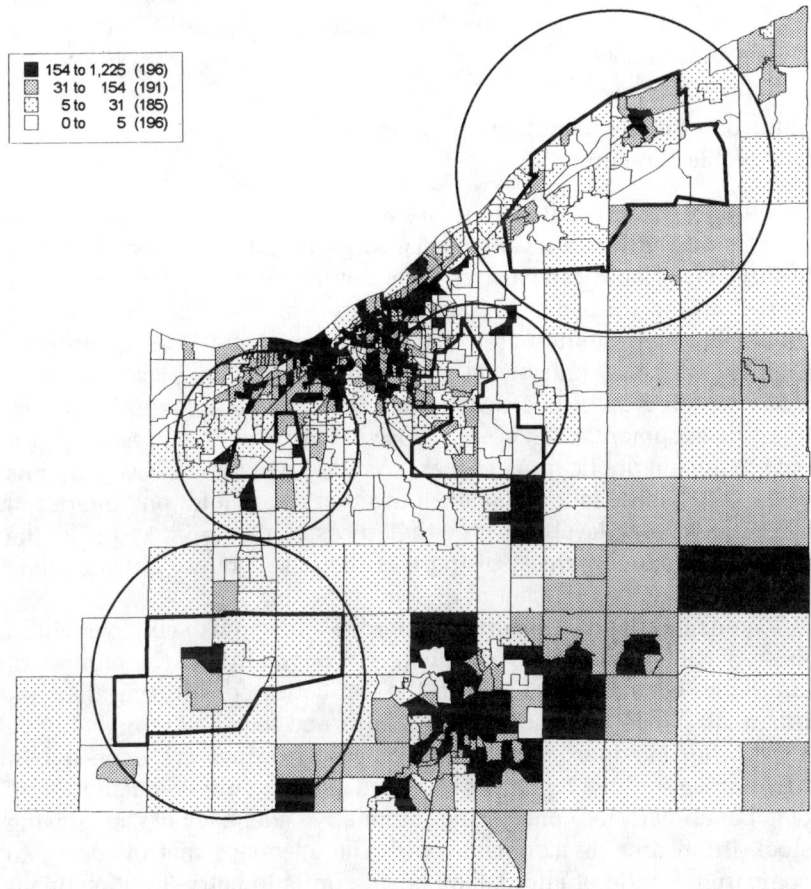

■ 154 to 1,225 (196)
▨ 31 to 154 (191)
▧ 5 to   31 (185)
□ 0 to   5 (196)

Source: Census data and authors' calculations.

Table 4.2 (above) compares the percentage of affordable housing in
different parts of the region with the geographic distribution of entry-
level job openings. The greatest mismatch is within the City of Cleveland, which accounts for 56.3 percent of affordable housing units but
only 11.8 percent of entry-level job openings. Conversely, within the
suburbs of Cuyahoga County, we find 35.6 percent of all area job
openings but only 14.2 percent of affordable housing units. Of course,

county lines are artificial geographic barriers. Perhaps of greater relevance is whether affordable housing lies within a reasonable commute distance of areas of employment concentration. To pursue this line of inquiry we turn to an analysis of several areas of suburban job concentration, their commute zones, and the availability of housing within those areas.

Suburban Employment Centers, Commute Zones, and Affordable Housing

Previously we identified four areas of concentrated suburban job growth: in southeastern Cuyahoga County, in the southwestern corner of Cuyahoga County, in western Lake County on the Cuyahoga County border, and in the center of Medina County, in the southwestern portion of the metropolitan area. Each of these areas is forecast to have high levels of new entry-level job openings in coming years. In each case, the job growth is at least partly attributable to significant new retail development. Each area is close to interstate freeways but without significant public transit access. As shown in the first two columns of table 4.5, these four areas taken together account for one-quarter of all annual entry-level job growth forecast for coming years in the region. The single largest of these is the Lake County cluster, alone accounting for 11.3 percent of area job growth.

To consider the relationship of affordable housing to employment in these particular suburban job clusters, we look first at the number of affordable housing units within the zip codes constituting the suburban job cluster. As shown in the third and fourth columns of table 4.5, while one-quarter of entry-level job openings are expected in these areas, only 4.2 percent of affordable housing is located there. One benchmark for considering the relative adequacy of the housing stock in an area, as compared with the adequacy metrowide, is to compare the ratio of affordable housing units to entry-level job openings for a particular area with that same ratio for the entire metropolitan area.[13] While the affordable housing stock of the metropolitan area may or may not be adequate to house all low-income families, the ratio of housing units to job openings provides us with a general standard for the area. We can then measure whether the adequacy of the housing stock in particular subareas deviates from this standard.[14] The ratio of affordable housing units to entry-level job openings for the entire metropolitan area is 7.4 (77,130 affordable housing units to 10,413 openings). The same ratios for suburban job cluster areas lie between 1.0 and 2.0. This mismatch is partially the result of a lack of

Table 4.5 JOBS AND THE PROXIMITY OF AFFORDABLE HOUSING TO SUBURBAN EMPLOYMENT CENTERS, CLEVELAND–AKRON METROPOLITAN AREA

Job Cluster	Entry-Level Job Openings by Cluster		Affordable Housing Units within Cluster Area			Affordable Housing Units within Average Commute Time		
	Number	Percent of Metro Area Openings	Number	Percent of Metro Area Units	Housing Unit to Job Opening Ratio	Number	Percent of Metro Area Units	Housing Unit to Job Opening Ratio
Southeast Cuyahoga County (Zip codes 44122, 44128, 44146, 44139)	779	7.5	940	1.2	1.2	8,331	10.8	10.7
Southwest Cuyahoga County (Zip code 44130)	311	3.0	531	0.7	1.7	11,448	14.8	36.8
Lake County (Zip codes 44060, 44077, 44094)	1,178	11.3	1,379	1.8	1.2	1,824	2.4	1.6
Medina County (Zip code 44256)	320	3.1	426	0.6	1.3	1,303	1.7	4.1
TOTAL	2,588	24.9	3,276	4.2	1.3	22,906	29.7	8.9
Total For Metro Area	10,413	100.0	77,130	100.0	7.4	77,130	100.0	7.4

affordable housing. But it is also a function of the segregation of residences and places of business within small areas. To pursue this further, we extend our analysis of housing to include the affordable housing within the commute zones associated with each area.

Commute zones are defined, as described in our methodology sec-tion, to encompass the majority of residential areas in which a com-mute into the job cluster can be accomplished (by car) within an average time. These zones are centered on the centroid of each job cluster, and are shown in figure 4.4. The zones have radii ranging from 7 to 12.5 miles, implying that an average commute driving speed of between 20 and 40 miles per hour would be required to travel from the edge of the circle to the center. The number of affordable housing units within each commute zone is shown in the sixth and seventh columns of table 4.5. Here the results depend on the suburban job cluster. A significant number of affordable housing units are reachable within an average length commute from the two job clusters located within Cuyahoga County. These job clusters are in inner-ring suburbs; thus, their commute zones contain significant portions inside the City of Cleveland. The commute zone around the southeast Cuyahoga County area contains 8,331 affordable housing units. The commute zone around the southwest Cuyahoga County area contains 11,448 affordable housing units. Together, the two areas are accessible, within an average length commute, from one-quarter of all affordable housing units in the metropolitan area. The ratio of housing units to job open-ings is 10.7 in the southeast and 36.8 in the southwest, both well above the metropolitan area average.

We see a significantly different picture of housing accessibility in the two outlying suburban areas, Lake County and Medina County. In the commute zones associated with these job clusters we see only marginally more affordable housing units than are located in the job clusters themselves. In Lake County, with over 10 percent of area entry-level job openings, only 1,824 affordable housing units (2.4 percent of the area total) are available within the commute zone. In Medina County, only 1,303 units (1.7 percent of the area total) are available. The ratio of housing to job openings in both instances is well below the areawide average.

DISCUSSION AND IMPLICATIONS

Our study looks at the feasibility of large numbers of welfare recipi-ents becoming employed in entry-level jobs in the Cleveland area, from the perspectives of both commute times and the possibility of moving to be closer to available jobs. We find that welfare recipients living in inner-city neighborhoods who rely on public transportation will be restricted from accessing many of the available job openings in the region. To the extent that they can access suburban job openings, they will have commute times exceeding those of most area workers in similar occupations. Further, their concentration near only one area of major job openings, the downtown, may lead them to displace existing workers in the city. In addition, the possibility that welfare recipients, now highly concentrated in a few city neighborhoods, could relocate to mostly white, middle- and upper-income suburbs seems quite limited. The current supply and location of housing that such job applicants could reasonably afford is mainly in the neighborhoods where they already live. Other unmeasured barriers to movement (such as racial discrimination and preferences) are additional factors that further impede large-scale relocation.

Furthermore, we find transportation barriers that are difficult to overcome using traditional mass transit. Over one-half of the anticipated job openings are served by transit authorities other than the one that serves inner-city Cleveland residents. New collaboration among transit authorities is needed for public transit to cross county lines. Even within areas of employment concentration, firms are dispersed and often not amenable to large-vehicle modes of transportation. This necessitates combined modes of transport. The distances themselves are considerable and, unless high-speed transit is used, average commuting times will well exceed those for the region.

Finally, residential moves to outlying communities with higher concentrations of jobs will not eliminate transportation problems for low-income workers. Mass transit within suburban residential neighborhoods is much less frequent and accessible than it is in the central city. However, it is possible that private solutions such as car pooling, employer vans, and purchases of used vehicles would provide adequate transportation for the shorter distances when work and home are in closer proximity.

This study is limited in that it only looks at spatial locations of people, jobs, housing, and mass transit. It does not take into consideration the role that improved information flows, social supports, or collective action might play in reducing barriers to work for welfare recipients. These are undoubtedly as important as space, and are intricately intertwined with it. Welfare recipients may, in many instances, be "outsiders" in distant communities where considerable numbers of entry-level job openings are located. Social networks between suburban employers and residents of central city neighborhoods can be fostered and strengthened by community-building efforts, though. Such efforts may lead to both improved transportation and the creation of housing options that allow more entry-level workers to live in the communities in which they work.

Notes

The authors acknowledge the support of the Cuyahoga County Department of Entitlement Services, The Summit County Department of Human Services, and The Cleveland and Gund Foundations.

1. GED captures "those aspects of education that contribute to the workers' reasoning development and ability to follow instructions; and the acquisition of 'tool' knowledge such as languages and mathematical skills" (U.S. Department of Labor 1956). The SVP scale indicates (in ranges of months) the total training time needed to perform in an occupation at an average level. Despite limitations, many have argued that the GED and SVP are still the richest available sources of information on the job content of the U.S. economy (e.g., Spenner 1983; Miller et al. 1980).

2. The skill content index is the first factor in a principal factor analysis and the only factor retained. The standardized scoring coefficients for this factor are .696 for GED, .196 for SVP, and .113 for the lower quartile of education. The correlations between GED and SVP, SVP and the lower quartile of education, and GED and the lower quartile of education are 0.85, 0.58, and 0.75, respectively.

3. These figures are consistent with Holzer's (1996) findings that a substantial fraction of noncollege jobs pay less than $6.00 (during the period 1992–1994) and provide no health care or pension benefits.

4. Ohio's occupation and industry employment projections are derived from the national projections prepared by the U.S. Bureau of Labor Statistics. Rosenthal (1992) finds the level of Bureau of Labor Statistics occupation projections for the period 1980–90 to be quite accurate, with actual employment in 1990 totaling 1 percent more than projected employment. Differences between actual and projected employment for the aggregate occupational groups were also generally quite small, with five out of eight major groups exhibiting projection errors of less than 6 percent. At the detailed occupational level, projections of the magnitude of occupational growth and decline exhibited a conservative bias, where the projected degree of growth or decline was smaller than that actually experienced. Less (1992) evaluates Ohio's industry employment projections for the period 1985–1990. Detailed industry employment projections during this period exhibited a weighted mean absolute projection error of 14.4 percent at the 1-digit level of disaggregation. Much of the error in these estimates resulted from failing to forecast Ohio's longer than average recovery from the 1981–82 recession and the associated structural shift from manufacturing to services that occurred in Ohio during this time period.

5. Zip code was chosen as the unit because of the concern about inaccuracies in the street addresses of the ES202 data.

6. When transfers were required, we left a minimum of five minutes to make connections. If a short walk was involved we assumed a walking speed of 3.5 miles/hour.

7. This measure is flawed because it does not take into account housing quality (Lerman and Reeder 1987) or other family needs (Stone 1994).

8. Turner and Edwards (1993) studied four metropolitan areas and concluded that the rental vacancy rates for low-cost housing were as high as 15 percent in some cases. However, these high vacancy rates were concentrated in central city, high-poverty neighborhoods and were largely due to housing that was becoming uninhabitable and close to being removed from the market. The vacancy rates in suburban areas can be assumed to be much smaller, closer to the commonly accepted level of 5 percent that is needed for normal turnover. In fact, in Chicago suburbs, Turner and Edwards (1993) found only a 2 percent vacancy rate among low-cost housing units.

9. The TAZ is a geographic unit approximately equivalent in size to a census tract.

10. Twenty minutes is the average length automobile commute for entry-level workers in the metropolitan area (computed by the authors from the 1990 PUMS).

11. We limit the analysis here to single-person, rush hour automobile commutes for several reasons. First, public transit ridership to these suburban job clusters is small, and sample sizes are too limited to use for analysis. Second, non-rush-hour commute data include middle of the night trips, the times of which can significantly lower the average commute time. Third, car pool commutes are eliminated due to the variability of time associated with collecting all members of the car pool.

12. The total number of openings shown in this table (10,413) includes only those which fall within the county lines of the counties listed. Openings that were attributable to special zip codes (those assigned to individual organizations but not associated with an actual street address, for example) and those located in the portions of zip codes that cross over county boundaries increase the total to 11,233.

13. Of course, one would not expect a 1:1 ratio across the metropolitan area: (1) we are comparing the flow of job openings here with the stock of housing units, (2) many entry-level jobs are held by individuals living in higher-cost housing units with other wage earners (for example, teenagers, partially retired individuals, individuals in two-earner families), and (3) some individuals hold multiple jobs.

14. Of course, this measure is only applicable at a level of aggregation where one expects a mix of both residences and employment. For example, a purely residential block would have an infinitely high ratio of jobs to housing, while a purely commercial block would have an infinitely low ratio.

References

Apgar, W. C., Jr. 1993. "An Abundance of Housing for All but the Poor." In *Housing Markets and Residential Mobility*, edited by G. T. Kingsley and M. A. Turner (99–123). Washington, D.C.: Urban Institute Press.

Bogdon, A. S., and A. Can. 1997. "Indicators of Local Housing Affordability: Comparative and Spatial Approaches." *Real Estate Economics* 25: 43–80.

Carlson, V. L., and N. C. Theodore. 1995. *Are There Enough Jobs? Welfare Reform and Labor Market Reality.* Unpublished manuscript, Center for Urban Economic Development, University of Illinois at Chicago.

Coulton, C. J. 1996. "Poverty, Work and Community: A Research Agenda for an Era of Diminishing Federal Responsibility." *Social Work* 41: 509–520.

Coulton, C. J., J. Chow, E. C. Wang, and M. Su. 1996. "Geographic Concentration of Affluence and Poverty in 100 Metropolitan Areas, 1990." *Urban Affairs Review* 32: 186–216.

Coulton, C., N. Verma, and S. Guo. 1996. "Time Limited Welfare and the Employment Prospects of AFDC Recipients in Cuyahoga County." Center on Urban Poverty and Social Change, Working Paper 96-01. Cleveland: Case Western University.

Ellwood, D. T. 1986. "The Spatial Mismatch Hypothesis: Are Teenage Jobs Missing in the Ghetto?" In *The Black Youth Unemployment Problem*, edited by R. Freeman and H. Holzer (147–185). Chicago: University of Chicago Press.

Galster, G. C., and R. B. Mincy. 1993. "Understanding the Changing Fortunes of Metropolitan Neighborhoods: 1980 to 1990." *Housing Policy Debate* 4: 303–348.

Holzer, H. J. 1991. "The Spatial Mismatch Hypothesis: What Has the Evidence Shown?" *Urban Studies* 28: 105–122.

Holzer, H. J. 1996. "Employer Skill Needs and Labor Market Outcomes by Race and Gender." University of Wisconsin, Institute for Research on Poverty, Discussion Paper 1087-96.

Hughes, M. A. 1991. "Employment Decentralization and Accessibility. A Strategy for Stimulating Regional Mobility." *Journal of the American Planning Association* 57(3): 288–298.

Hughes, M. A. 1995. "A Mobility Strategy for Improving Opportunity." *Housing Policy Debate* 6(1): 271–297.

Ihlanfeldt, K. 1994. "The Spatial Mismatch between Jobs and Residential Locations within Urban Areas." *Cityscape: A Journal of Policy Development and Research* 1(1): 219–244.

Ihlanfeldt, K., and D. Sjoquist. 1989. "The Impact of Decentralization on the Economic Welfare of Central City Blacks." *Journal of Urban Economics* 16: 110–30.

Ihlanfeldt, K., and D. Sjoquist. 1990. "Job Accessibility and Differences in Youth Employment Rates." *American Economic Review* 80: 267–76.

Kasarda, J. D. 1993. "Inner-City Concentrated Poverty and Neighborhood Distress: 1970 to 1990." *Housing Policy Debate* 4: 253–302.

Kingsley, G. T., and P. Tatian. 1997. "Housing and Welfare Reform: Geography Matters." Presented to the Fannie Mae–Johns Hopkins University Institute for Policy Studies Research Roundtable, Baltimore.

Kirschenman, J., and K. M. Neckerman. 1991. "'We'd Love to Hire Them, but . . .': The Meaning of Race for Employers." In *The Urban Underclass*, edited by C. Jencks and P. E. Peterson (203–233). Washington, D.C.: The Brookings Institution.

Lazere, E. B. 1995. *In Short Supply: The Growing Affordable Housing Gap*. Washington, D.C.: Center on Budget and Policy Priorities.

Leete, L., and N. Bania. 1995. *Assessment of the Geographic Distribution and Skill Requirements of Jobs in the Cleveland–Akron Metropolitan Area: Report to Summit County.* Cleveland: Center on Urban Poverty and Social Change, MSASS, Case Western Reserve University.

Leete, L., and N. Bania. 1997. "The Impact of Welfare Reform on Local Labor Markets." *Journal of Policy Analysis and Management* 18(1).

Lerman, D. L., and W. J. Reeder. 1987. "The Affordability of Adequate Housing." *The Journal of the American Real Estate and Urban Economics Association* 15: 389–404.

Less, L. 1992. "An Evaluation of Industry Projections: A Case Study of the Ohio Economy." *Economic Development Quarterly* 6(3): 334–338.

Massey, D. S., and N. A. Denton. 1993. *American Apartheid: Segregation and the Making of the Underclass.* Cambridge, Mass.: Harvard University Press.

Miller, A., D. Treiman, P. Cain, and P. Roos. 1980. *Work, Jobs and Occupations: A Critical Review of the Dictionary of Occupational Titles.* Washington D.C.: National Academy Press.

Mishel, L., and J. Schmitt. 1995. "Cutting Wages by Cutting Welfare." Briefing paper, Economic Policy Institute, Washington, D.C.

Newman, S. J. 1995. "The Implications of Current Welfare Reform Proposals for the Housing Assistance System." *Fordham Urban Law Journal* 22: 1231–1253.

Ohio Bureau of Employment Services. 1993. *Ohio Labor Market Information: Labor Market Projections—Ohio Projections, 1991–2000.* February.

Ong, P. M. 1997. "Work and Automobile Ownership among Welfare Recipients." In *Social Policy*, edited by P. L. Ewalt, E. M. Freeman, S. A. Kirk, and D. L. Poole. Washington, D.C.: NASW Press.

Pastor, M., and A. R. Adams. 1996. "Keeping Down with the Joneses: Neighbors, Networks and Wages." *Review of Regional Economics* 26: 115–145.

Popkin, S. J., J. E. Rosenbaum, and P. M. Meaden. 1993. "Labor Market Experiences of Low-Income Black Women in Middle-Class Suburbs: Evidence from a Survey of Gautreaux Program Participants." *Journal of Policy Analysis and Management* 12(3): 556–573.

Rosenthal, N. 1992. "Evaluating the 1990 Projections for Occupational Employment." *Monthly Labor Review* 115: 32–48.

Spenner, K. 1983. "Deciphering Prometheus: Temporal Change in the Skill Level of Work." *American Sociological Review* 48(6): 824–837.

Stone, M. E. 1994. "Whose Shortage of Affordable Housing? Comment." *Housing Policy Debate* 5: 443–458.

Turner, M. A., and J. G. Edwards. 1993. "Affordable Rental Housing in Metropolitan Neighborhoods." In *Housing Markets and Residential Mobility*, edited by G. T. Kingsley and M. A. Turner (125–160). Washington, D.C.: Urban Institute Press.

U.S. Bureau of the Census. 1993. *Poverty in the United States: 1992.* Washington, D.C.: U.S. Government Printing Office.

U.S. Department of Labor. 1956. *Estimates of Worker Trait Requirements for 4,000 Jobs as Defined in the Dictionary of Occupational Titles.* Washington, D.C.: U.S. Government Printing Office.

U.S. Department of Labor. 1977. *Dictionary of Occupational Titles,* 4th ed. Washington, D.C.: U.S. Government Printing Office.

Chapter Five

WHAT CAN WE LEARN FROM PREVIOUS HOUSING-BASED SELF-SUFFICIENCY PROGRAMS?

Amy S. Bogdon

Efforts to move low-income individuals into jobs and welfare recipients into work have been ongoing for at least 30 years. Figure 5.1 illustrates the timing of selected self-sufficiency, welfare-to-work, and job training programs. States have been required to operate employment and training programs for Aid to Families with Dependent Children (AFDC) recipients since 1967, when Congress created the Work Incentive (WIN) program. Welfare recipients not exempt from work requirements had to register for WIN services before they could receive benefits, and welfare recipients who refused to work could be sanctioned. However, the WIN program proved ineffective, despite repeated reforms. The federal government did not set employment or training goals for states and the requirements became just a paper process for many (Lurie 1996). The goal of the Job Training Partnership Act of 1982 (JTPA) was to help economically disadvantaged adults and out-of-school youth with barriers to employment increase their earnings and employment. Although welfare recipients and low-income individuals were not the primary focus of JTPA, they were often among the program's target population. Important features of JTPA were involvement of the private sector in the development and implementation of job training programs though Private Industry Councils (PICs) and creation of a series of performance measures that focused on outcomes. An extensive research effort documented the impacts of JTPA programs (Orr et al. 1996), one of the first evaluations of a major national job-training program that employed an experimental design with random assignment of individuals to treatment and control groups. Passage of the Family Support Act (FSA) in 1988, which created the Job Opportunities and Basic Skills (JOBS) program, was another important milestone in "welfare reform." Passage of the FSA was influenced by a number of state welfare waivers that tested changes in welfare policy (Wiseman 1996).[1] With the help of case managers, JOBS participants were required to develop individual service plans that prescribed the education, training, job search assistance, and support services they needed to obtain jobs that should lead to self-sufficiency.

In the past decade and a half, the U.S. Department of Housing and Urban Development (HUD) has also run a number of demonstrations intended to help low-income households become self-sufficient. Although a great deal has been written about the welfare-to-work and job training programs, much less is known about these HUD-sponsored housing-based, self-sufficiency efforts. This chapter examines HUD's three major national self-sufficiency programs—Project Self-Sufficiency (PSS), Operation Bootstrap, and Family Self-Sufficiency (FSS)[2]—to determine what can be learned and applied to future self-sufficiency efforts. It also looks at the Gateway Transitional Families Program, a demonstration authorized by Congress in 1988 to allow the North Carolina Public Housing Authority to experiment with some changes to the PSS program.

Figure 5.1 TIME LINE FOR SELECTED SELF-SUFFICIENCY, WELFARE-TO-WORK, AND JOB TRAINING PROGRAMS

HUD and Housing Programs		Welfare and Job Training Programs
	1967	Work Incentive Program (WIN)
	1982	Job Training Partnership Act (JTPA)
Project Self-Sufficiency Round 1 funding	1984	
	1988	Family Support Act creates Job Opportunities and Basic Skills (JOBS) Program
Operation Bootstrap First funding round	1989	
National Affordable Housing Act creates Family Self-Sufficiency	1990	
Family Self-Sufficiency First programs	1991	
	1996	Personal Responsibility and Work Opportunity Reconciliation Act ends AFDC and creates Temporary Assistance for Needy Families (TANF)

PROGRAM DESCRIPTIONS

The HUD programs reviewed in this chapter (see figure 5.2 for administrative characteristics) used housing assistance along with other services to promote participants' self-sufficiency. They also promoted cooperation among public and private sector entities and sought community involvement. They were initiated during the same period that several of the welfare-to-work and job-training programs were beginning or under way. The initial sites for the PSS demonstration were selected in 1984. As described below, some of the services used for PSS participants came from JTPA and WIN programs. The creation of Operation Bootstrap—initially funded in 1989—was influenced by passage of the Family Support Act. Bootstrap programs again relied on services provided through other programs, including the JOBS program. The FSS program, created by the Cranston-Gonzalez National Affordable Housing Act of 1990, coordinated services from various local programs, including JTPA and JOBS.

Project Self-Sufficiency

Project Self-Sufficiency was designed to encourage communities to develop mechanisms for integrating public and private support services to enable unemployed or underemployed single parents with low incomes to become economically self-sufficient. Although HUD required that PSS programs follow the same basic model and include certain standard elements, the demonstration was intended to be flexible enough to meet the needs of individual communities. Certain program elements were mandated, but communities were given discretion in other aspects of program design. HUD provided participating housing authorities with a special allocation of Section 8 certificates, but did not include any additional funding for the support services included in the design.

A total of 154 communities—out of 400 applicants—participated in the PSS demonstration. HUD announced the selection of the first 77 demonstration sites in September 1984.[3] In the second round, 108 communities received funding, including 31 communities already selected in round I. The factors used in selecting public housing authorities (PHAs) for participation in the demonstration included PHA diversity, past PHA performance in administering Section 8, and program resources and planning.[4] The PSS program utilized nearly 10,000

Figure 5.2 ADMINISTRATIVE CHARACTERISTICS OF SELF-SUFFICIENCY PROGRAMS

	Project Self-Sufficiency	Operation Bootstrap	Family Self-Sufficiency
PHA participation	Optional, by proposal	Optional, by proposal	Optional in 1991 and 1992; mandatory in 1993 for incremental Section 8 or public housing
Eligibility	Section 8 applicants	Section 8 applicants	Current Section 8 certificate or voucher holders or public housing residents
Targeted participants	Low-income single-parent households from Section 8 waiting lists	Low-income single- and two-parent households from Section 8 waiting lists	Current residents of public and assisted housing
Participant incentive	Section 8 certificate	Section 8 certificate	Rent increases are deposited to interest-bearing escrow account
Participant selection	Programs encouraged to screen for motivation	Local screening criteria permitted	Only limited screening for motivation permitted
Participant sanctions?	None	None	Section 8 (but not public housing) may be terminated for failure to comply with contract of participation; may also forfeit escrow account
Individual plans?	Only in round II	Individual action plans	Participants enter contracts of participation up to 5 years; "graduation" when they leave welfare or when 30% of income exceeds the fair market rent

Source: Adapted from Blomquist et al. 1994, Appendix A.

Section 8 Existing Housing Certificates totaling about $48 million in contract authority. Federal oversight of the Project Self-Sufficiency demonstration ended in May 1988.

Program design. The design of the PSS program was influenced by the operation of two prior pilot programs.[5] Important program features included the use of housing assistance in a self-sufficiency program, utilization of existing local services and resources, involvement of public and private entities, participation of local elected officials, and screening for participant motivation. Because housing assistance is not an entitlement, the provision of a Section 8 certificate could provide an incentive to enter the self-sufficiency program. Housing assistance could also provide financial security and stability, facilitating family efforts to become self-sufficient. Further, the Section 8 certificate could enable families to locate housing near employment opportunities or move to better neighborhoods.

Since the program provided housing authorities with additional Section 8 certificates but did not include any funding for other services to participants, a key design feature was the involvement of the community. Communities were expected to develop a comprehensive approach to coordinate public and private resources to meet the multiple needs of participating families. Local elected officials were expected to participate in the program to emphasize its importance, help coordinate local services, and mobilize local resources. The local private sector was to be involved in identifying prospective jobs, determining the types of training programs needed, and assisting in job placement. Public and private agencies were to provide existing services and find resources to augment them as necessary.

Another feature of the program, applicant screening to ensure the selection of motivated single parents, also was intended to ensure that resources were utilized effectively. The selection of motivated participants was intended to limit the dropout rate, because housing assistance provided a powerful incentive to apply and there were no sanctions for quitting the program once the certificate was issued.

Program management and operation. Each PSS program was directed by a local task force. The task force was responsible for conducting the local needs assessment, developing program objectives and an action plan, identifying and securing commitments of public and private sector resources, selecting program participants, monitoring participant progress, and evaluating program success. The task force's chief elected official—typically a local mayor, county executive, city manager, or county commissioner—appointed task force members and the task force chair. HUD required the task force to include representatives from the local PHA, public and private agencies with resources or programs to assist the single-parent population, the business community, educational or training facilities, and the low-income single-parent population. HUD also encouraged communities to include other representatives, such as those from state agencies, local private industry councils, Chambers of Commerce, religious institutions, financial institutions, or transportation authorities. A project director or coordinator was typically hired to operate the program. Additional staffing and other needs were to be met using volunteers, loaned staff from local agencies, and additional resources obtained from gifts or donations. The local PHA was required to participate on the task force, to help select program participants, and to administer the Section 8 component of the PSS program. HUD provided guidance and technical assistance.

Participant eligibility and selection. Within the targeting and screening guidelines, the actual selection process was allowed to vary. Some sites only required applicants to submit short written forms while other sites developed more elaborate procedures (the completion of detailed forms, attendance at meetings, interviews, and the accomplishment of other tasks) to screen out the less motivated. PSS sites also considered one or more additional criteria in selecting participants, although they differed in whether these criteria were used to select the easiest to serve or those most in need. One-half of the task forces gave special consideration to applicants with relatively greater housing needs, more than half considered relative economic needs, and more than half considered applicants' current wage earning potential (HUD 1987).

Program services. At minimum, HUD mandated that programs provide housing assistance, child care services, counseling and personal development training, development of job skills, job placement assistance, access to public transportation, and monitoring of individual progress. Other suggested but not required services included general educational development (GED) training, support group discussions, preventive health care training, financial counseling, and housing maintenance training.

Participant incentives and sanctions. Although they may have had other motivation, applicants on the Section 8 waiting list had clear incentives to participate in Project Self-Sufficiency. Participants who did not continue to participate in the PSS program did not face any sanctions. If a recipient dropped out of the PSS program, the Section

8 certificate was lost to the PSS program but not to the PHA. The current recipient and, with turnover, any future recipient of the certificate became part of the regular Section 8 program.

Gateway Transitional Families Program

The Gateway Transitional Families Program is a demonstration run by the Charlotte, North Carolina, Public Housing Authority.[6] In addition to the PSS requirements described above, the Gateway program instituted escrow accounts for participants to help them buy their homes and held AFDC and food stamp benefits constant for a two-year "remediation phase" so participant earning gains would not be offset by benefit reductions.

Current public housing residents or families on the Section 8 waiting list are eligible for the program. Participants enter a contract with the housing authority for a period of up to two years, specifying the services the family will receive and the requirements they must fulfill to remain in the program. During the two-year remediation phase, participants are expected to learn skills that will eventually allow them to become economically self-sufficient. Applicants requiring more than two years of remediation were not accepted into the program. After the two-year contract period, there is a transitional stage, lasting up to five years, during which rents rise to 30 percent of the participant's income. The portion of rent that exceeds $274 per month goes into the escrow account that is intended to help families save for a down payment on a home. Participants also receive services to help them purchase a home.

Operation Bootstrap

Operation Bootstrap's design largely followed the Project Self-Sufficiency model. The major differences were inclusion of two-parent families in Bootstrap, a requirement that participants develop individual action plans,[7] and somewhat greater local flexibility. As in PSS, PHA participation was optional and participating PHAs received a special allocation of Section 8 certificates. Bootstrap programs, like PSS programs, coordinated access to services provided by other public and private agencies. The core functions of Bootstrap programs were recruitment and selection of eligible participants, assessment of service needs, development of individual action plans, issuance of Section 8 rental housing assistance, referral to core services, and ongoing case management. HUD awarded two rounds of Operation

Bootstrap funding, with 2,842 Section 8 certificates awarded to 61 communities in 1989 and 9,086 additional certificates awarded to 292 communities in 1990.[8]

Coordinating Councils were to plan and implement programs, much as did the PSS task forces. Coordinating Councils were to include representatives from the public, nonprofit, and private sectors, although requirements for council composition were less strict than for the PSS task force.[9] The chief elected official was also encouraged to be on the Coordinating Council, although in practice direct involvement was not common.[10] As in PSS, the PHA was not required to be the lead agency. In the first round of Bootstrap funding, PHAs were the lead agency in one-third of programs, multiple agencies in another third, nonprofits in one-fifth, and welfare or JTPA agencies in the remainder (Frees et al. 1994a).

Bootstrap Eligibility was restricted to low-income families eligible for Section 8.[11] Given Bootstrap's focus on self-sufficiency and the example of PSS, many programs screened participants for motivation, with interviews, written applications, or tests used in a number of sites as screening methods.[12]

With some guidance from program regulations, local Bootstrap programs were given the authority to offer the mix of services that would best meet the needs of their clients. Four core types of services were identified: education and vocational training; personal development, including support groups and job readiness skills; job search assistance; and support services such as child care and transportation assistance. Participant incentives were the same as under Project Self-Sufficiency. There were no sanctions for dropping out, although some programs delayed certificate issuance until participants had begun their self-sufficiency efforts.

Family Self-Sufficiency

The Family Self-Sufficiency program, still in operation, borrowed a number of features from its predecessors discussed above, but also included important changes related to PHA participation and to participant eligibility, incentives, and sanctions. In fiscal years 1991 and 1992, PHAs could receive funding under FSS incentive award competitions.[13] Starting with the 1993 fiscal year, FSS programs became mandatory for PHAs receiving incremental Section 8 or public housing units. PHAs may request a waiver of this requirement for specified reasons.[14]

The basic requirements for FSS programs include a minimum program size, an action plan for the housing authority, establishment of a program coordinating committee, contracts of participation with families in the program, and FSS escrow accounts for participants. Program size must be at least equal to the number of incremental Section 8 certificates or vouchers or public housing units reserved beginning with the 1993 fiscal year plus any units reserved under the FY 1991 and FY 1992 incentive award competitions.[15] The housing authority, in consultation with a Program Coordinating Committee and the appropriate local elected official, must develop an action plan to describe the policies and procedures of the FSS program. The action plan is required to include the number and demographic characteristics of expected participants, family selection procedures, incentives to be used to encourage participation, outreach efforts, certification of coordination with appropriate agencies, services to be provided, timetable for implementation, and policies regarding participant sanctions for noncompliance. Recommended membership on the Coordinating Committee includes local elected officials; JOBS and JTPA agencies; and other service providers, local businesses, and other local organizations. Housing authority and assisted housing residents must be represented. The committee's primary goal is to secure commitments of public and private resources for the operation of the FSS program.

Like PSS and Operation Bootstrap, FSS programs are permitted to screen for participant motivation. PHAs may require potential participants to attend FSS orientation sessions or preselection interviews for this purpose. They may also assign tasks that indicate the family's willingness to undertake the obligations required by the FSS contract. However, unlike the predecessor programs, factors such as education and job history cannot be used in the FSS screening process.[16] In selecting participants, PHAs may give preference for up to half their slots to eligible families who have one or more members currently enrolled in an FSS-related service program.

FSS regulations require that local programs provide "appropriate supportive services" to participating families but do not require specific services. Potential services that might be provided under an FSS program include child care; transportation assistance; remedial education and general education/high school completion; job training and preparation; substance abuse treatment and counseling; home management, parenting skills, and money management training; case management; and other services deemed appropriate by the housing authority.[17]

The motivation and incentives for individual participation are different from those in PSS and Operation Bootstrap. FSS is limited to current holders of Section 8 certificates or vouchers or current residents of public housing. In addition, each family in the FSS program must enter into a contract of participation with the housing authority operating the program. This contract includes an individual training and services plan, interim goals for measuring progress, a requirement for complying with the terms of the Section 8 lease, and an employment obligation for the head of the family. The maximum length of an FSS contract is five years, although the contract can be extended under certain circumstances if the family is making progress toward self-sufficiency. FSS participants face sanctions—in some local programs they may lose their Section 8 assistance—if they fail to comply with their contract of participation.[18] The FSS program also adds an escrow savings account as an incentive for participants. PHAs deposit rent increases that result from participant employment into interest-bearing accounts. Participants can access these accounts upon successful completion of the program or, in the interim, to pay for job-related expenses. As in the previous programs, participation is voluntary.

PARTICIPANT CHARACTERISTICS AND SELF-SUFFICIENCY OUTCOMES

The design and implementation of the programs limit what can be learned from these demonstrations, as discussed in more detail in chapters 6 and 7. Most importantly, none of the three major programs followed a true experimental design. Participants were not randomly selected into the programs; most sites screened out less motivated participants, and some sites used educational attainment and/or job experience to select participants. For this reason we can only learn about what happened after program implementation (outcomes). We can say nothing about what happened as a result of the program (impacts), because we have no way of measuring what would have happened without the program. (The evaluation of the Gateway program is a partial exception to this because it did incorporate a quasi-experimental design that used a comparison group of applicants who did not participate in the program as a measure of what would have happened in its absence.) Another limitation is that flexibility in program regulations led to local variation in program design so that outcomes could not readily be compared across sites. Data collection and follow-up were also limited. A further difficulty in assessing self-sufficiency outcomes arises from the time frames for the programs and the studies. In order for self-sufficiency program participants to earn wages high enough to become independent of all types of assistance, most will need significant education or training.[19] Interim follow-up studies done after two years of program participation may observe individuals making progress in educational or training programs or initial employment, but longer-term follow-up will yield better information on actual outcomes. Unfortunately, the typical follow-up period was only about two years in the PSS and Operation Bootstrap studies. While the longer duration of FSS contracts of participation—up to five years—means that participants may remain in the program longer, no findings are yet available on longer-term program outcomes.

Despite these drawbacks, it is important to understand what can be learned from these demonstrations. The following discussion is based largely on the formal research studies of these programs that have been published. HUD prepared two reports on the findings from PSS (HUD 1987, 1988) and contracted with Abt Associates, Inc., for a study of Operation Bootstrap (Blomquist et al. 1994; Frees et al. 1994a, 1994b). Rohe and Kleit (1997a) conducted a longitudinal evaluation of the Gateway Transitional Families Program. The U.S. General Accounting Office (GAO) completed a briefing report on the early stages of FSS (GAO 1992), and Rohe and Kleit (1997b) have completed a recent assessment of the program.

Project Self-Sufficiency

HUD's initial study of PSS examined program outcomes through September of 1986 for a random sample of 40 of the 77 programs initiated in 1984 (HUD 1987). Data and information sources for the report included participant applications and tracking forms, discussions with project directors and PSS task forces, and visits to selected sites. Participant data were aggregated to the site level, and the aggregate data were updated through September of 1986, so the report covers about two years of local program operation. In August 1988, HUD produced an additional brief summary report containing project directors' observations about the program (HUD 1988). As of May 1988, project directors from 134 PSS programs reported that 9,928 out of 29,660 applicants had been accepted into PSS programs. At that time, the local demonstration phase was not yet completed in 35 percent of respondent communities.

Participant characteristics. PSS participants were, on average, some-what better off than AFDC recipients. Some of the difference may be accounted for by the fact that about one-quarter of PSS participants were not receiving AFDC at the time of application. Figure 5.3 sum-marizes differences between PSS participants and AFDC recipients. Average household income for PSS participants was slightly over $5,500, compared with less than $4,000 for AFDC recipients. About one-third of PSS participants' income came from sources other than AFDC, while AFDC recipients relied on AFDC for 95 percent of their income. However, education and training levels for PSS participants were still much below those of the general population.

PSS families were generally small, headed by young mothers with young children. The average participant's age was 27, three years younger than the average AFDC participant. The average number of children was slightly below that for AFDC families (1.8 for PSS com-pared to 2.0 for all AFDC families). About half of PSS households included one child, and one-third included two children. About two-thirds of PSS households contained children under age 5, compared with 60 percent of AFDC households. Nearly all participants were female; only about one percent of PSS participants were male.

Outcomes. Although the program results were generally interpreted positively by HUD and by local program directors, the lack of exper-imental design and the limited availability of comparative data make it difficult to assess the effects of the program itself. Figure 5.4 sum-marizes some of the interim outcomes of PSS, including comparisons with JTPA outcomes and with preprogram conditions. Employment rates nearly doubled, rising from 25 percent at application to 48 per-cent by September 1986. Average hourly wages for employed partici-pants also rose, increasing from $4.20 to $4.94. It is worth noting that

Figure 5.3 CHARACTERISTICS OF PROJECT SELF-SUFFICIENCY PARTICIPANTS

	Project Self-Sufficiency Participants	AFDC Recipients
Average household income	$5,529	less than $4,000
Share employed	25%	5%
Share of income from non-AFDC sources	about 33%	5%
Average age	27	30
Number of children	1.8	2.0
Share of households with children under age 5	66%	60%

Source: HUD (1987).

Figure 5.4 PROJECT SELF-SUFFICIENCY INTERIM OUTCOMES
(As of September 1986)

	At Application	September 1986
A. Average Employment Rates and Wage Rates		
Employment Rates	25.0%	48.0%
Hourly Wage Rates*	$4.20	$4.94

Note: Average wage rates include only working participants.
*As a comparison, the minimum wage was $3.35 per hour from January 1981 through April 1990.

B. Comparison with Job Training Partnership Act Outcomes

PSS employment rates:	80% of the final JTPA level
PSS employment rates:	90% of the final level for AFDC recipients in JTPA
Average PSS wage rate:	6 cents higher than the average JTPA wage

Note: Comparisons are made for each site in relation to the state JTPA outcomes.

C. Attainment of Self-Sufficiency

AFDC independence:	Working participants earned over twice the income needed to be ineligible for AFDC and Medicaid
Section 8 independence:	Working participants earned over half the income needed to become independent of Section 8 assistance.

Note: Comparisons are made for each site in relation to local thresholds.

Source: HUD (1987).

even preprogram average wages were 25 percent above the prevailing federal minimum wage of $3.35.

Interim employment rates were 80 percent of the final level achieved by JTPA participants and 90 percent of the final level achieved by AFDC recipients in JTPA programs. The average PSS wage was nearly the same as the average wage achieved by JTPA participants. In terms of the attainment of self-sufficiency, working participants earned over twice the income needed to be ineligible for AFDC but only about half the income needed to become independent of Section 8 assistance.

Participant housing outcomes also improved. About 80 percent of recipients used their Section 8 certificates to move to a different housing unit. This is markedly higher than in the regular Section 8 program, in which about half of participants move. Rent burden decreased for about one-third of participants, but increased for others. Those paying more for rent may have previously been doubled up or living in substandard housing, so even with an increase in rent burden they chose to use the certificate. Just over 40 percent of households moved from substandard to standard housing, 26 percent moved from higher- to lower-crime neighborhoods, and 21 percent moved from less to more job-accessible locations (HUD 1987). As a result of improved housing circumstances, over two-thirds of PSS project directors concluded that the housing component was among the most important factors in helping participants move toward self-sufficiency.

The 1987 HUD report also provides cross-tabulations of outcomes by various program characteristics. Because of the small sample size and the timing of the report—only interim outcomes were available—these findings should be interpreted cautiously. Project directors from nonprofit organizations headed programs that had a higher share of employed recipients and a higher average wage. Nonprofit directors' greater experience coordinating resources and their greater linkages to other agencies may have led to more rapid program implementation. Programs with wage goals above $4.50 per hour had a lower than average share of employed participants, but higher average wages. Perhaps surprisingly, programs with a greater share of high school graduates did not have the highest employment rates, although they did report the highest average wages. Programs that started with a higher share of employed participants continued to have a greater share employed. Sites with more intensive training had lower employment rates and slightly lower average wages, perhaps reflecting continuing training and the acceptance of lower-paid jobs in the interim. Also surprising was the fact that communities with higher unemployment rates achieved higher PSS employment rates.

According to HUD's 1988 report, 42 percent of participants had completed the PSS program, meaning that they either obtained full-time jobs with growth potential or were enrolled in a two-year or four-year college degree program. Wages for employed participants with full-time jobs averaged over $5.00 per hour. Fully 88 percent of participants were still in PSS programs or had completed them as of May 1988.

Gateway

In their Gateway evaluation, Rohe and Kleit (1997a) employed a comparison group that included those who applied for the program but either did not complete the application process or declined participation once accepted. Except for preapplication education levels, the comparison group's characteristics were similar to those of the Gateway participants. However, because participants were not randomly assigned to treatment and control groups, there remains some selection bias in the estimate of program impacts, even after controlling for differences in education levels.[20]

Differences between program graduates and the comparison group indicated statistically significant improvements in the share with full-time employment, increases in wages, and reduced reliance on AFDC and food stamps.[21] Of those who finished the program, 93 percent achieved full-time employment. Program graduates earned 22 percent more per hour than did the comparison group. Only 10 percent of graduates were dependent on AFDC at the end of the observation period, compared with 41 percent of the comparison group. Graduates were also much more likely than comparison group members to become homeowners. Eleven of the 41 participants who completed the program became homeowners, 20 moved on to private rental housing, and 10 continued to rely on subsidized housing.

A major difficulty with the Gateway program was that only 32 percent of entrants completed the program. The high dropout rate may be partially attributable to problems with the program, which included insufficient program staffing, high staff turnover, program emphasis on nontraditional occupations, the length of the program, and the fact that some participants only signed up so they could obtain public housing. Participant characteristics also contributed to the high dropout rate; some participants were terminated from the program because they used drugs, did not pay their rent, or failed to follow through on program obligations.

Operation Bootstrap

The study of participant outcomes from Operation Bootstrap relied on a survey of participants from a sample of 26 programs.[22] The survey was necessary because HUD did not require any specific data items to be recorded or reported and the available data were not consistent across sites.[23] The 26 survey sites were not selected randomly; the intent was to choose sites with interesting programs and a willingness to cooperate with the study.[24] Survey questions covered the time period from six months prior to program enrollment through the date of the interview.[25] About half—47 percent—of respondents had entered the program at least two years prior to the interview.

Participant characteristics. The initial characteristics of Operation Bootstrap participants differed from nonelderly Section 8 recipients nationwide (figure 5.5). Fully 91 percent of Bootstrap participants

Figure 5.5 CHARACTERISTICS OF OPERATION BOOTSTRAP PARTICIPANTS

	Operation Bootstrap Participants	Nonelderly Section 8 Recipients
Percent female	91%	75%
Share under age 36	70%	55%
Average household size	3.3 people	2.5 people*
Share of households with children under age 18	94%	77%
Share of households with children under age 6	62%	Not available
Received AFDC within 6 months prior to Bootstrap enrollment	49%	Not applicable
Received food stamps in the 6 months prior to Bootstrap enrollment	55%	62%**
Share completing 12 or more years of schooling	78%	63%

Source: Blomquist et al. (1994).
Note: The comparison group is a nationwide sample of Section 8 recipients.
*Average includes elderly households.
**Share of nonelderly Section 8 households receiving food stamps.

were female—slightly less than the 99 percent share of PSS participants but still higher than the 74 percent share of Section 8 recipients
overall. Bootstrap participants were also younger and more likely to
have children under age 18. Nearly all Bootstrap participants had
children under age 18 (94 percent), and 62 percent had children under
age 6. About half of Bootstrap participants received AFDC, and a
similar share (55 percent) received food stamps in the six months
before they enrolled in the program. As a comparison, about 62 percent of nonelderly Section 8 recipients nationwide reported receiving
food stamps. Over three-quarters of Bootstrap participants completed
at least 12 years of schooling, compared with 63 percent of nonelderly
Section 8 recipients nationwide.

Outcomes. Bootstrap participants made mixed progress toward self-
sufficiency. Figure 5.6 compares preprogram characteristics with outcomes 19 to 24 months and 25 to 30 months after program enrollment
for two subsamples of those surveyed. The sample size is much
smaller for the longer-term follow-up group because the interviews
took place in early 1993 and not all the surveyed participants had
been in the program 30 months by that time. Preprogram characteristics are reported separately for each group because they differ
slightly across subsamples.

Figure 5.6 OPERATION BOOTSTRAP—PARTICIPANT PROGRESS TOWARD
SELF-SUFFICIENCY

	Subsample with at least 24-month follow-up		Subsample with at least 30-month follow-up	
	Six months before entry	Months 19–24	Six months before entry	Months 25–30
Number of respondents	337	337	158	158
Looked for work	15%	25%*	13%	24%*
In school or job training	40%	50%*	35%	49%*
Employed	35%	41%	38%	49%*
Employed full time—at least one month at the same job	15%	24%*	18%	26%*
Employed at same job 6 or more months	27%	32%	28%	39%*
Earning an hourly wage over $4.25	28%	32%	30%	42%*
High overall satisfaction with employment	24%	33%*	26%	41%*
Receiving AFDC	45%	48%	44%	47%
Receiving food stamps	45%	53%*	42%	56%*

Source: Blomquist et al. (1994).
*Indicates that the change since program entry is statistically significant at the 10 percent level.

Involvement in employment and training generally increased from preprogram levels, although not all differences were statistically significant. The share who looked for work was about 10 percentage points higher in the follow-up period and the share in school or training was also at least 10 percentage points higher after two or more years in the program. Those enrolled in Bootstrap for at least 30 months showed increases of 8 to 11 percentage points in the share employed, employed full time, or employed at the same job for at least 6 months. Increases for the 24-month follow-up group tended to be smaller or insignificant, with the exception of the share employed full time, which increased by 9 percentage points from the preprogram level. Forty-two percent of the 30-month follow-up group reported earning more than the $4.25 minimum wage. Both subsamples reported increased overall satisfaction with their jobs.

Earlier follow-up periods showed markedly different outcomes, however, with statistically significant *declines* in most employment activities in the 6-month and 12-month follow-up periods as compared with preprogram levels.[26] The share of participants in school or training was higher in the initial follow-up periods than later. The observed pattern of initial decline and later improvement in employment outcomes may be a result of the program—in that more reliance on training in the early months of program involvement might limit employment opportunities initially and improve them over time. However, other factors could also have been responsible for this pattern.

While participants appeared to be making slow progress toward self-sufficiency on the employment front, their reliance on AFDC and food stamps did not decline. The share receiving AFDC was slightly higher in the two follow-up periods than prior to program enrollment, although the differences are not statistically significant. The share relying on food stamps rose above 50 percent, a statistically significant increase over preenrollment levels. Some increase in participant reliance on public assistance may have been a result of greater awareness of these programs.

Participants also improved their housing outcomes, although not as dramatically as in PSS. Fully 84 percent of participants were the sole tenants of private apartments at the start of the program. Based on participant self-rating of housing and neighborhood characteristics, the Section 8 assistance led to improvements in unit quality, neighborhood safety, school quality, and neighborhood appearance and quality. Improvements were larger for the 42 percent of participants who moved sometime between program enrollment and the interview date.

Family Self-Sufficiency

Because FSS is the most recent of the programs and has the longest period of participation, few outcomes have been reported to date. Rohe and Kleit (1997b) report on the results of a survey they mailed to the 1,039 PHAs that had at least 250 units of assisted housing and that were identified as having received incremental Section 8 vouchers or certificates or public housing units after FY 1991.

Larger public housing authorities (those with 1,250 or more units) were more likely to have an active FSS program than were smaller authorities. Fully 84 percent of the largest authorities that received incremental housing assistance in FY 1993–95 reported operating an FSS program. In comparison, 76 percent of medium-sized programs (with between 500 and 1,249 units of assisted housing) and 69 percent of the small programs (between 250 and 499 units) reported active FSS programs. Because most incremental housing assistance has been in the form of Section 8 certificates or vouchers, most FSS programs (67 percent) are exclusively for Section 8 recipients.

Rohe and Kleit (1997b) estimate that there have been slightly over 59,000 participants in FSS programs begun in 1995 or earlier, making this a much larger effort than previous programs (Figure 5.7). As in both PSS and Bootstrap, nearly all FSS participants (91 percent) are female. Nearly half (48 percent) receive welfare, and 64 percent receive food stamps. Fully 69 percent of the participants were still enrolled in FSS programs as of the survey date. Just over 6 percent of participants had already completed an FSS program; 7 percent had dropped out; and 17 percent had withdrawn for reasons such as moving to another city, getting married, or moving out of public housing. Thirty-one percent of participants had established escrow accounts as of the survey date, suggesting that they had increased their incomes above preprogram levels.[27]

PHAs responding to Rohe and Kleit's survey cited a lack of interest in the program by potential participants, understaffing, and a lack of job opportunities when participants graduate as large problems they encountered in the past year. Over 40 percent of responding PHAs cited lack of participant interest in the program as a large problem, and only 24 percent stated that it was not a problem. Potential participants appear to be concerned about leaving public housing or Section 8 or losing other benefits, are more interested in caring for their families, have a cynical attitude toward social programs, are unwilling to sign a 5-year contract, or face other difficulties. Just over 40 percent of local programs indicated that understaffing was a large problem, and 33 percent found a lack of job opportunities to be a large problem.

IMPLICATIONS AND CONCLUDING THOUGHTS

These limited findings are open to both optimistic and pessimistic interpretations. On the optimistic side, given certain incentives, re-

Figure 5.7 ESTIMATED NUMBER OF FAMILY SELF-SUFFICIENCY PARTICIPANTS

	Participants	Percentage Distribution
Program graduates	3,792	6.4%
Dropouts/terminations	4,268	7.2%
Withdrawn from program	10,274	17.3%
In program as of survey date	40,971	69.1%
Total number ever in program	59,305	100.0%

Source: Rohe and Kleit (1997b).
Note: Counts participants in programs begun in 1995 or earlier.

cipients have volunteered to participate in self-sufficiency programs and are making progress toward self-sufficiency. The receipt of Section 8 certificates improved the housing outcomes (and possibly the neighborhood outcomes) for many participants, enabling them to pursue their self-sufficiency goals. Also, local programs have been reasonably successful in coordinating a wide range of services to assist participants. In the Gateway program, program graduates had a high full-time employment rate; had higher wages than the comparison group; and relied less on AFDC, food stamps, and housing assistance than did the comparison group.

On a more pessimistic note, the early program findings do not show participants becoming completely independent of all assistance programs, despite progress. Even the limited progress that participants have made is based largely on a selective, highly motivated subsample of housing assistance recipients. In the same vein, there was even more "creaming" of the most able participants in PSS and Bootstrap than in FSS, since local sites were allowed to determine their own selection criteria and many selected those with more education or job experience. The difficulties associated with participant recruitment for FSS are also troubling. The understaffing of FSS programs is also likely to limit their effectiveness. And Gateway's high dropout rate, which is attributable partially to the difficulties inherent in serving public housing–eligible households, illustrates another difficulty for self-sufficiency efforts.

On the evaluation side, it is not possible to state definitively that the programs were successful, let alone cost-effective, in moving participants toward self-sufficiency, since the program design precluded the possibility of estimating program impacts, except in the Gateway evaluation. Another evaluation goal, to learn more about the potential role that housing assistance could play in increasing prospects for self-sufficiency, also remains elusive.

Even so, since it is clear that a large number of participants benefited from their access to self-sufficiency programs, it is important to understand better the magnitude of these benefits for the individuals and the program as a whole. In pursuing such understanding, designers of future programs should consider the following recommendations:

- If program regulations permit, consideration should be given to limited program experiments incorporating treatment and control groups. If this is not feasible, a quasi-experimental design should be considered. The Jobs-Plus demonstration, for example, incorporates a quasi-experimental design to capture differences in outcomes for treatment and control sites.

- Require collection of program data in a standardized (preferably computerized) format at the start of the program (participant application) and at selected intervals (e.g., annually).
- Since a major cost of coordinating services and other resources from multiple sources is the difficulty of collecting complete information on participants, fund technology experiments that enhance data gathering from multiple service providers. This could benefit both program evaluators and service providers.
- Test a mandatory program, even though this would require a statutory change. One possibility would be to make the program mandatory for a random sample of new housing assistance recipients.
- Use new or existing data to make some estimates (or a range of estimates under varying assumptions about impacts) of the cost-effectiveness of the programs.
- In line with the welfare-to-work literature's testing of different income disregards, test the incentive effect of different variants of the escrow account, possibly combined with other incentives.
- Given the obstacles faced by many assisted households, continue some services after participants become independent of AFDC and food stamps. A follow-up study of long-term job retention should then consider which transitional services are most effective in helping participants remain employed.

The most fundamental conclusion is that the potential role of housing assistance in the long-term process of attaining self-sufficiency still needs to be addressed. In different programs, housing assistance has served as an incentive for entering a self-sufficiency program, as a means of providing stability and security to families on their way toward self-sufficiency, and as a means to locate near employment opportunities or move to better neighborhoods. In the PSS and Bootstrap programs, the receipt of housing assistance clearly improved housing outcomes and probably improved neighborhood outcomes. Since FSS participants are already receiving housing assistance, the self-sufficiency program is not the source of any improvements in housing conditions resulting from the receipt of housing assistance. One suggestion made in the evaluation of the Gateway program was to cluster participants in a single public housing site so they could provide encouragement to one another (Rohe and Kleit 1997a). This will be done implicitly in the Jobs-Plus demonstration, since the program aims to saturate a single public housing site with a wide variety of employment-related and other supportive services.

However, the fact that housing is not an entitlement and the existence of waiting lists for Section 8 assistance means that households may hesitate to give up their housing assistance, knowing that they cannot readily get it back.[28] Beyond some point, this may serve as more of a disincentive to increasing earnings than the Section 8 program's implicit 30 percent "tax" on increases in income. Since housing assistance typically has higher income limits for continued eligibility than do the "welfare" programs, the potential stabilizing role of housing assistance needs to be studied further.

Housing programs will also be affected by the local outcomes of "welfare reform." Most recipients of Temporary Assistance for Needy Families will face work requirements and time limits. One possibility is that demand for FSS will increase as participants become aware of impending time limits for welfare assistance. If so, then programs that are already understaffed may become oversubscribed, further limiting their effectiveness.

Notes

I would like to thank Bill Rohe and Mark Shroder for their insights and for their help in obtaining unpublished information on the programs discussed in this article. I would also like to thank Robert Kornfeld, Sandra Newman, Barbara Sard, Felicity Skidmore, participants at the July 1997 Roundtable, and two anonymous reviewers for their helpful comments.

1. The Omnibus Budget Reconciliation Act of 1981 granted states more discretion in the operation of welfare employment and training programs, thus initiating the welfare waiver process. The approval of program waivers was often contingent on the inclusion of an evaluation component that relied on classical experimental design, comparing the outcomes of treatment and control groups

2. HUD and local housing authorities have also supported other self-sufficiency efforts. Current HUD programs and demonstrations that have employment and training or self-sufficiency components include HOPE VI, Moving-to-Work, Jobs-Plus, Bridges to Work, the Economic Development and Supportive Services Grant program, Campus of Learners, Neighborhood Networks, Youthbuild, and the Tenant Opportunity program.

3. The Notice of Funds Availability was published in the Federal Register on May 21, 1984 (HUD 1985).

4. HUD aimed for PHA diversity in terms of geographic location, population, and level of government (city, county, or other locality). The selection process also took into account HUD field office comments regarding the past performance of the PHA in administering Section 8 and other programs. In evaluating the proposed PSS program, HUD considered the extent of local public sector resources committed to the program;

the extent to which the task force represented a broad spectrum of the community capable of marshaling the necessary public and private sector resources; the extent to which the application reflects an understanding of the PSS concept; the degree of cooperation between local government, the PHA, and the private sector; and the ability of the applicant to implement the program in a reasonable period of time (HUD 1985).

5. The pilot programs were Project Independence in Prince George's County, Maryland, and Warren Village in Denver, Colorado (HUD 1985).

6. Rohe and Kleit (1997a) provide a more detailed description of the program and an appraisal of its success.

7. Similar plans were required in round II of Project Self-Sufficiency.

8. 1,053 of these additional certificates went to 39 of the communities who participated in the 1989 funding round.

9. Only 10 of the 26 sites in the Bootstrap evaluation (see further below) actually included representatives from private business on their Coordinating Council (Frees et al. 1994a).

10. The involvement of elected officials or their representatives appeared to be associated with greater success in obtaining public resources. However, it seems reasonable to assume that both the amount of involvement in the program and the extent of resources made available would be related to the degree of the chief elected official's interest in it.

11. Twenty-one of the 26 sites included in the Abt study further restricted their targeting. Nine of the programs focused on particularly vulnerable populations; 12 targeted individuals with a greater likelihood of becoming self-sufficient, using education and/ or job experience as selection criteria.

12. In the Abt study, 21 of 26 sites relied on interviews, 16 used written applications, and 7 used tests to screen for motivation.

13. The criteria used to select PHAs for participation in 1991 and 1992 included the successful implementation of an existing self-sufficiency program (for Section 8 programs), or PHA efforts to establish/support resident councils, resident management, and similar initiatives (for public housing programs). Other selection criteria were similar to those used to select PHAs for Project Self-Sufficiency. For public housing, separate competitions were held for FY 1991 and 1992 incentive awards. For Section 8 assistance, there was a single combined FY 1991/1992 competition.

14. Reasons include lack of supportive services in the area, lack of support from state or local officials, lack of funds for administering the program, or lack of interest on the part of the assisted tenants (Rohe and Kleit 1997b).

15. HUD may grant exceptions to the minimum program size requirement. The reasons for granting exceptions are similar to reasons for allowing housing authorities not to operate a program.

16. Prohibited screening factors include education level or educational or standardized motivational test results, previous job history or performance, credit rating, marital status or number of children, manual or sensory skills, or any factors that may result in discriminatory practices or treatment.

17. Although not explicitly mentioned in the Code of Federal Regulations (CFR) or the National Affordable Housing Act, a significant share of programs include community college and university programs among the services offered. Rohe and Kleit (1997b) find that 77 percent of responding agencies include community college programs and 59 percent include four-year university programs among their list of services.

18. However, public housing residents cannot lose their housing assistance for failing to meet the terms of their contract. In practice, most local programs do not withdraw Section 8 assistance for FSS dropouts.

19. According to U.S. General Accounting Office (GAO) calculations for FY 1992, a family renting a two-bedroom unit would need earnings of at least $1,533 to $3,022 a month to become independent of housing assistance (GAO 1993). The income required in the median state was $1,955 a month—a wage rate of about $13.00 an hour for an individual working 150 hours a month.

20. Those who participated in the program may have unobservable characteristics that predisposed them to succeed in comparison with those who did not complete the application process. However, those who declined participation in the program could potentially have more (or less) motivation than those who actually participated. While the direction of the bias is therefore not certain, it seems likely that the net results would overstate any positive program impacts and understate negative ones.

21. The results reported here control for the differences in characteristics between the program participants and the comparison group. For more details, see Rohe and Kleit (1997a).

22. A major drawback of relying on participant surveys is the potential for participant recall error. This may be a more serious issue for the longer recall periods.

23. In particular, systems of aggregation were limited and variable across sites. The various agencies providing core services keep fairly detailed case records but could not always identify Bootstrap participants separately from others using the same services. It was also not possible in most cases to compile service delivery information from all agencies to create a pooled database.

24. Seven characteristics—lead agency, participant selection requirements, previous self-sufficiency experience, geographic region, urban/rural location, size, and local labor market conditions—were considered in final site selection. Details about the selection process are described in Frees et al. (1994a).

25. Telephone interviews were conducted with 798 of the 2,109 participants at the sample sites; outcomes are reported for various subgroups of the 723 responses deemed usable.

26. More detailed outcome tables are included in chapter 5 of Blomquist et al. (1994).

27. Although most participants do not have escrow accounts, the accounts appear to be a major motivating factor for a minority of participants. Among participants with escrow accounts, the average balance is $1,600 and monthly contributions average $225 (Internal HUD memorandum made available by Mark Shroder).

28. In the current Section 8 program, participants may already face an income "cliff" if the Fair Market Rent (FMR) is less than 30 percent of their increased income. At this point, they receive no subsidy even if they are still within the income eligibility limits. Section 8 includes a one-year suspension feature through which a family's Section 8 assistance can be reinstated—without going through the waiting list and application process—if their income drops so that their rental contribution is less than the FMR.

References

24 CFR, Subtitle B, Chapter IX, Part 984. *Section 8 and Public Housing Family Self-Sufficiency*.

Blomquist, John D., Ingrid Gould Ellen, and Stephen H. Bell. 1994. *Documentation of Operation Bootstrap, Volume II: Report on Project Outcomes*. Project report prepared for the U.S. Department of Housing and Urban Development, HUD-1484-PDR.

Cranston-Gonzalez National Affordable Housing Act. Public Law 101-625. November 28, 1990.

Frees, J. W., Ingrid Gould Ellen, and Gretchen Locke. 1994a. *Operation Bootstrap, Volume I: Program Administration*. Project report prepared for the U.S. Department of Housing and Urban Development, HUD-1483-PDR.

Frees, J. W., Gretchen Locke, Ingrid Gould Ellen, and Christian Holm. 1994b. *Operation Bootstrap, Volume III: Case Studies*. Project report prepared for the U.S. Department of Housing and Urban Development, HUD-1485-PDR.

Lurie, Irene. 1996. "A Lesson from the JOBS Program: Reforming Welfare Must Be Both Dazzling and Dull." *Journal of Policy Analysis and Management* 15(4): 572–586.

Newman, Sandra, and Ann Schnare. 1988. *Subsidizing Shelter: The Relationship between Welfare and Housing Assistance*. Washington, D.C.: The Urban Institute.

Newman, Sandra, and Ann Schnare. 1994. "Back to the Future: Housing Assistance Policy for the Next Century." In *New Beginnings Project: A First Report* (1–24). Washington, D.C.: Center for Housing Policy.

Orr, Larry L., Howard S. Bloom, Stephen H. Bell, Fred Doolittle, Winston Lin, and George Cave. 1996. *Does Training for the Disadvantaged Work?* Washington, D.C.: Urban Institute Press.

Rohe, William M., and Rachel Garshick Kleit. 1997a. "From Dependency to Self-Sufficiency: An Appraisal of the Gateway Transitional Families Program." *Housing Policy Debate* 8(1): 75–108.

Rohe, William M., and Rachel Garshick Kleit. 1997b. "Returning Public Housing to Its Roots: An Assessment of the Family Self-Sufficiency Program." Working paper, Center for Urban and Regional Studies, University of North Carolina at Chapel Hill.

U.S. Department of Housing and Urban Development. 1985. *Project Self-Sufficiency Guidebook*, Washington, D.C.: U.S. Government Printing Office.

U.S. Department of Housing and Urban Development. 1987. *Project Self-Sufficiency: An Interim Report on Progress and Performance*. Washington, D.C.: U.S. Government Printing Office.

U.S. Department of Housing and Urban Development. 1988. *Project Self-Sufficiency: A Summary*. HUD-5323. Washington, D.C.: U.S. Government Printing Office.

U.S. Department of Housing and Urban Development. 1996. *Promoting Self-Sufficiency in Public Housing*. Urban Policy Brief Number 2, August.

U.S. General Accounting Office. 1992. *Public and Assisted Housing: Linking Housing and Supportive Services to Promote Self-Sufficiency*. GAO/RCED-92-142BR, April.

U.S. General Accounting Office. 1993. *Self-Sufficiency: Opportunities and Disincentives on the Road to Independence*. GAO/HRD-93-23, August.

Wiseman, Michael. 1996. "Welfare Reform in the United States: A Background Paper." *Housing Policy Debate* 7(4): 595–648.

LESSONS FROM WELFARE-TO-WORK EXPERIMENTS AND THEIR IMPLICATIONS FOR HOUSING-BASED SELF-SUFFICIENCY PROGRAMS

James Riccio

Compared to mainstream welfare-to-work and job training programs, similar programs intended explicitly for residents of public and assisted housing have operated on a much smaller scale and, as discussed in the previous chapter, little is known about their effectiveness. Yet, their fundamental goal—to help poor families advance toward self-sufficiency—is shared by their mainstream cousins, a number of which have been subjected to careful evaluation as part of large-scale social experiments. This chapter discusses findings from some of the most important welfare-to-work and job training experiments conducted in recent years and the lessons they hold for housing-based initiatives. Although the context differs, these lessons can inform the debate over how best to structure and operate self-sufficiency programs for residents of public and assisted housing. The chapter then describes Jobs-Plus, an ambitious new employment initiative for public housing residents in seven cities that builds upon the lessons of the past and also charts new directions. It incorporates strategies found in the most effective welfare-to-work programs to date but also includes new approaches designed to overcome the limitations of even the best-performing programs of the past. In addition, Jobs-Plus will be rigorously evaluated to determine whether the program dramatically increases residents' employment outcomes and quality of life. To do so with a high degree of credibility, the evaluation must surmount the special challenges inherent in attributing causality in evaluations of community- or place-based initiatives.

HOUSING-BASED SELF-SUFFICIENCY PROGRAMS

Major housing-based self-sufficiency programs are relatively recent inventions, dating back to 1984, when the Department of Housing and

Urban Development (HUD) launched its first major initiative of this type. In more recent years, the goal of helping residents of public and assisted housing advance toward self-sufficiency has taken on a new urgency and has become critical in the wake of recent welfare legislation that imposes time limits and other new restrictions on access to welfare. Many observers fear that these restrictions will reduce many residents' income and, hence, their ability to pay rent. For public housing authorities, this would exacerbate the financial strain they are already feeling from reductions in HUD operating subsidies that help fill the gap between rent revenues and operating costs.

The main housing-based self-sufficiency initiatives of the past (described in chapter 5 of this book) have been decidedly modest interventions, unlikely to suffice in moving large numbers of residents to economic independence.[1] Despite a number of important differences in their design and operation, some or all of these programs share certain assumptions or theories about how best to promote self-sufficiency for recipients of government housing assistance.[2]

One assumption, at least as the programs have been put into practice, appears to be that employment and training services should give priority to building residents' human capital through education and training activities before encouraging recipients to enter the labor market. This is expected to help residents qualify for better-paying jobs that will enhance their chances of becoming self-supporting. A second assumption is that program effectiveness is enhanced by choosing participants very selectively, with preference given to those volunteers who appear to be highly motivated. The rationale appears to be that more motivated individuals will make better use of the services offered and, therefore, be more likely to benefit from the program. A third assumption, pertinent to the Family Self-Sufficiency and Gateway programs, is that stronger financial incentives for residents to work are essential to achieving that goal, and that an escrow savings plan is an effective incentive strategy.

As discussed in the foregoing chapter, none of these programs has been subjected to the types of evaluation than can reliably determine its effectiveness. If it is not possible to know from existing research whether these programs have been effective, it is worth considering whether the assumptions on which they rest are supported by other research. Studies accumulating over the past two decades that rigorously evaluate welfare-to-work and job training programs offer a number of pertinent lessons. These findings cannot, of course, be used to infer in any convincing way whether the housing-based programs are likely to have been effective. However, they can provide a useful basis for thinking critically about that issue, and for thinking creatively about possible ways of designing more effective housing-based programs in the future.

LESSONS FROM WELFARE-TO-WORK PROGRAMS

The research on welfare-to-work programs paints a mixed picture. The good news is that some initiatives are indeed effective: they increase employment and earnings, reduce welfare payments, and are well worth investing in. At the same time, even the best-performing programs have important limitations. In particular, they have had little success in reducing poverty and job turnover remains high.

Much of the evidence for these conclusions comes from a series of social experiments over the last two decades involving initiatives targeted toward recipients of cash assistance (mostly single mothers) under the former Aid to Families with Dependent Children (AFDC) program, which has since been replaced by the Temporary Assistance for Needy Families (TANF) program. In assessing the programs' effectiveness, the studies relied on random assignment designs, the gold standard of evaluation research and a method that (as noted earlier in this book) has rarely been used to evaluate self-sufficiency programs for residents of public or assisted housing. Welfare recipients were assigned on a random basis (though a computerized "coin flip") either to a program group that got the special program or to a control group that did not. Both groups were followed over time, and a program was judged effective only if the accomplishments (e.g., average earnings) of its enrollees were above and beyond what the control group achieved without the special program intervention. What has been learned from these studies?[3]

Short-Term, Low-Cost, Mandatory Jobs Search Programs

In the early 1980s, a number of states launched demonstration programs that established a tighter connection between the receipt of welfare and participation in work-related activities. They required participation in individual job search activities or job search classes, or "job clubs," that taught welfare recipients how to look for work, how to prepare resumes, and how to present themselves favorably to employers. In some cases, the programs also included a small-scale unpaid work experience or "workfare" component. Participation in the programs was mandatory for single parents with school-age children. Failure to comply with the participation requirement could result in a financial sanction in the form of a reduced monthly welfare check, unless one had a good excuse for not complying. Through these efforts to establish a mutual obligation—with government providing the opportunities and residents being required to take advantage of them—welfare was to be transformed from a pure entitlement to a "conditional entitlement."

Overall, the programs were modestly effective. They typically raised employment rates above and beyond those of the control group by about 4 to 6 percentage points, and increased earnings by 12 to 28 percent (although the average dollar value of the gain was not large).[4] They also achieved small reductions in welfare payments. However, the programs were not successful in raising earnings of long-term welfare recipients, who seemed to require more intensive assistance to prepare them for work. These findings helped pave the way for a more ambitious approach (Gueron and Pauly 1991).

A Mix of Services: Job Search, Education, Training, and Workfare

In 1988, the federal government passed a new law establishing the Job Opportunities and Basic Skills (JOBS) training program. The goal was to achieve larger effects than the earlier programs by investing heavily in "human capital development" through education and training in addition to job search and workfare. Special attention was to be given to improving the basic reading and math skills of welfare recipients, in the belief that recipients without those skills would have an increasingly difficult time finding jobs in America's post-industrial economy—especially jobs paying a decent wage and offering fringe benefits. Again, participation in the program was mandatory.

Two of the largest studies of these reforms reveal important successes but also limitations. Findings covering a five-year follow-up period are available from a six-county study of California's version of this program, the Greater Avenues for Independence (GAIN) program, the largest welfare-to-work program in the nation. These are the most complete and longest-term results from studies of programs operating under the 1988 law.

Overall, the findings on GAIN are positive (Riccio, Friedlander, and Freedman 1994; Freedman et al. 1996). The program, with its mix of services and ongoing participation mandate, increased employment and earnings and reduced welfare payments in most of the study counties. Moreover, the earnings effects were sustained or grew over time. This contrasts with the pattern found in studies of the mostly job search programs of the early 1980s. In those earlier studies, the control group tended to "catch up" to the program group, with little difference in outcomes remaining between them by the end of the fifth year of follow-up.

Other important findings are emerging from a large, cross-state study of programs in seven locations in six states, known as the National Evaluation of Welfare-to-Work Strategies and sponsored by the U.S. Department of Health and Human Services (HHS). This study is still under way, but short-term results covering two years of follow-up are currently available from four of those sites and point to early positive effects (Hamilton et al. 1997; Scrivener et al. 1998).

Emphasizing Quick Job Entry within a Mixed-Service Strategy

Evidence from GAIN and other studies suggests that a pervasive program emphasis on moving recipients into the labor market quickly may be a key element in producing large impacts on earnings and welfare payments across a wide variety of subgroups in the welfare caseload. In the GAIN study, for example, a county-by-county comparison shows that one county taking this approach—Riverside—had considerably larger impacts than all the others. It increased the program group's earnings by 42 percent over the control group average, and reduced AFDC payments by 15 percent.[5] Riverside's performance is especially impressive because the county both increased earnings *and* reduced welfare payments—and did so for a broad cross-section of the welfare caseload, including school dropouts and long-term welfare recipients.

Like all GAIN counties, Riverside provided a mix of job search assistance and basic education (i.e., remedial instruction in basic reading and math skills and English as a Second Language instruction or ESL) for those lacking a high school diploma or general educational development (GED) certificate or proficiency in the English language. However, it differed in the messages it presented to recipients about work and welfare and in the relatively lower priority it gave to education and training. Recipients were pressed to participate in job search workshops and look seriously for employment *before* moving on to education or training activities. Those assigned to education and training programs were not permitted to languish there. All recipients were encouraged to view any job, even a low-paying job, as having value and offering a stepping stone to better paying jobs in the future. The program complemented these messages and instruction with direct job development assistance, whereby staff scoured the community for job openings and gave participants the names of employers who were actually looking for workers. Other counties, which did not perform as well as Riverside (they did not consistently achieve both welfare savings and earnings gains across a wide range of subgroups) took a different approach. Several of them, in varying degrees, more strongly embraced and organized their programs around a human capital development—or an *upfront* "skills-building"—philosophy, which stressed "education first."

Another mandatory, mixed-service program similar to Riverside's, in many respects, has been operating in Portland, Oregon, and is being studied as part of the National Evaluation of Welfare-to-Work Strategies. Like Riverside's GAIN program, Portland's program emphasized quick job entry and made heavy use of upfront job search activities. A smaller but still substantial proportion of recipients participated in education, training, and work experience activities, but these assignments tended to be short-term in order to facilitate rapid employment. In support of the program's employment focus, job developers helped recipients locate job openings. In contrast to Riverside, however, Portland staff, mindful of the region's very strong labor market, were more likely encourage recipients to look for and take "good" jobs—full-time positions that paid more than the minimum wage and offered fringe benefits and opportunities for advancement. Interim research findings indicate that, after two years of follow-up, the program group had substantially better outcomes than the randomly assigned control group. Employment rates for the program were 11 percentage points higher than they were for the control group, earnings were 35 percent higher, and welfare payments were 17 percent lower.

Basic Education for School Dropouts

Research suggests that policymakers' high expectations of the value of making basic education a central feature of welfare-to-work programs have not been realized. For example, several of the counties in the GAIN evaluation attempted to maximize the proportion of dropouts who entered such activities when they began the program. However, those recipients did not achieve levels of employment and earnings higher than the levels obtained by school dropouts in the control group. This may be because many of those who participated in these classes did not want to be there, did not complete the course of instruction, or did not end up with an educational degree.

Early results from three sites in the National Evaluation of Welfare-to-Work Strategies also raise questions about the wisdom of making basic education the initial program activity for most nongraduates (Hamilton et al. 1997). They indicate that a "labor force attachment" approach, stressing more rapid employment, was somewhat more effective in improving dropouts' average earnings—at least during the first two years of follow-up—than a strategy that requires basic education classes first. Longer-term follow-up data, which are not yet available, will be key to drawing firmer conclusions.

It is important to note that none of these findings means that basic education does not help *some* people. Rather, they suggest that making this the *first* activity for *most* recipients who are school dropouts is unlikely to produce the best results. A better approach for this group may be to provide basic education to some recipients but also to encourage as many or more to try job search first, as in the Riverside and Portland programs, which achieved substantial earning gains and welfare savings for them. Other ways of enhancing recipients' basic skills (e.g., by continuing basic education instruction with skills training or employment) should also be considered.

Vocational Training and Post-secondary Education

Less evidence is available on the contributions of vocational training and post-secondary education in welfare-to-work programs. Some evidence suggests that a strong emphasis on vocational training for recipients who enter the program with a high school diploma or GED in hand may help some in that group *who would have worked and left welfare anyway* get *better* jobs, but may not lead to an overall increase in the proportion of recipients getting jobs or to welfare savings. This pattern was discovered, for example, in the GAIN evaluation's analysis of Alameda County's GAIN program, which strongly encouraged recipients with a diploma or GED to participate in vocational training and post-secondary education before looking seriously for a job. In contrast, the Riverside GAIN program's less costly rapid employment approach, which did not stress vocational training or post-secondary education, increased employment as well as earnings among recipients in this group, and also reduced welfare payments. However, it did not help recipients who did work get better jobs than workers in the control group.

Short-term findings from two sites in the National Evaluation of Welfare-to-Work Strategies offer some corroborating, though still preliminary, evidence. In that study, for recipients who already had a high school diploma or GED, less costly rapid employment strategies were about as effective in boosting their earnings (relative to control groups) as were more expensive interventions stressing human capital development through upfront education and training. (It may, of course, take longer for the human capital development approach to show an impact, so the early findings may not be indicative of the longer-term trends.)

Findings from a study of Job Training Partnership Act (JTPA) programs are also worth noting. One part of that study focused on JTPA applicants who volunteered for services and were recommended for a service strategy that emphasized classroom occupational skills training. These applicants were randomly assigned to a program group that got those services or to a control group, which did not receive any JTPA services. For adult women (many but not all of whom were AFDC recipients), the study found that the classroom training service strategy produced no statistically significant impacts on earnings within a 30-month follow-up period. The study also examined the effects of a service strategy that emphasized on-the-job training and job search assistance. Adult women recommended for that service strategy were randomly assigned either to a program group that got it or to a control group. The study found that this service strategy *did* produce impacts on earnings for adult women. The study also found earnings impacts for adult women who were recommended for a services strategy that provided a mix of job search assistance and miscellaneous services (e.g., job-readiness training, customized training, vocational exploration among other services) (Orr et al. 1994).

As with basic education, none of these findings demonstrate that vocational training and post-secondary education "don't work" for some people. However, they do suggest that directing *most* welfare recipients into long-term classroom-based education and training as their *initial* program activity may not achieve as broad-based earnings gains and welfare savings as a more mixed approach—one that does not exclude education and training but that encourages many or most recipients to look for work first and assists them in those efforts.

Other evidence showing more promising effects of vocational training on earnings of low-income young adults, including many single mothers on AFDC, comes from two studies of the Center for Employment and Training (CET) in San Jose, California (Cave et al. 1993; Zambrowski and Gordon 1993).[6] However, this training program was distinguished from traditional programs in several respects. With the goal of helping most participants enter the labor market relatively quickly, most training was short term (lasting approximately six months). The curricula emphasized "hands-on" instruction. And basic education instruction, when needed, was integrated into the vocational instruction rather than required as a separate activity prior to immersion in training. Training was followed by intensive job placement assistance, aided by the program's well-developed connections with private sector employers in the community.[7]

Case Management and Participation Mandates

Day-to-day case management practices that strongly promote work, diligently enforce a participation requirement, and make serious efforts to monitor and assist more than just the most job-ready recipients may also be critical for success. The GAIN Evaluation and the National Evaluation of Welfare-to-Work Strategies both suggest that what makes a successful program involves more than just what job search, education, and training services it offers. Broader implementation practices may also matter. When case managers strongly promote work and diligently enforce a participation requirement, and when the program seeks—and has adequate resources—to work with *all* enrollees, not just those who seem most ready to work, the chances of success may be enhanced.

Economic Costs and Benefits

Mandatory, mixed-service programs like GAIN can be cost-effective. They can pay for themselves within a few years and even produce a net financial gain for the government and taxpayers. However, this may be more difficult to achieve in programs emphasizing long-term education and training. Riverside's program, which was cheaper to operate relative to the other counties' programs, largely because of its lower use of education and training, more than paid for itself in less than five years. In fact, for every public dollar invested per person assigned to GAIN, government budgets (federal, state, and local combined) got back an impressive $2.78. In contrast, the counties that placed the strongest emphasis on longer-term education and training did not pay for themselves.

The GAIN benefit-cost analysis also showed that in all but one of the study counties, welfare recipients were made somewhat better off by the program (by almost $1,900 per program group member in Riverside during the five-year follow-up period). However, it is clear from this and other analyses that GAIN did not dramatically improve family income or produce large reductions in poverty.

Job Turnover

Mandatory, mixed-service programs like GAIN have not solved the problem of high job turnover, which is partly why they did not substantially improve family incomes. Even in Riverside, many people who were assigned to this best-performing program and who worked during the follow-up period did not work continuously. For example, although 72 percent of the program group in Riverside worked at some point during the five-year follow-up period, only 39 percent worked at some time during Year 5. Moreover, a substantial proportion of recipients—31 percent—were receiving AFDC at the end of Year 5.

In response to this common limitation of welfare-to-work programs, an HHS research demonstration in several states is testing what are referred to as post-placement services (Haimson and Hershey 1997). Case managers in these programs continued to monitor and advise recipients *after* they were placed into a job. This included counseling them on how to adjust to the demands of the workplace and how to handle disputes with supervisors or coworkers. If the job were just not working out, the case managers would try to help them find new jobs quickly. They would also help individuals find solutions to child care or personal problems that emerged after the job began and that threatened to interfere with success on the job or make referrals to other appropriate agencies or programs. Post-placement assistance also included efforts to help resolve problems relating to continued eligibility for welfare, food stamps, child care assistance, and Medicaid; urging workers to take advantage of the Earned Income Tax Credit; and helping those who were performing well at a low-paying job find better job opportunities as they acquired more work experience—in other words, helping them move up a career ladder. The HHS evaluation now under way will help determine whether strategies like these make any difference. However, preliminary findings show small to modest improvements after one year in new workers' job retention, earnings, and other welfare and employment outcomes compared to a randomly selected control group (Rangarajan, Meckstroth, and Novak 1998).

Combining Services, Mandates, and Stronger Financial Incentives to Work

One reason why the GAIN program—and others like it—may not have done better in reducing job turnover is that the low-paying jobs recipients typically got may not have paid enough to make it financially attractive to continue working, considering what recipients gave up in AFDC and other benefits and the costs of transportation and child care expenses. A more effective approach might be to combine services and mandates with enhanced financial incentives to work.

A dual approach like this is currently being tested in Minnesota and is showing promise for long-term, single-parent, welfare recipients in urban areas (Miller et al. 1997). Long-term data are not yet available, but early findings on the Minnesota Family Investment Program (MFIP) indicate that after a year and a half of follow-up, long-term recipients living in urban areas who were randomly selected to receive the full MFIP treatment—a combination of mandatory employment services *plus* enhanced financial incentives—had substantially higher earnings than a randomly selected control group that received only the incentives and services available under traditional AFDC rules. The full MFIP group also had higher earnings than an alternative program group that offered the enhanced incentives without the mandatory services. At the same time, this combination of services and incentives has not produced any substantial effect on earnings for welfare applicants (i.e., single parents who were entered into the study at the time they applied for welfare, and who tend to be a more job-ready group). In addition, as discussed below, its earnings impacts were concentrated in a subgroup of recipients who were living in government-subsidized housing.[8]

EFFECTS OF MAINSTREAM WELFARE-TO-WORK PROGRAMS ON WELFARE RECIPIENTS LIVING IN PUBLIC OR ASSISTED HOUSING

Some of the programs cited above included among their participants welfare recipients living in public and assisted housing. Did the programs work for *them*? The evidence is limited, and the results are mixed.

In the Atlanta site of the National Evaluation of Welfare-to-Work Strategies, two-year employment, earnings, and welfare outcomes were compared for single-parent welfare recipients randomly assigned to one of two treatment streams (one emphasizing labor force attachment and the other stressing human capital development through education and training) or to a control group. As part of that study, program effects were examined separately for the subgroup of welfare recipients living in public housing.[9] The results show that over the two years of follow-up, both treatment groups in public housing had substantially higher employment rates and average earnings and lower average welfare payments than the control group in public housing. Moreover, the earnings effects were somewhat larger for the labor force attachment group than the human capital development group. At the same time, high job turnover remained a problem in both groups.

In the MFIP study cited above, a special analysis found that most of the impacts on long-term recipients achieved by the combination of enhanced incentives and mandatory services were concentrated in the subgroup of long-termers who were living in public or assisted housing. (Over 80 percent of this group resided in assisted housing.) The effects were large. Among recipients in this subgroup who were enrolled in MFIP, the proportion who ever worked during the year and a half follow-up period was 26 percentage points higher (79 percent versus 53 percent) than for comparable people in the control group. MFIP also increased the average earnings for this subgroup by 52 percent (compared to the average for those in the control group). The program appears to have had much less effect, so far, on long-term recipients living in private housing, or for welfare applicants living in either assisted or private housing. The reasons for the differences in program effectiveness between groups are uncertain at this time.[10]

The JTPA study discussed above also examined program effects for public housing residents, although the sample for this analysis was not restricted to AFDC recipients and the follow-up period covers only a year and a half (Bloom et al. 1993). For women as well as men who were public housing residents and volunteered for JTPA, those randomly assigned to JTPA programs had no higher earnings than those assigned to a control group. However, earnings gains were detected for JTPA assignees who did not live in public housing (a group that included people living in both private and assisted housing).

Overall, then, some evidence suggests that welfare-to-work programs outside the public and assisted housing systems may have positive effects for welfare recipients who happen to live in publicly subsidized housing, but that success is limited in important ways, such as by the continuing high job turnover (as in the Atlanta study) or by not extending to other important subgroups (e.g., the applicant group in the Minnesota study). Also, the JTPA study, which targeted a broader group of public housing residents, found no effect of this mainstream program.

IMPLICATIONS FOR HOUSING-BASED SELF-SUFFICIENCY PROGRAMS

The studies of non-housing-based self-sufficiency programs reviewed above challenge a number of the assumptions on which Project Self-Sufficiency (PSS), Operation Bootstrap, and Family Self-Sufficiency (FSS) rest, raising concerns about their potential effectiveness.

Concerns about the Programs' Recruitment Strategies

In recruiting and selecting participants, the housing-based programs have explicitly sought to weed out individuals deemed to be less motivated to work. This contrasts with the mandatory approach of effective welfare-to-work programs. One risk of selective recruitment (or creaming) is, of course, that many participants who get jobs and leave welfare might have done so on their own, even without a program's help. In addition, it might cause a program to miss a chance to help individuals who need the program more and for whom the program might make a big difference. The housing-based programs have banked heavily on their selective recruitment processes to get the "right" people into the program. But it is not at all clear that the people who do enter are the "right" ones—that is, the ones for whom the program really can make the biggest difference. It is at least arguable that recipients who do not step forward on their own, or who seem less prepared for and motivated to work, may be precisely the ones that self-sufficiency programs in public and assisted housing must reach if they are to propel large numbers of residents into steady work.[11]

Concerns about the Programs' Service Focus

Federal regulations that apply to FSS and its predecessor programs require that "appropriate" employment-related activities and support services be made available, but they allow localities discretion over the choice and sequencing of specific services. Consequently, FSS and earlier programs have varied considerably in their specific service offerings and delivery strategies. At the same time, many appear to have stressed longer-term, classroom-based education and training.

If the findings from the welfare-to-work and JTPA evaluations are any guide, this may not be the best approach. From the evidence available, there is reason to suspect that housing-based self-sufficiency programs may have given too little attention to upfront job search activities, strong work-promoting messages, aggressive job development to help residents locate job openings, and connecting education and training activities more closely to well-guided job search efforts. Providing a mix of job search, education, and training activities, helping many recipients enter the labor market relatively quickly—and not assuming that *most* residents must take part in long-term education and training as their initial activity—may be a more effective strategy, on average, for a diverse group of residents. Research on the Gateway program reinforces this perception. Rohe (1995) found that some participants dropped out of Gateway's long-term education and training activities because they were anxious to work, or wanted to leave part-time jobs for full-time work rather than spend two years taking community college courses.

It also appears that housing-based self-sufficiency programs have paid little attention to what happens *after* residents get jobs. Whether the post-placement employment services now being tested in several states actually reduce job turnover remains to be seen, but the case for trying such strategies as part of housing-based self-sufficiency programs seems compelling.

Concerns about the Absence or Limited Scope of Financial Work Incentives

PSS and Bootstrap did not include special financial incentives to work, while FSS introduced a new work incentive in the form of escrow accounts—a long-term savings plan whereby the rent increase that would normally follow a rise in income is instead diverted into a savings account, the proceeds of which one can get after becoming free of public assistance. The earlier Gateway program also instituted an escrow savings plan, but the monies diverted to those accounts were earmarked for purchasing a home. Gateway also included a freeze on welfare and food stamp benefits during its two-year remediation stage.

As noted previously, the Minnesota study suggests that financial incentives by themselves will not necessarily boost earnings among welfare recipients. However, the study also suggests that certain financial incentives can contribute to poverty reduction for some subgroups of welfare recipients when packaged with mandatory employment services and strong work-promoting messages, and when repeatedly "marketed" to recipients.

These findings add some empirical backing to arguments to include financial incentives as part of housing-based self-sufficiency programs. However, the favored strategy of those programs—diverting rent increases into escrow accounts—might not be the best approach for promoting and supporting work if many residents would prefer to see the benefit of their labor more immediately and with fewer conditions attached. It is also important to consider whether FSS programs—and housing authorities more broadly—have done enough to educate residents on other financial incentives from which they might benefit. Findings from the GAIN evaluation underscore the importance of this question. On a special survey of recipients, over half (55 percent) of those assigned to the GAIN program said they had never heard of the Earned Income Tax Credit (EITC). It is, thus, reasonable to ask: Do residents really understand the earnings and child care disregards available to them under existing housing and welfare rules? Do they know about and understand the EITC? Can housing authorities do more to promote these existing incentives?

THE JOBS-PLUS INITIATIVE: WILL IT DO BETTER?

The Manpower Demonstration Research Corporation (MDRC)—with financial support from and in partnership with HUD and the Rockefeller Foundation, and more recently from HHS, the U.S. Department of Labor, and the James Irvine, Joyce, Northwest Area, Surdna, and Annie E. Casey Foundations, has launched a new research demonstration in public housing developments. The demonstration, called Jobs-Plus, builds on the successes of past welfare-to-work programs and, at the same time, pushes beyond the limitations of those and past housing-based programs. Eight public housing developments in seven cities—Baltimore, Chattanooga, Cleveland, Dayton, Los Angeles (two developments), St. Paul, and Seattle—have been selected as the planning and implementation sites for Jobs-Plus. The program planning period began in each of the sites in the spring of 1997. Implementation began in 1998.

Each of these cities has formed a new partnership—or collaborative—to design and operate Jobs-Plus. These collaboratives include representatives of the public housing authority; the residents in the Jobs-Plus development; the welfare department; JTPA; other employment, training, and education agencies; and, in some cases, private sector employers. MDRC and a team of consultants are providing intensive technical assistance to these collaboratives to help them build strong partnerships and programs.[12] The collaboratives will tailor their program strategies to local circumstances. However, they must include the following three broadly defined features:

Work incentives and requirements. Jobs-Plus communities will develop a new system of financial incentives for residents to go to work even in low-paying jobs. This is to be achieved through changes in public housing authority (PHA) rent rules and, possibly, changes in welfare department rules for calculating welfare grants. The objective is to ensure that employment is positively rewarded, and that working more yields a higher family income than does working less. The program may also include new requirements for residents to take advantage of the employment-related services and assistance that Jobs-Plus will offer through its other components, with certain penalties applying to those who refuse to comply without "good cause."

Best practices in preparing residents for sustained employment and in linking them with jobs. A second element of Jobs-Plus involves "best practice" employment-related activities that take heed of the lessons on "what works" and "what doesn't" from careful evaluations of welfare-to-work and job training programs, such as those described previously in this chapter. Jobs-Plus will adapt what appear to be the most effective approaches, and at the same time introduce new strategies that hold promise of overcoming the known limitations of previous efforts. Thus, in contrast to past housing-based programs, Jobs-Plus is likely to give more emphasis to moving people into the labor force quickly. Although it will not assume that all or most nonworking residents need longer-term education and training before seeking employment, neither will it ignore the potential value of education and training activities for some residents. It will also make special efforts to improve job retention and help working residents build a career ladder.

Enhanced community support for work. The third component of Jobs-Plus encompasses a variety of actions to increase "community support for work" among and on behalf of residents of the Jobs-Plus housing development. These actions can be classified into two broad categories: (1) *strengthening residents' social networks* inside and outside the development in ways that support and promote work, and (2) *changing institutions* in ways that support work among residents. The assumptions behind the community support for work component are that many public housing residents are isolated from the kinds of informal job information and referral networks through which other members of society learn about and get access to employment opportunities; that they live in an environment that does not actively encourage or facilitate work or accurately communicate the benefits of working; and that they face institutional impediments that make it very difficult for them to work. Typical welfare-to-work and job-training programs do little to address these types of social and institutional constraints on work. Consequently, the community support for work component promises to be one of the most innovative—and challenging— features of Jobs-Plus.[13]

Previous research from welfare-to-work programs suggests that neither services nor incentives alone could reasonably be expected to enable housing developments to increase employment dramatically among residents. But successful *simultaneous* implementation of best-practices employment and training services and financial incentives, combined with efforts to build community support for work, may create a synergy that achieves results that far exceed the effects of even the best-performing programs of the past. That, at least, is a central theory of Jobs-Plus.

Also important is the program's broad targeting scheme. In contrast to the highly selective recruitment policies of earlier housing-based programs, Jobs-Plus will attempt to serve *all* working-age residents in the housing developments hosting the program. In effect, the program will "saturate" these developments with enough opportunities for services, financial work incentives, and community support for work so that no working-age adult is untouched by the program. This intensive concentration of assistance and resources in a single housing development is expected to contribute greatly to the power of the intervention. Consequently, the demonstration provides a rare opportunity to test the notion that a comprehensive, intensive, place-based employment intervention can dramatically transform public housing developments from communities of nonworkers to communities of workers and, in turn, improve the quality of life within those communities.

THE RESEARCH AGENDA AND APPROACH FOR THE JOBS-PLUS DEMONSTRATION

The Jobs-Plus demonstration includes a comprehensive knowledge development agenda, the goals of which are to determine the program's feasibility, effectiveness, costs, benefits, and best practices. The research is intended to provide highly credible evidence with which to judge the merits of the program and its potential for replication. Toward this end, it is attempting to break new ground in the field of community initiative evaluations. A key challenge is to determine reliably the impacts of a place-based intervention that cannot be studied using a research design involving the random assignment of individuals.

A Study of the Program's Feasibility and Implementation

Jobs-Plus is an unusually ambitious program that presents formidable implementation challenges. Consequently, questions concerning the sites' implementation strategies and experiences will be a major focus of the research. For example: Do the interagency and resident collaboratives become *true and effective partnerships*, with agencies other than the housing authority demonstrating that they have an important stake in the success of the program, and with residents achieving a *real* voice and decisionmaking influence within the collaboratives? How successful are the demonstration cities in *integrating* the program's three main components and operating them at *saturation levels*? How do residents respond to the combination of services, incentives, and community support for work offered to them? What strategies and local conditions help or hinder implementation? Overall, though, the goal of the implementation study is much broader than answering these particular questions. It aims to assess whether Jobs-Plus achieves substantial and enduring institutional change—that is, change in the ways in which institutions make and implement policies and practices on behalf of the shared population they serve, and in the opportunities and capacity of that population to influence decisions intended to help them.

A Study of the Program's Effectiveness

The bottom-line questions for the Jobs-Plus demonstration are: Does the program achieve its ambitious goal of dramatically increasing employment and earnings among public housing residents? And does it lead to a better quality of life for residents? To answer these questions, an effort is under way to design an impact analysis that combines experimental and quasi-experimental methods. If it succeeds, it will provide unusually credible evidence on the impacts of a place-based social intervention.

Determining the effectiveness of Jobs-Plus with a high degree of certainty poses a special challenge. The program's goal of reaching all working-age residents in the treatment development rules out the opportunity to randomly assign some residents to a control group unaffected by Jobs-Plus. As an alternative, the program will be studied using a research design that combines some elements of a social experiment with quasi-experimental methods. In each of the cities, several housing developments that were reasonably well-matched on demographic and selected other criteria were identified as potential candidates for hosting Jobs-Plus. One of these developments was then randomly selected to be the Jobs-Plus development, and one or two were randomly selected to be comparison sites. With the samples from all the demonstration cities combined, it will be possible to provide unbiased estimates of the program's impacts. This is because, on average, the Jobs-Plus sites were not systematically chosen to favor housing developments where residents were more likely (or less likely) to increase their employment and earnings than residents in the comparison developments.

Within this overall framework, the evaluation will include a comparative interrupted time-series analysis. Through this technique, trends in earnings and welfare receipt will be measured for the Jobs-Plus and comparison developments using administrative records. These trends will be examined beginning five years *before* the start of Jobs-Plus and continuing for five years *after*. If residents' employment trends after the start of Jobs-Plus deviate sharply (in a positive direction) from their historical trends, and by a much larger amount than in the comparison developments, this will lend weight to a conclusion that Jobs-Plus—and not other factors—caused the increase in employment. The same logic would apply in analyzing trends in welfare receipt. (For a detailed discussion of the impact research design, see Bloom 1996).

Before-and-after resident survey data will also be analyzed, especially to determine whether changes in various dimensions of residents' life experiences within public housing and their quality of life in general occur in conjunction with the changes in employment, earnings, and welfare receipt.

The study will investigate whether the program's impacts are robust—whether, in other words, Jobs-Plus can achieve large, positive impacts across a diverse set of cities and local environments and for very different types of people living in public housing. As one illustration of these differences, it is noteworthy that among the demonstration sites are some developments whose residents are almost all African-Americans, some where a majority are Latino, and some with a large number of Southeast Asian and other immigrant groups as well as whites. And although all sites are located in large urban areas, those areas are themselves quite diverse, ranging, for example, from a West Coast metropolis (Los Angeles) to a much smaller city of the South (Chattanooga). The study will also investigate whether certain program strategies (e.g., particular ways of providing and integrating employment and training services, work incentives, and community support for work) yield better results.

A Study of the Program's Costs and Benefits

Jobs-Plus will not be cheap, and different public agencies will share in its cost. Politicians and agency administrators will therefore want to know just how much it costs and how these costs are distributed across agencies. They will also want to know whether the economic benefits of operating the program outweigh its costs, and whether residents themselves are made financially better off by the program. To answer these questions, the evaluation will include comprehensive cost and benefit-cost analyses.

The evaluation of Jobs-Plus is expected to continue through the year 2003.

CONCLUSION

Public housing authorities hoping to move large numbers of their residents into steady employment face an enormous challenge. Strategies tried in the past, as exemplified in programs such as Operation Bootstrap, PSS, and FSS, are unlikely to be sufficient.

Evaluations of welfare-to-work and job training programs offer some direction for building more effective housing-based self-sufficiency programs. These studies suggest that future housing-based programs ought to give high priority to helping residents enter the labor market quickly. Although there is a role for education and training, programs should not assume that most residents should be placed in longer-term education and training as their *first* step toward self-sufficiency. The research also shows that effective rapid employment strategies often involve participation requirements, efforts to avoid creaming, substantial case management (to monitor participation, aggressively promote work, and assist in addressing situational problems that can impede work), and substantial job development efforts that help participants locate job openings and make connections to employers.

The studies also highlight the limitations of past welfare-to-work programs, especially the continuing challenge of reducing job turnover and poverty. They point to the need for more effective strategies to help participants who enter jobs keep those jobs and move up a career ladder. More recent evidence, although still preliminary, suggests that combining employment and training activities with improved financial work incentives may enhance a program's effectiveness, especially in reducing poverty.

This growing body of research provides a useful foundation on which to build new employment strategies for residents of public and assisted housing. Dramatic change, however, requires bolder interventions that can draw only partial guidance from past research. Moreover, no single agency is likely to accomplish big changes in employment and quality of life by itself. The Jobs-Plus demonstration represents one attempt to meet these challenges. It will carefully test an employment initiative created by committed local stakeholders (with guidance from national partners). The program will provide a scope and intensity of assistance to public housing residents that is unprecedented. Success is not guaranteed, of course, but the stakes are too high not to make bold efforts to outperform programs of the past.

Notes

1. For other relevant studies or summaries of these programs see Blomquist et al. (1994); Frees et al. (1994); Shroder and Khadduri (1992); Newman and Schnare (1994); Rohe (1995); Rohe and Kleit (1997); and Shlay (1993).

2. Each of the programs has attempted to motivate and prepare public or assisted housing residents to work. Other approaches, not yet tried on a large scale, attempt to increase directly the demand for residents' labor. They are not discussed in this chapter because they are so different from the kinds of welfare-to-work and job training programs that have been rigorously evaluated and from which this chapter is attempting to draw lessons relevant for public housing initiatives. These include, for example, the apprenticeship training program known as Step-Up and HUD "Section 3 initiatives." The latter typically involve (but are not limited to) efforts to get private contractors who are performing construction or rehabilitation work on public housing authority (PHA) properties to hire residents for those projects [see Bailey and Lynn (1996) for more information on these initiatives]. Also not discussed are Family Investment Centers in public housing developments, about which little has been written, and the newer Moving to Opportunity programs that attempt to relocate inner-city residents in public or assisted housing in high-poverty census tracts to suburban areas that are perceived to offer better job opportunities.

3. In addition to the reports cited in the text, see Bloom (1997) for an excellent summary of this research.

4. These findings pertain to evaluations in five states that found that the programs raised the proportion of sample members who ever worked during the follow-up period (which ranged from 6 to 12 quarters).

5. In dollars, Riverside increased average earnings for the program group by $5,038 (roughly $1,000 during each year of follow-up) above and beyond the average earnings for the controls. (It is important to stress that this is the *average* effect—some people in the program did not work at all and so did not have any earnings gain, while for others the impact was much larger than this average.) Riverside also produced the largest reduction in average AFDC payments: $2,705 per program group member.

6. The latter study found that results held up through a fifth year of follow-up. In that year, the program group, on average, earned $95 per month more than the control group, although the proportion employed was comparable.

7. See Melendez (1996).

8. A demonstration project taking place in Canada, called the Self-Sufficiency Project (SSP), is showing early positive effects of a pure wage supplement for lone parents receiving income assistance. The program offers them a generous wage supplement—some see their wages effectively doubled. But they must take a full-time job of at least 30 hours per week, and the supplement lasts only for up to three years. Early results show that by the second year of follow-up, earnings for the eligible group as a whole were over 50 percent higher than the average earnings of similar people in a control group not offered the supplement, and the proportion working full-time was twice as high (Lin et al. 1998). The important open question, of course, is: What will happen when the supplement ends? Will people launched into work continue working or will they return to welfare? The evaluation will address these issues in future reports. A study of the New York State Child Assistance Program also found positive effects of financial incentives offered to welfare mothers who had court orders for child support (Hamilton et al. 1993).

9. Unpublished analyses conducted by the Manpower Demonstration Research Corporation (MDRC).

10. Unpublished analyses conducted by MDRC.

11. See Riccio and Hasenfeld (1996) for a discussion of participation mandates in welfare-to-work programs and Shroder and Khadduri (1992) for a discussion of these issues as they pertain to housing-based self-sufficiency programs.

12. Partnerships like this, which require agencies that do not normally work together to begin doing so in intimate ways and to share decisionmaking power with residents, do not just happen, and do not happen quickly. Recognizing this, MDRC, in conjunction with consultants who bring expertise in building relationships across community groups and agencies (the Consensus Organizing Institute) and in organizing residents (The Empowerment Network), has made strengthening the collaboratives a central focus of its early technical assistance to the sites. Of particular concern is that residents not only be given a real voice in these partnerships but also develop the *capacity* to exercise that voice effectively. Thus, empowering residents to play key roles in the design and management of Jobs-Plus is a top priority for the demonstration.

13. The Gateway program includes some attempts to foster mutual support among residents by congregating about half of them in the same housing development. However, this strategy broke down as some residents dropped out of the program but remained in the Gateway-targeted units (Rohe 1995).

References

Bailey, Maxine, and Suzanne Lynn. 1996. *Employment Opportunities for Public Housing Residents: Lessons from the Field on the Implementation of Section 3*. Prepared by the Manpower Demonstration Research Corporation. Washington, D.C.: U.S. Department of Housing and Urban Development, Office of Policy Development and Research.

Bogdon, Amy S. 1979. "What Can We Learn from Previous Housing-Based Self-Sufficiency Programs?" In *The Home Front: Implications of Welfare Reform for Housing Policy*, edited by Sandra J. Newman. Washington, D.C.: The Urban Institute Press.

Blomquist, John D., Ingrid Gould Ellen, and Stephen H. Bell. 1994. *Operation Bootstrap, Volume II: Outcomes of Participation*. Prepared by Abt Associates, Inc. Washington, D.C.: U.S. Department of Housing and Urban Development, Office of Policy Development and Research.

Bloom, Dan. 1997. "After AFDC: Welfare-to-Work Choices and Challenges for States." *ReWORKing Welfare: Technical Assistance for States and Localities*. New York: Manpower Demonstration Research Corporation.

Bloom, Howard. 1996. "Building a Convincing Test of a Public Housing Employment Program Using Non-Experimental Methods: Planning for the Jobs-Plus Demonstration." Paper prepared for the Manpower Demonstration Research Corporation and presented at the Annual Research Conference of the American Association for Public Policy and Management (APPAM), Pittsburgh, PA, October 31–November 2, 1996.

Bloom, H., L. Orr, F. Doolittle, V. Hotz, and B. Barnow. 1993. *The National JTPA Study. Title II-A: Impacts on Earnings and Employment at 18 Months*. Bethesda, Md.: Abt Associates, Inc.

Cave, George, Fred Doolittle, Hans Bos, and Cyril Toussaint. 1993. *JOBSTART: Final Report on a Program for School Dropouts*. New York: Manpower Demonstration Research Corporation.

Freedman, Stephen, Daniel Friedlander, Winston Lin, and Amanda Schweder. 1996. "Five-Year Impacts on Employment, Earnings, and AFDC Receipt." Paper. New York: Manpower Demonstration Research Corporation.

Frees, J. W., Ingrid Gould Ellen, and Gretchen Locke. 1994. *Operation Bootstrap, Volume I: Program Administration*. Prepared by Abt Associates, Inc. Washington, D.C.: U.S. Department of Housing and Urban Development, Office of Policy Development and Research.

Friedlander, Daniel, David H. Greenberg, and Philip K. Robins. 1997 (December). "Evaluating Government Training Programs for the Economically Disadvantaged." *Journal of Economic Literature* 35: 1809–1855.

Gueron, Judith M., and Edward Pauly. 1991. *From Welfare to Work*. New York: Russell Sage Foundation.

Haimson, Joshua, and Alan Hershey. 1997. *Getting Help to Stay Employed: The Use of Postemployment Services*. Princeton, N.J.: Mathematica Policy Research, Inc.

Hamilton, Gayle, Thomas Brock, Mary Farrell, Daniel Friedlander, and Kristen Harknett. 1997. *Evaluating Two Welfare-to-Work Program Approaches: Two-Year Findings on the Labor Force Attachment and Human Capital Development Programs in Three Sites*. Prepared by the Manpower Demonstration Research Corporation. Washington, D.C.: U.S. Department of Health and Human Services, Administration for Children and Families and Office of the Assistant Secretary for Planning and Evaluation.

Hamilton, William L., et al. 1993. *The New York State Child Assistance Program: Five-Year Impacts, Costs, and Benefits*. Cambridge, Mass.: Abt Associates, Inc.

Lin, Winston, Philip K. Robins, Kristen Harknett, Susanni Lui-Gurr, Elsie C. Pan, Tod Mijanovich, Gail Quets, and Patrick Villeneuve. 1998. *When Financial Incentives Encourage Work: Complete 18-Month Findings from the Self-Sufficiency Project*. Ottawa: Social Research and Demonstration Corporation.

Melendez, Edwin. 1996. *Working on Jobs: The Center for Employment and Training*. Boston, Mass.: The Mauricio Gaston Institute.

Miller, Cynthia, Virginia Knox, Patricia Auspos, Jo Anna Hunter-Manns, and Alan Orenstein. 1997. *Making Welfare Work and Pay: Implementation and 18-Month Impacts of the Minnesota Family Investment Program*. New York: Manpower Demonstration Research Corporation.

Newman, Sandra, and Ann Schnare. 1994. "Back to the Future: Housing Assistance Policy for the Next Century." Paper prepared for the Center for Housing Policy, *New Beginnings Project: A First Report*. Washington, D.C.

Orr, Larry, et al. 1996. *Does Training for the Disadvantaged Work? Evidence from the National JTPA Study*. Washington, D.C.: The Urban Institute Press.

Rangarajan, Anu, Alicia Meckstroth, and Tim Novak. 1998 (January). *The Effectiveness of the Postemployment Services Demonstration: Preliminary Findings*. Princeton, N.J.: Mathematica Policy Research, Inc.

Riccio, James. 1997. "A Research Framework for Evaluating the Jobs-Plus Demonstration: A Saturation and Place-Based Employment Initiative for Public Housing Residents." Paper prepared for the Manpower Demonstration Research Corporation and presented at the Annual Research Conference of the American Association for Public Policy and Management (APPAM), Washington, D.C., November 6–7, 1997.

Riccio, James, Daniel Friedlander, and Stephen Freedman. 1994. *GAIN: Benefits, Costs, and Three-Year Impacts of a Welfare-to-Work Program*. New York: Manpower Demonstration Research Corporation.

Riccio, James, and Yeheskel Hasenfeld. 1996. "Enforcing a Participation Mandate in a Welfare-to-Work Program." *Social Service Review* 70: 516–542.

Riccio, James, and Alan Orenstein. 1996. "Understanding Best Practices for Operating Welfare-to-Work Programs." *Evaluation Review* 20(1): 3–28.

Rohe, William M. 1995 (Autumn). "Assisting Residents of Public Housing Achieve Self-Sufficiency: An Evaluation of Charlotte's Gateway Families Program." *Journal of Architectural and Planning Research* 12:3.

Rohe, William M., and Rachel Garshick Kleit. 1997 (June). "Returning Public Housing to Its Roots: An Assessment of the Family Self-Sufficiency Program." Working Paper. Chapel Hill: The Center for Urban and Regional Studies, The University of North Carolina.

Scrivener, Susan, Gayle Hamilton, Mary Farrell, Stephen Freedman, Daniel Friedlander, Marisa Mitchell, Jodi Nudelman, and Christine Schwartz. 1998. *Evaluating Two Welfare-to-Work Program Approaches: Implementation, Participation Patterns, Costs and Two-Year Impacts of the Portland (Oregon) Welfare-to-Work Program.* Washington, D.C.: U.S. Department of Health and Human Services, Administration for Children and Families, and Office of the Assistant Secretary for Planning and Evaluation.

Shlay, Anne B. 1993. "Family Self-Sufficiency and Housing." Paper prepared for 1993 Fannie Mae Annual Housing Conference.

Shroder, Mark, and Jill Khadduri. 1992. "Housing Subsidies and the Underclass: The Family Self-Sufficiency Program as a Test of Social Contract Welfare Reform." Unpublished paper. Washington, D.C.: U.S. Department of Housing and Urban Development, Office of Policy Development and Research.

Zambrowski, Amy, and Anne Gordon. 1993. *Evaluation of the Minority Female Single Parent Demonstration: Fifth-Year Impacts at CET.* Prepared by Mathematica Policy Research, Inc. New York: The Rockefeller Foundation.

INCREASING THE POLICY VALUE OF EVALUATION RESEARCH ON HOUSING AND SELF-SUFFICIENCY

Craig Thornton, Robert G. Wood, and Pamela M. Jones

Weak evaluation designs undermined the policy value of the large-scale housing and self-sufficiency demonstrations of the 1980s and early 1990s. As described in earlier chapters, these demonstrations failed to produce the types of evidence policymakers require in order to judge whether the approaches tested in the demonstration made a difference in the lives of participants. The demonstrations did provide evidence that the various program models are feasible to implement, some estimates of possible participation rates, and a general sense of participants' success in becoming self-sufficient. However, the impact estimation methods and supporting data cannot provide evidence that would convince skeptics about the value of housing-based self-sufficiency programs compared to their absence.

The situation has improved with the current round of housing-related self-sufficiency studies, including the evaluations of Moving to Opportunity and Jobs-Plus. These studies have learned from the methodological problems of the past and have adopted more rigorous evaluation designs that should provide evidence of greater value to decisionmakers. This chapter begins by reviewing the major determinants of an evaluation's policy value. It then examines the methods used in the earlier demonstrations, the policy value those methods generated, and the "salvage value" of the demonstrations—that is, whether and to what extent a reanalysis of the data might increase their policy value. This is followed by a discussion of the greater promise of the new round of Department of Housing and Urban Development (HUD)-sponsored demonstrations. We close with some suggestions for ensuring the value of future evaluation research.

DETERMINANTS OF POLICY VALUE

An evaluation has policy value if it helps the people who set policy identify and choose between alternative courses of action in a way

that promotes effective decisionmaking. Four primary elements underlie the policy value of evaluations:

1. *Relevance.* An evaluation has policy value if it addresses choices
   faced by decisionmakers. These choices include how to target available assistance to different population groups, what types of assistance to provide, and over what period.
2. *Validity.* An evaluation has policy value if it provides a sound basis
   for judging the effects of an intervention. Validity includes *internal
   validity*, the extent to which what we observe—for example, a difference in a specific measure of housing adequacy or resident self-
   sufficiency—is in fact caused by the policy or program under
   study. Validity also encompasses *external validity*, the extent to
   which the observed program effects, if implemented in broader
   settings and/or on a larger scale, would be the same. The absence
   of either aspect of validity weakens the evaluation results as a
   guide for policy.
3. *Timeliness.* To have the greatest value, evaluation findings must be
   available at the time decisions are being made. This factor does
   not preclude long-term evaluation efforts, because the persistence
   of most social issues forces policy and program decisions to be
   continually made or revisited. Furthermore, well-designed studies
   can create their own timeliness by drawing attention to effective
   policy options.
4. *Accessibility.* An evaluation cannot have policy value unless it can
   be understood by the people who must use it. Accessibility encompasses the quality of the writing and presentation as well as the
   extent to which policymakers can understand the validity of the
   underlying research methods.

While all these dimensions are crucial to an evaluation's policy
value, evaluation methodology primarily affects the second element—
validity. Validity requires that an evaluation make accurate comparisons between situations that represent each option being considered.
This is generally no easy matter. The choices being evaluated are often
multidimensional and involve changing human behaviors influenced
by myriad factors in addition to the program or policy under study.
Furthermore, program implementation varies over time and place and
is influenced by many factors in addition to the decisions of policymakers. Evaluators must sort through this mix of interacting factors
to identify the extent to which events, actions, and characteristics
differ *because of* the policy or program under study.

Policy debates (and hence policy choices) emerge when policymakers disagree about the most effective course of action. In this context, anecdotal evidence and "quick and dirty" evaluations can have only a limited impact. Both sides of the debate are likely to have such studies available and will use them to illustrate the potential effects of the respective policies. However, these types of studies can easily be dismissed by opponents as flawed or irrelevant. Methodologically rigorous studies that have statistical validity cannot be so easily ignored. By providing a solid basis for understanding the effects of a policy, such studies can help bridge the gap between sides of the debate and thereby foster policy action.

All program evaluation methods strive to make systematic comparisons of alternative programs or policies. In essence, the designs contrast what happens under a specific program/policy with a counterfactual situation that represents what would have happened under an alternative program or policy. This counterfactual is typically the status quo representing the current mix of programs and policies, but it can also be a specific alternative program or policy. The designs differ with respect to the precision of the estimates and the time and resources required to produce the estimates.

An experiment creates a counterfactual through random assignment. A comparison-group study, in contrast, creates this group through nonrandom methods. Prior studies have identified comparison groups on the basis of (1) space (creating a comparison group from a similar population outside the intervention area), (2) eligibility (creating a comparison group from a set of "near-eligibles" for the program who are similar to the eligibles in other relevant dimensions), (3) enrollment (creating a comparison group from those who are eligible for the program but choose not to enroll), or (4) time (creating through a pre-post design a comparison group that is actually the treatment group during the period before entry into the program).

In the realm of internal validity, the strongest designs are based on random assignment. Well-designed randomized experiments have established their clear superiority over comparison group and other methodologies (Boruch 1997; Metcalf and Thornton 1992). Only with random assignment do evaluators have a basis for attributing what we observe to the impact of an intervention with a known degree of statistical precision. While other methods can produce credible impact estimates, those estimates are generally surrounded by uncertainty stemming from whether the evaluation has effectively isolated program impacts from other influences. As typically implemented, experiments do less well with external validity, leaving the analyst to employ non-experimental, often judgmental, methods to establish generalizability and policy relevance. But only a carefully crafted, randomized design is likely to produce the robust and internally valid measures of intervention impacts that are the best starting point of policy interpretation. The inconclusive or even misleading results of weaker designs risk the loss of the opportunity to learn.

Experiments tend to have greater accessibility as well. As one former staff member at the General Accounting Office put it:

> Congress tends to divide research studies into two types. Studies that use random assignment are referred to as "scientific" studies and are generally believed. Studies that use other methods are referred to as "unscientific" and everyone feels free to ignore them.

The tension in applying randomization is to ensure that the evaluation addresses a policy-relevant question. Randomization often changes program intake processes or other aspects of program implementation in order to ensure a structured comparison. In many cases, these changes are minor and have, at most, a trivial effect on behaviors. In some cases, however, efforts to structure the comparison change the environment to such an extent that the results cannot be generalized beyond the group directly involved in the study. Evaluators must often deal with the tension of addressing the "right question" with weak methods or the "wrong question" with sound methods.

Other designs have their place, of course, particularly when random assignment is infeasible. Designs that do not use random assignment can often save money and simplify implementation, but also tend to compromise the confidence that can be placed in the findings. Policymakers who fund these research studies should assess carefully whether this trade-off is appropriate and whether the resulting study will produce findings that will enable them to make the associated choices. Typically, these weaker designs will be inappropriate when the choices are controversial, when decisions involve very large amounts of money, or when policies once established would be difficult to reverse. In these cases, the consequences of poor decisions can be substantial, and decisionmakers are poorly served by designs that do not provide the best possible guidance.

Regardless of the specific design used to estimate program impacts, all evaluations require information about program operations. A robust and valid impact evaluation would have little policy value if it could not fully describe the program or policy that produced the impacts. Thus, evaluations must describe accurately the specific program being tested, the alternative with which that program is being compared, and the context in which the program operated (including general economic conditions and historical practices or attitudes that might influence program implementation and effectiveness). This descriptive information enables policymakers to assess external validity and to understand the specific policy choice for which the results are relevant.

Even when evaluations fail to provide much policy value, the underlying programs and demonstrations can produce considerable policy value. In particular, the processes of developing a demonstration intervention, selecting communities or organizations to implement a demonstration, and operating the demonstration intervention all help focus policy attention on an issue, population group, or community. Demonstrations often represent a small first step that will enable diverse parties to begin a longer-term policy process to address large problems. Demonstration funding for new pilot programs around the country can also create a constituency for an initiative among demonstration staff and participants. Finally, demonstrations provide direct services that can benefit needy individuals.

The challenge for evaluations is to build on this underlying value of demonstration activity in order to provide a firm base for future decisionmaking. Clearly, policy decisions can (and will) be made without strong evaluation evidence. Often, demonstration operations can provide testimonials and anecdotal evidence that policymakers can use to advance a particular position. But decisions based on such haphazard information can easily miss unintended consequences or fail to take advantage of more effective policy options. Evaluators must combine systematic data collection with rigorous analysis in order to make the most of the precious opportunities that demonstrations represent to learn about the social problems and effective interventions. In this way, evaluators add value by transforming the inherent short-term value of a demonstration into a clear guide for longer-term action.

THE POLICY VALUE OF PSS, OPERATION BOOTSTRAP, AND FSS EVALUATIONS

Since 1984, HUD has undertaken a series of demonstrations and evaluations intended to help policymakers understand how to alleviate housing deficiencies and simultaneously promote self-sufficiency. Chapter 5 describes these efforts in some detail and makes the point that, although many participants benefited in a variety of ways, these evaluations cannot yield the impact estimates necessary to conclude that the programs actually improved participant outcomes.

This experience is similar to that of the U.S. Department of Labor (DOL) in the late 1970s, when it conducted a series of demonstrations to address the problem of youth unemployment. DOL spent several billion dollars on these programs to assist young adults. But weak evaluation designs and flawed data collection strategies yielded very little information about what programs were effective in promoting youth employment (Betsey et al. 1985). Many of the designs used pre-post methods and followed participating youth for relatively short periods of time. This failure to implement strong evaluations left policymakers with little lasting value from the demonstrations.

History repeated itself with the first HUD demonstrations to test housing and self-sufficiency. (The evaluation situation has improved considerably with the latest round of housing and self-sufficiency demonstrations: Moving to Opportunity and Jobs-Plus. Both of these demonstrations involve rigorous evaluations and should produce valuable policy information about housing-based self-sufficiency programs.)

The PSS Research Design

Project Self-Sufficiency (PSS) operated in 154 communities from 1984 to 1988 and offered housing and employment services to low-income, single-parent households on waiting lists for Section 8 housing vouchers. As described in chapter 5, PSS was voluntary and participants could not lose their housing assistance for failure to comply with program requirements. To minimize the dropout rate from the program, HUD encouraged PSS sites to screen applicants and target program services to those who appeared to be highly motivated to succeed.

PSS used a pre-post research design to estimate program impacts. In a pre-post design, program participants are used as their own comparison group. Participants' employment levels, degree of housing stability, and other outcomes from the period prior to program entry (the "pre" period) are compared to outcomes after program entry (the "post" period). Any differences in program outcomes between the "pre" and "post" periods are attributed to the effect of the program. In the case of PSS, program evaluators point to the fact that employment levels and wage rates of participants increased after they entered the program as a sign of the program's success (HUD 1987).

The PSS demonstration examined a relevant policy option for addressing the employment barriers facing public housing recipients. It also demonstrated that it was feasible to operate PSS at a policy-relevant scale and provided information about participation patterns and outcomes for the people who enrolled. But it did not provide policymakers with useful evidence about whether or not this option was effective compared with the status quo or other policy alternatives. The reason is that, as with all pre-post designs, the results rest entirely on an assumption that may well be invalid: that in the absence of the intervention, employment levels, wage rates, and other key outcomes would be the same in the "pre" and "post" periods.

Consider the evidence (see figure 7.1) from a recent random assignment evaluation of a job training program for Supplemental Security Income (SSI) recipients (Decker and Thornton 1995). The program had substantial and sustained impacts on employment and earnings, as illustrated by differences in average earnings between treatment- and control-group members. However, control-group members, as well as treatment-group members, experienced earnings growth over the follow-up period. This pattern indicates that substantial improvement in earnings would have occurred among participants even if they had not received program services. Therefore, if this evaluation had relied on a pre-post design, which implicitly assumes that earnings levels

Figure 7.1 AVERAGE MONTHLY EARNINGS FOR DEMONSTRATION
PARTICIPANTS AND NONPARTICIPANTS

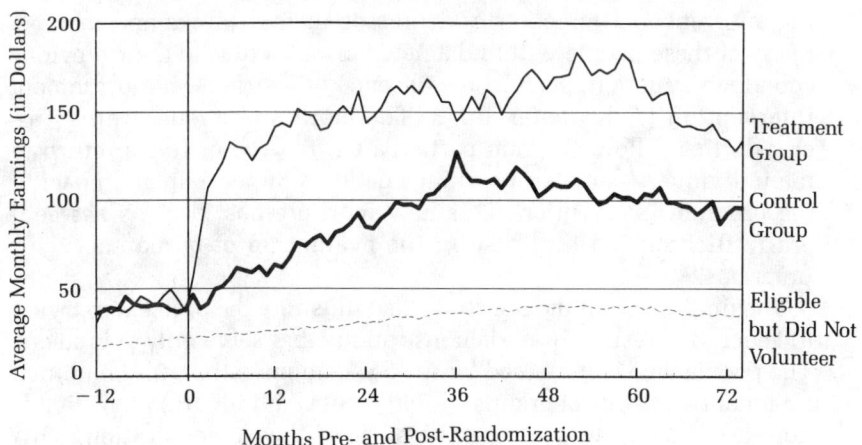

Figures expressed in 1986 dollars

Source: Decker and Thornton 1995.

during the "pre" period would have remained unchanged in the absence of the intervention, it would have substantially overestimated impacts. In this case, the pre-post design would have yielded an impact estimate that was over 100 percent greater than the estimate based on the treatment-control difference in earnings.

The possibility of overestimating impacts with a pre-post design is a particular concern when evaluating a voluntary program that targets highly motivated people, as was the case in the PSS demonstration. Highly motivated volunteers to a job training program may be even more likely than other individuals to experience earnings growth, even without having access to the program's services. For example, in the study of SSI recipients noted earlier, control-group members (who volunteered for the training program but were not offered its services) experienced substantial earnings growth over the follow-up period. In contrast, eligible program participants who did not volunteer for the program experienced little earnings growth over this period (see figure 7.1 again). These patterns suggest that people who volunteer for training programs are looking to improve their economic status and would pursue that goal even if the program were not available.

The basic flaw with pre-post designs is that they bet against the resiliency and motivation of people who have volunteered for a program designed to help them help themselves. A program may bolster people's efforts to achieve self-sufficiency, but many of these people would have had improvement anyway. This is particularly true for people who enter a program after losing a job or otherwise experiencing an event that temporarily depresses their earnings and income. Many of these people will find a new job and return to their previous economic situation, even in the absence of a structured government intervention (Ashenfelter 1978). Therefore, observed earnings increases that follow program participation may be merely a return to the individuals' long-term earnings patterns rather than an impact of the program intervention. This flaw with pre-post designs has generally discredited their use in the evaluation of human services programs.

The findings from the SSI study also illustrate the problem in trying to generalize results from demonstrations that serve only volunteers. The people who volunteered for the SSI demonstration (the combined treatment and control groups) differed substantially from the eligible nonparticipants even before the start of the demonstration. This difference is illustrated (see figure 7.1 again) by the higher average earnings among the volunteers relative to nonparticipants prior to enrolling in the demonstration. The difference suggests that the experiences of volunteers are likely to misrepresent what program outcomes would be if a broader eligible population were enrolled (which would happen if a program became mandatory rather than voluntary). This problem of external validity affects the evaluations of any program offered only to volunteers, regardless of whether the design relies on random assignment or pre-post comparisons.

Given the problems with pre-post designs, the fact that PSS participants experienced wage growth during the initial period in PSS provides no credible evidence that PSS caused the earnings increase. PSS participants may have experienced increases in earnings even if they had not been in the program. In fact, it is possible that they would have experienced even greater earnings gains if they had not been in the program.[1] Thus, the pre-post estimates available from the PSS evaluation fail to provide policymakers with any concrete sense of the extent to which the intervention affected participant self-sufficiency.

These limitations are inherent in the pre-post design and cannot be overcome by using alternative analytical methods. Accurately measuring the effect of PSS on earnings and other outcomes requires information for a group of people who were very similar to PSS participants, except that they did not receive PSS services. The pre-program experiences of participants do not provide this information, and there is no way to simulate the information statistically using only the information collected in the pre-post study.

The PSS evaluators tried to address this issue by supplementing their pre-post analysis with information on the earnings of participants in Job Training and Partnership Act (JTPA) programs from the same states. While this approach has some promise, it can never provide the level of accessibility that would be provided by an experiment or well-designed comparison group design. Furthermore, the comparison of PSS and JTPA participants is compromised by the lack of detailed information. The PSS participants were selected, in part, because they were thought to be highly motivated. Without similar information about the JTPA participants, it is impossible to know whether any observed differences between the two groups are due to the two programs or to differences in motivation levels. Finally, a comparison of PSS and JTPA participants does not address the policy choice tested in the PSS demonstration. An appropriate comparison of participants in these two programs would illustrate the relative effectiveness of those programs, not the impact of introducing PSS as a service for people on Section 8 waiting lists who would otherwise not receive any systematic self-sufficiency intervention.

The Operation Bootstrap Research Design

Operation Bootstrap, HUD's next major self-sufficiency demonstration after PSS, began in 1989; the program eventually operated in 314 communities. Like its predecessor, PSS, Operation Bootstrap offered employment support services to low-income households on waiting lists for Section 8 housing vouchers. It also targeted applicants who appeared highly motivated to succeed. Operation Bootstrap also introduced two new features. Unlike PSS, both two-parent and single-parent households were eligible for Operation Bootstrap. In addition, Operation Bootstrap participants were required to develop individual action plans.

Like the PSS evaluation, the Operation Bootstrap evaluation used a pre-post research design (Blomquist, Ellen, and Bell 1994). Program evaluators tracked employment, public assistance, and other outcomes of program participants over time. They then compared the levels of these outcomes from the period before participants were in the program to the levels after program entry. The researchers explicitly state that this design does not allow them to measure program impacts. However, they go on to write that "Even so, documenting participant progress will provide evidence on how well the program, in conjunction with other factors, accomplished its stated objectives."

As with the PSS study, the options being tested by the Operation Bootstrap evaluation were policy relevant and sought to help policymakers decide whether to institute this type of service package more broadly among public housing residents. In addition, as with the PSS study, the evaluation produced useful descriptive information about the program and the population served. However, the pre-post research design for Operation Bootstrap suffers from the same problems as the PSS design. Individuals who voluntarily enter support programs are motivated to improve their circumstances. Therefore, their pre-intervention activities levels are poor predictors of what would have happened in the "post" period if they had not participated in the program.

The researchers evaluating Operation Bootstrap found that participants were more likely to engage in education and training activities after program entry than before program entry. In addition, after an initial decline, Operation Bootstrap participants were more likely to be employed after program entry than they had been prior to program entry. The researchers caution those interpreting their results, writing that "Operation Bootstrap was one among possibly many factors" that led to these improved outcomes. This is an understatement. The increased levels of employment and training may have been due entirely to other factors unrelated to the program. Furthermore, as with the PSS evaluation, the pre-post information does not rule out the possibility that earnings increases might have been even larger if participants had pursued activities other than Operation Bootstrap. Because Operation Bootstrap evaluators collected data only on program participants (and not on a comparison group who did not receive program services), it is not possible to reanalyze evaluation data to get a more accurate estimate of program impacts.

The FSS Research Design

Like the earlier programs, Family Self-Sufficiency (FSS) offers éducation, job training, child care and transportation assistance, and other support services. Unlike PSS and Operation Bootstrap, however, FSS is available only to current recipients of housing assistance. A key component of FSS is that participants have a portion of any earnings increases deposited into an escrow savings account. Participants can access these savings once they are no longer receiving government housing assistance or any other forms of public assistance. As a condition for participation in the program, participants must sign a self-sufficiency contract. Failure to comply with this contract can result in forfeiture of the participant's escrow savings. Continued noncompliance can result in the loss of the participant's housing assistance.

The evaluation information on FSS consists primarily of a mail survey of public housing authorities (PHAs); no survey of participants was conducted (Rohe and Kleit 1997). Therefore, the focus of the FSS evaluation was to document how PHAs were implementing FSS, not to provide detailed information on participant outcomes or to estimate program impacts.

The only participant outcome data that are available through the PHA surveys are aggregate reports about the proportion of participants who are still enrolled in the program at the time of the survey, the proportion who had dropped out of the program, and the proportion who had "successfully completed" the program. No information is available to indicate how participants would have fared in the absence of FSS, making it impossible to derive any impact estimates using the data being collected as part of the evaluation.

A NEW GENERATION OF HUD-SPONSORED DEMONSTRATIONS

In 1994, HUD launched a new initiative, Moving to Opportunity for Fair Housing (MTO), which represents a different strategy for improving the economic status of public housing residents from the strategies used by the earlier HUD initiatives. Rather than providing training and other employment-related services for public housing residents, MTO seeks to improve the economic outcomes of participants by relocating them to a low-poverty neighborhood. MTO offers Section 8 certificates to public housing residents with the condition that they use these certificates to obtain private housing only in low-poverty neighborhoods. In addition, the program provides housing search assistance and counseling services to program participants.

The Jobs-Plus initiative, which is being directed by the Manpower Demonstration Research Corporation and funded by HUD, the Rockefeller Foundation, and other charitable foundations, is scheduled to be implemented in 1998. As discussed in chapter 6, Jobs-Plus will operate in eight public housing developments in seven cities nationwide. Local collaboratives will design the intervention in each site. These collaboratives will consist of representatives of the public housing authority; the local welfare department; and JTPA and other employment, training, and education agencies, as well as public housing residents. While individual sites will have a high level of control over the design of the intervention, each site's Jobs-Plus program must include three main features. First, programs must increase the financial incentives to work by changing PHA rent rules and changing how welfare departments calculate welfare grants. Second, programs must include employment-related services, such as job search and job placement assistance, education and training, and job-retention services. Third, programs must attempt to promote the "community support for work," through promoting social networks both inside and outside the development that support and promote work.

Both these initiatives hold the promise of providing valuable policy guidance for decisionmakers interested in the possibility of promoting economic self-sufficiency through housing-based strategies.

The MTO Research Design

An experimental research evaluation of MTO is currently under way. Public housing residents from high-poverty neighborhoods who apply to the program are randomly assigned to one of three research groups:

a *primary treatment group* who receive the full set of MTO services; a *secondary treatment group* who receive regular Section 8 certificates (that can be used in any neighborhood) but who do not receive any special housing search or counseling services; and a *control group* who do not receive Section 8 certificates. Random assignment is occurring in five cities: Baltimore, Boston, Chicago, Los Angeles, and New York City. All three research groups will be tracked for a 10-year period.

The MTO evaluation's strong research design will allow program evaluators to conduct a rigorous examination of several important policy questions. The use of random assignment will create research groups that are very similar at baseline and will allow researchers to attribute (with a known degree of statistical precision) any differences among the research groups to the effect of the housing policies. Furthermore, having three research groups will allow program evaluators to measure the impact of multiple policy options. First, by comparing the outcomes of the primary treatment group (who receive the full MTO program) to the control group (who receive no housing vouchers or extra services), evaluators will be able to measure the impact of MTO on program volunteers. Second, by comparing the secondary treatment group (who receive regular Section 8 certificates and no extra services) to the control group, evaluators will be able to measure the impact of offering regular Section 8 housing vouchers to program volunteers in public housing. Finally, by comparing the outcomes of the primary and secondary treatment groups, program evaluators can measure the effect of both restricting the housing voucher to low-poverty neighborhoods and offering the housing search and counseling services.

A possible criticism of the MTO evaluation is that, if program evaluators find that MTO has positive impacts on the economic status of participants, it will be unclear exactly which MTO component led to this effect. For example, the improved economic circumstances could be the result of moving from a high-poverty to a low-poverty neighborhood. But they could be the result of moving from a large public housing project to private housing financed by Section 8 vouchers (regardless of neighborhood). And they could be the result of MTO's counseling and support services. Or they could be due to some combination of any of these three factors.

The secondary treatment group will be of some help in disentangling the importance of these different factors. For example, suppose evaluators find big differences in outcomes between the secondary treatment group and the control group and small differences between the primary and secondary treatment groups. This result would suggest that support services and the requirement to move to a low-poverty neighborhood are not the key factors that improved outcomes, but that the switch from congregate public housing to scattered privately owned housing is most important. Alternatively, suppose evaluators found little difference between the secondary treatment group and the control group but large differences in outcomes between the primary and secondary treatment groups. This result would suggest that it is the low-poverty neighborhood requirement and the support services that are key and not the rent voucher for private housing. The MTO design does not, however, make it possible to separate the effects of offering public housing residents a rent voucher that is restricted to low-poverty neighborhoods from the effect of MTO counseling and housing search services.

Comparing outcomes among the five cities may also disentangle the relative effects of different program components. This is because MTO implementation is likely to differ among the cities because of differences in operations or in the context in which the programs operate. Comparing city-specific impact estimates is inherently less certain than estimating overall impact. First, sample sizes are smaller. There are only 600 to 1,100 people in each city spread among the three research groups. Second, there are potentially hundreds of reasons why impacts might differ among the cities, which are impossible to disentangle with only five cities. However, these limitations can be offset somewhat by having good information about program implementation and context. This operational information can help to explain the observed differences among sites and provide a basis for developing more refined hypotheses about the links between program structure and impacts.

The value of this combination approach is well illustrated in the evaluation of the Minority Female Single Parent Demonstration (Burghardt et al. 1992). That study used random assignment to estimate the impact the four participating programs had on the employment and earnings of the single mothers who enrolled. Those estimates indicated that only one of the four programs generated a significant increase in average earnings. While this pattern of site-specific results could have reflected many different factors (including chance), the implementation analysis indicated that the one successful program had followed a distinct approach in providing education, training, and support services. Furthermore, the successful site provided a theory behind its approach that explained why it had succeeded while the others had not. This mix of impact and operational evidence does not constitute a formal test of the relative effect of the successful program's strategy, but it does provide valuable policy information that policymakers can use for making decisions. In this case, DOL decided to rigorously evaluate replications of the approach used by the successful program.

Regardless of the methods used to evaluate MTO, the results will pertain only to a program that served volunteers because the research sample includes only those who apply for MTO. The effect of the intervention might be very different if applied to those who choose not to apply. Therefore, it will not be possible to use the evaluation results to determine the effect of the change in housing policy on *all* public housing residents, including those who chose not to apply to the program. This will be a serious limitation if there are efforts to make the intervention mandatory.

In spite of this limitation, the MTO research design represents a vast improvement over the designs used by the earlier HUD studies. The evaluation's experimental research design should provide clear and reliable results on the effectiveness of a specific housing policy option.

The Jobs-Plus Research Design

Jobs-Plus has been planned as a "saturation" initiative, designed to serve all working-age residents of a public housing development. By involving all working-age residents in the program, it is hoped that community attitudes can be changed in ways that promote work and self-sufficiency. However, serving all residents within a particular public housing development makes it impossible to use a research design that relies on random assignment of individuals into treatment and control groups. Therefore, the design of Jobs-Plus will rely on a design that uses both random assignment and comparison-group methods.

Before Jobs-Plus was implemented, participating sites identified pairs of (or, in some cases, sets of three) public housing developments that were considered similar to each other based on the demographics of their residents and other factors. From among each set of two or three developments, program evaluators then randomly selected one development where the Jobs-Plus program will operate. The residents of the randomly selected developments will serve as the treatment group for the evaluation. Residents in the one or two developments in the set that were not randomly selected will remain ineligible for Jobs-Plus services and will serve as the comparison group. The random assignment of matched groups of developments helps to ensure that the treatment and control groups will be similar even though there are only a small number of developments included in the study.

Using administrative records data, researchers will track employment outcomes for treatment- and comparison-group members for the five years prior to implementation of Jobs-Plus, as well as for the five years after program implementation.[2] Program evaluators will analyze these data to determine whether the employment trends of treatment- and comparison-group members begin to diverge at the point at which Jobs-Plus is implemented. If a substantial divergence does occur, program evaluators will attribute this divergence to the effect of the program.

The Jobs-Plus evaluation will use an innovative research design to evaluate a saturation initiative. A design that randomly assigns individuals to the program is not feasible. Therefore, program evaluators must rely on a design in which housing developments (and not individuals) are assigned randomly to the treatment or comparison groups. Randomly selecting the housing developments that will operate the program is an improvement over the typical methods used in matched comparison designs. Comparison sites are typically chosen after the program sites have been selected, making it possible that sites selected for the program are systematically different from the comparison sites not selected. These initial differences in treatment and comparison sites may, in turn, lead to later differences in outcomes that will bias impact estimates. Choosing program sites (or in this case Jobs-Plus housing developments) randomly ensures that the evaluators can measure impacts with a known degree of statistical precision.

If evaluators are able to pool the data across the sites, then random differences between particular treatment and comparison developments should cancel each other out to a large extent. The fact that local agencies are being granted broad flexibility in designing the Jobs-Plus intervention in their area may limit the ability and appropriateness of pooling across sites, however. If Jobs-Plus is a very different program in the different sites, then the evaluation may have to be treated as eight separate studies, researchers will not be able to combine data across the various sites, and the power of the Jobs-Plus research design will be substantially reduced.

PROMOTING THE POLICY VALUE OF EVALUATION RESEARCH

As the nation seeks to improve the economic and social circumstances of the millions of people who reside in government-subsidized housing, policymakers must make the most of every program dollar. In particular, they must find ways to alleviate current housing problems while promoting long-term self-sufficiency. Such policymaking requires a strong empirical basis for designing and assessing policies. The resources available to evaluate alternative programs and policies are extremely limited, so evaluation projects must produce the greatest possible increase in policymaking capacity. Only then can the evaluation effort justify diverting funding from direct service efforts.

Overall, policymakers will pursue a strategy that includes a mix of theoretical, descriptive, and evaluation studies designed to promote informed decisions about how best to help people with limited self-sufficiency. As in the past, the mix will include a few large-scale demonstrations that provide excellent opportunities to learn about the effects of pursuing different policies or programs. It will be essential to continue the pattern set with the Moving to Opportunity and Jobs-Plus demonstrations by using rigorous evaluation designs to produce valuable policy analysis.

The past two and a half decades of social science research have shown that large-scale demonstrations have the potential to create tremendous policy value, but only if they are accompanied by rigorous evaluations. Early successes include the negative income tax experiments (Munnell 1986) and the health insurance experiment (Manning et al. 1987). More recent successes include the series of welfare-to-work demonstrations (Gueron and Pauly 1991). Such demonstration programs represent precious opportunities to inform future policy decisions. But they use scarce public funding and involve the efforts of many individuals and program operators. They also use up political "capital" as the demonstration supporters seek to find the funding and operational support required to mount it. Thus, completing such a demonstration without producing substantial policy value creates serious problems.

The successful demonstrations bear several hallmarks. First, the demonstration sponsors started planning the evaluations at the same time they started planning for the demonstrations. This planning included specifying the demonstration goals, determining how progress toward those goals would be measured, and developing rigorous evaluation and data collection designs. Second, the demonstrations tested important policy issues that could ultimately affect billions of dollars of public expenditures and millions of people. Therefore, this justified the considerable resources necessary to make the evaluations of the demonstrations thorough. Third, the demonstrations took place over a period of years, enough time for large numbers of participants to be recruited and for longer-term outcomes such as self-sufficiency and family formation to be observed. Finally, the evaluations succeeded in providing valid and accessible findings. By using large samples of individuals, detailed information about individual outcomes and characteristics, and rigorous analytical methods, the evaluations produced information that could convince skeptics. This information did not resolve policy debates about priorities or the social value of various impacts, but it did enable the debate to focus on those issues rather than on whether or not there were positive impacts.

In the end, the key lesson the successful demonstrations provide for the future is to take full advantage of the precious opportunities that large-scale demonstrations represent. The issues of self-sufficiency, adequate housing, and poverty are too important for society to waste opportunities to learn about effective policy responses to these issues. The lost opportunities to clearly understand whether PSS, Operation Bootstrap, or FSS can increase self-sufficiency are the largest costs of those demonstrations. Those lost opportunities mean that policymakers will struggle for an extra decade without knowing whether the policies fielded in those demonstrations are better or worse than the other options. Seen from this perspective, any short-term savings from the use of simplistic evaluation designs seem pitifully small.

Notes

1. Such a negative program impact might occur if participation in the program activities prevented participants from gaining useful on-the-job training or other experience that would increase long-term employment and earnings.

2. The Jobs-Plus evaluation will also collect data on some other outcomes through surveys of residents conducted before and after the intervention was implemented.

References

Abt Associates, Inc. 1993. *Documentation of Operation Bootstrap: Report on the Outcomes of Participation.* Cambridge, Mass.: Abt Associates, Inc.

Ashenfelter, Orley. 1978. "Estimating the Effect of Training Programs on Earnings." *The Review of Economics and Statistics* 60(1, February).

Betsey, Charles L., Robinson G. Hollister, and Mary R. Papageorgiou (eds). 1985. *Youth Employment and Training Programs: The YEDPA Years.* Washington, D.C.: National Academy Press.

Blomquist, John D., Ingrid Gould Ellen, and Stephen H. Bell. 1994. *Operation Bootstrap, Volume II: Outcomes of Participation.* Washington, D.C.: U.S. Department of Housing and Urban Development, Office of Policy Development and Research.

Boruch, Robert F. 1997. *Randomized Experiments for Planning and Evaluation: A Practical Guide.* Thousand Oaks, Calif.: Sage Publications.

Burghardt, John, Anu Rangarajan, Anne Gordon, and Ellen Kisker. 1992. "Evaluation of the Minority Female Single Parent Demonstration." Princeton, N.J.: Mathematica Policy Research.

Decker, Paul T., and Craig V. Thornton. 1995. "The Long-Term Effects of Transitional Employment Services." *Social Security Bulletin* 58(4): 71–81.

Gueron, Judith M., and Edward Pauly. 1991. *From Welfare to Work.* New York: Manpower Demonstration Research Corporation.

Manning, W. G., J. P. Newhouse, and N. Duan. 1987. "Health Insurance and the Demand for Medical Care: Evidence from a Randomized Experiment." *American Economic Review* 77(3): 251–277.

Metcalf, Charles E., and Craig Thornton. 1992. "Random Assignment." *Children and Youth Services Review* 14(1/2): 145–156.

Munnell, Alicia H. 1986. *Lessons from the Income Maintenance Experiments.* Boston, Mass.: Federal Reserve Bank of Boston.

Rohe, William M., and Rachel Garshick Kleit. 1997. "Returning Public Housing to Its Roots: An Assessment of the Family Self-Sufficiency Program." Chapel Hill, N.C.: University of North Carolina at Chapel Hill, Department of City and Regional Planning, June.

U.S. Department of Housing and Urban Development. 1996. "Rental Housing Assistance at a Crossroads: A Report to Congress on Worst Case Housing Needs." [http://www.huduser.org/publications/hsgpolicy/plcyrpts/rental.html]. March 14.

U.S. Department of Housing and Urban Development. 1987. *Project Self-Sufficiency: An Interim Report on Progress and Performance.* Washington, D.C.: U.S. Government Printing Office.

Chapter Eight

FROM THE EYE OF THE HOUSING PRACTITIONER

Sandra J. Newman

Whatever the impacts of welfare reform on the housing assistance system, the housing practitioners who staff the more than 3,000 local public housing authorities (PHAs) across the nation will play a critical role. These individuals are, in effect, the implementers of housing assistance policy.[1] They have always been responsible for ensuring that assisted housing properties are in sound physical and financial shape and for tenant income certifications.[2] More recently, they have taken on responsibility for the tenants as well, connecting them with employability and other services or actually providing such services themselves. It will fall to these housing professionals to manage the impacts of welfare reform not only on their physical housing assets and budgets, but on their tenants.

Their position on the front lines gives housing practitioners a unique vantage point for explaining how housing programs actually are implemented on the ground, identifying key policy questions to be addressed, and speculating on what the evidence is likely to show. While their speculations are not the hard evidence repeatedly called for throughout this book, they provide a good empirical foundation for generating hypotheses about the role of assisted housing in achieving economic independence, and for expanding the research agenda.

DISINCENTIVES TO WORK

A core question for practitioners, as for researchers, is the disincentive effects of housing assistance. As noted in chapter 1, under current housing policy, when housing assistance recipients increase their incomes, the sliding-scale rent calculation imposes the equivalent of a tax on their housing benefit. And in the certificate and voucher programs, if earnings increase to the point that the housing subsidy drops to zero and remains there for six months, the family becomes ineligible for housing assistance. Housing assistance practitioners suspect, as economic theory predicts, that these "taxes" on housing assistance have tended to deter families who receive both housing and welfare from increasing their earnings. But the way this occurs is not always straightforward. Some certificate and voucher households "game" the rules. They get jobs, in spite of the effect of earnings on their assistance amount. But when they get close to the end of their six-months zero benefit period, some reduce their work hours rather than give up their certificate or voucher, which one PHA director characterizes as "housing insurance."

Unless there are compensating incentives to increase earnings or sanctions that force recipients to leave the housing or welfare rolls, the argument goes, some families will accept the standard of living these subsidies provide rather than work to increase their chances of economic independence. "It may not be a great life, but it beats the risks associated with the alternatives." Work-related risks include low wages, employment uncertainty, child care problems, restricted free time, and being under regular supervision. The housing risk is that increased earnings will either lose the family its eligibility for housing assistance in the certificate and voucher programs, or have them paying market rents in the public housing program. Since the waiting lists for this nonentitlement benefit are very long in most communities, if increased earnings remove the family from the housing assistance rolls, it could be a very long time, if ever, before they receive assistance again if their labor market success should prove temporary.

DISINCENTIVES TO REPORT AND INVESTIGATE EARNED INCOME

The disincentives to earn income also discourage tenants from reporting such income, as required by program regulations. There is at least some hard evidence that underreporting occurs because even PHAs that pursue such fraud aggressively—presumably deterring the practice over time—report a large number of cases. But other PHAs see no reason to investigate these cases because the expensive investigation is likely to cost more than the value of the back rent to be collected. Thus, there are disincentives for both tenants to report earned income and PHAs to pursue underreporting.

There is no systematic information on either the receipt of underground income or the extent to which it is investigated by the PHAs. Such information would provide additional insights into the workings of housing assistance that could affect program administration and possibly the number of housing assistance recipients. If more families are working and receiving earnings than either conventional wisdom or survey data suggest, then the development of better approaches to enforcing current regulations could increase the pool of housing assistance dollars and open housing assistance access to more eligible families. Even in the absence of welfare reform, such improvements are warranted as part of the general Department of Housing and Urban Development (HUD) "house cleaning." But if the enforcement costs more than the revenues it recoups, the outcome will be limited to more equitable treatment of tenants, not an increase in assisted households.

One model for improving income reporting is the Quality Control (QC) data collections that the federal government has required for Aid to Families with Dependent Children (AFDC), food stamps, and Medicaid.[3] Each state is required to review the income eligibility determination for a systematic probability sample of active cases. States with high error rates receive financial sanctions, though apparently some welfare commissioners find it cheaper to pay the penalty than to implement costly changes to improve their accuracy. Perhaps the stronger incentive to improve performance has been the federal government's publication of "report cards" for the 50 states, which are released to the press. An additional benefit of the QC data is their usefulness for profiling cases most prone to error, which allows states to target their quality control activities (Nightingale 1998). Although the QC program focuses on income calculations, not verification, one could envision a program that covered both. An important challenge in designing such an effort is balancing the goal of detecting errors with the goal of protecting individual privacy rights.

DISINCENTIVES TO DISREGARD EARNED INCOME

An entirely different option could also encourage families to report and, more importantly, to have earned income, namely, earned income disregards. Such disregards, which have been allowed for a long time in the AFDC program and are now included in many state welfare reform plans, have been required in housing programs since 1990.[4]

But few PHAs have implemented these disregards. There are three possible reasons why the PHAs have not done so: loss of operating subsidies; loss of excess rent payments; or malfeasance, ignorance, or confusion.

The Loss of Operating Subsidies

The first possibility is that there is little incentive for PHAs to implement earned income disregards because they risk the loss of operating subsidies. In the case of public housing, a PHA's operating subsidy is based on the difference between its estimated expenses to operate a development and the rent receipts it projects for the development. This subsidy is set prospectively using the PHA's best estimate of its revenues and expenses for the next year. If the PHA were able to disregard only earned income above and beyond the income it used to project rents, then the effect on operating subsidies should be neutral. But if all earnings were disregarded, the PHA would lose some of its operating subsidy because the tenant's rent payment of 30 percent of income would decline. The difference between expenses and rents in the operating subsidy calculation would be larger than the amount the PHA projected and, therefore, that HUD used in setting the operating subsidy.

As it turns out, both types of disregards are required of PHAs. They must disregard *incremental* earnings for any assisted housing tenants participating in an employment training program, such as many of the initiatives launched under welfare reform. But they must disregard *all* income if the tenant is participating in a HUD-funded training program or programs covered by the Job Training Partnership Act (JTPA) (Bryson 1998a).[5] Under the full disregard, operating subsidies would decline, at least in the short run. Although PHAs who applied the full earned income disregard and lost money in the process can request a retrospective increase in their operating subsidy from HUD, there is always the chance that this request will be denied. While some of these problems might sort themselves out in the long run— for example, the PHAs would become more adept at projecting rents— most PHAs have apparently been unwilling to take the risk. This assessment is undoubtedly influenced by the fact that PHA operating subsidies have not been fully funded since fiscal year 1995.[6] Nor have they been willing to take the even longer-term gamble that authorizing earned income disregards would ultimately encourage large numbers of families to go to work, thereby generating rent increases that exceed the loss of operating subsidy.

PHAs also have not enthusiastically pursued earned income disregards in the Section 8 certificate and voucher programs. Here, the issue is not risking the loss of operating income but making the choice between encouraging work and increasing the number of households served. Because a decrease in tenant income results in an increase in the federal housing subsidy, the larger the subsidy to current tenants, the less money is available for additional eligible households. PHAs also have to weigh the uncertain connection between earned income disregards and long-term increases in income, on the one hand, and the certain relationship between the amount of subsidy and the number of households who can be served, on the other.

Since the main problem in both the public housing and certificate and voucher programs is PHA reluctance to risk uncertainty, one option is to limit, or eliminate, this risk. The most obvious approach would be for HUD to guarantee coverage of any shortfall in operating subsidies or reduction in certificate or voucher slots[7] caused by the earned income disregard. But to limit the risk for taxpayers, this should be tested carefully through a demonstration and research project to see whether the earned income disregards have any work incentive effects and how long it takes PHAs to break even.

The Loss of Excess Rent Payments

A very different disincentive for PHAs to implement the required earned income disregards is the loss of excess rent payments. While there is a risk of losing operating subsidies if the earned income disregards don't "work," the PHAs also risk losing money if the disregards do work—because the PHAs don't get to recapture the increases in incomes from earnings through increased rents either during the disregard period (during training or, in public housing, during the first 18 months of employment after training) or in the longer run when the tenant is steadily employed.

Any remedy that reinstates some or all earnings for calculating income and, therefore, rent, undercuts the disregard policy and its presumed work incentive effect. But current rules governing the type and amount of income that is to be disregarded are not based on a systematic analysis of where the incentive effect begins and ends. Without such information, any change in rules will be no less ad hoc than the current rules. But it will be no more ad hoc either. An argument could, therefore, be made that since current rules are also arbitrary, an adjustment that at least provides an incentive to the PHAs to follow the rules might be an improvement over the status quo, even if the effects on tenant work behavior are neutral.

Malfeasance, Ignorance, or Confusion

The most negative interpretation of why PHAs have not implemented mandatory disregards is that the risk of doing so—namely, the loss of operating subsidies or certificate or voucher slots—exceeds the risk of being detected by HUD. Because HUD has been almost continuously in the throes of reorganization, reinvention, and downsizing throughout the 1990s, some administrative details have inevitably fallen through the cracks. The PHAs may have been betting on the disregards being among these details. A more benign interpretation is that many PHAs have been reacting to the inherent unfairness of the earnings disregards policy, because it provides no additional benefits to those who are working when they enter housing programs while rewarding the unemployed.

Under the assumption that PHAs are not knowingly ignoring the disregards, it is possible that many PHAs are either unaware of the earnings disregards requirement or confused about it. The facts make it hard to accept the claim of ignorance. The requirement became law in 1990, and HUD published the rules on the statute several times between 1994 and 1996, including two special Notices sent to all PHAs alerting them to the publication of the new rules and attaching copies of them (National Housing Law Project 1998a).[8] But these same facts make it easy to accept an explanation of confusion. How were the PHAs supposed to implement the law, which is relatively vague, before the implementing regulations were published to fill in the holes? If regulations take four years to be published, doesn't that suggest some uncertainty about the proper way to interpret this statute? And how should a PHA proceed if *detailed* information on these complex rules is not published for eight years?[9] These facts suggest considerable confusion even within HUD about this statute. A PHA's choice in this situation is either to forge ahead and serve as a "test case" for HUD to sort out its confusion, or to wait until HUD has worked out the details. One knowledgeable commentator who supports this interpretation suggests that in all such cases of complex program rules, HUD needs to not only publish and distribute the rules but to train PHAs in these rules as well (Bryson 1998b).

The experience with earnings disregards is far from unique. The historical record of many features of housing assistance programs is a jigsaw puzzle for which the pieces either do not fit well or come together only slowly. The statutes, regulations, rules, and notices are sometimes so complex and convoluted that no one truly understands them, bringing to mind the Jarndyce lawsuit in the Dickens novel *Bleak House*. These problems are not restricted to arcane fine points; they include core elements such as how rents are set, how income is calculated, and what percentage of income is to be paid as rent—all key provisions for tenants covered by welfare reform. Such confusion suggests that there is probably much more variation in the implementation of housing programs across the country than is commonly recognized. If so, the typical approach researchers have followed, in which all housing programs—or even all sites implementing a single program—are pooled together for analysis, under the assumption that they are generally equivalent, may not be justified. This is a significant complication for studies aimed at isolating the impact of housing assistance on economic independence, because it suggests that variations are not limited only to different types of assistance programs (e.g., public housing vs. certificates), but are present within each program type as well. Methodologically, a time-varying, fixed-effects model would be the best way to account for these variations, but no data currently exist that could be used in this approach. Even the fallback strategy of controlling for the most common and major variations in program implementation could be accommodated by only a handful of existing databases. The main data source on housing across the nation, the American Housing Survey, for example, could not handle this approach. Neither could any of the other major surveys that include questions on assisted housing programs, including the Current Population Survey (CPS) and the Survey of Income and Program Participation (SIPP).

Disincentives to Comply with Welfare Reform

Inconsistencies in housing policy provide disincentives to comply with welfare reform in two major areas: sanctions and time limits.

SANCTIONS

Under current federal housing policy, if a family living in assisted housing has its cash grant reduced or eliminated because of noncompliance with the rules of welfare reform (i.e., sanctioned), its rent is reduced because of the lost welfare income. In other words, failure to meet program requirements in one welfare program reaps rewards from another assistance program, weakening the effects of the sanctions accordingly. The only exception to this is the case of alleged welfare fraud. If the PHA (or housing manager in the case of privately owned subsidized developments) chooses to document the fraud—which, as already noted, they typically do not—they can terminate the family's housing assistance or collect the subsidy overpayment from the tenant.

This fundamental inconsistency in program rules clearly sends mixed messages to the family, but it also may create perverse incentives for the welfare department. "If you are the welfare department and you know a family has a subsidized housing safety net and you are making no progress with them, you will certify that they've made a good-faith effort just so they can keep their housing and you do not have to worry about them becoming homeless."

At this writing, housing authorizing bills in both Houses of Congress (H.R. 2 and S. 462) contain provisions that would remove this core inconsistency between housing programs and welfare reform. Both bills would deny rent reductions to welfare tenants who lose part or all of their welfare grant because they are sanctioned. But it is impossible to predict whether either bill will become law and, if so, whether this particular provision will remain in the bill.[10]

TIME LIMITS

A second basic inconsistency between welfare reform and housing programs is that welfare now has time limits but housing assistance does not. This, too, is likely to attenuate the effects of welfare reform on families in assisted housing because when they reach the welfare time limit, their out-of-pocket rent payment will be reduced commensurately. Thus, the housing subsidy, once again, can cushion at least some of the blow of the loss of welfare income.

Neither H.R. 2 nor S. 462 disallows rent reductions when a family hits the welfare program time limit. Therefore, if these families cannot replace the income they were receiving from welfare before the time limit, they will have their rents reduced to the point at which they are not paying any more than 30 percent of their incomes for rent. This is not quite as inconsistent with welfare reform as it might at first appear, however. Although federal funds cannot be used to support welfare families after the five-year time limit specified in the federal statute, states are not restricted from using their own funds for this purpose. A number of states are doing so, using the same criterion as the two housing bills, namely, that the family made a good-faith effort to comply with work requirements but was unable to find employment.

HOW WOULD PRACTITIONERS FIX HOUSING PROGRAMS?

Although housing practitioners are no more likely to have a consensus view on all matters of policy in their field than any other group,[11] they do seem to share at least one position. When asked how housing programs should change to foster economic independence among tenants, their consistent answer is: "Government should get out of our way." The Moving-to-Work Demonstration (MTW) does just that. Under MTW, launched by HUD in 1997 and just getting under way, PHAs can combine their different streams of HUD subsidies[12] and use them in any way they think will best encourage tenants to enter the workforce, free of many of the rules and regulations otherwise governing housing programs.[13] MTW provides no additional funds, but PHAs can keep any savings their strategies generate.

The 24 PHAs competitively selected for MTW propose a variety of approaches to increase incentives for work.[14] These include delaying rent increases as income increases, reducing the rent-to-income ratio for a period of time, escrowing increases in income, setting flat rents or ceiling rents so that rents do not continue to increase with income, and excluding work-related expenses, including child care, from income calculations. A few proposals set aside housing assistance slots for welfare recipients who have no housing assistance but are making the transition to work, consistent with the "bonus" hypothesis of housing assistance. Beyond income and rent policies, which encompass the PHAs' typical purview, the MTW proposals also include strategies for assessing tenants' needs; obtaining education, training, health, and other skills acquisition and supportive assistance that is required; peer group support and counseling; job retention activities; and co-locating case managers and employment counselors in or near assisted housing developments. Many proposals also include plans to collaborate or at least coordinate with welfare agencies, local area employers, community colleges, and child care providers.

The MTW applications reflect essentially every bright idea about how to reduce or eliminate the disincentive effects of housing assistance that has been discussed since housing programs began. MTW, then, presented the greatest opportunity to date to address many of the fundamental policy questions about the role of housing assistance in achieving economic self-sufficiency that have been vexing researchers and practitioners alike for years. To achieve its potential for knowledge development, however, some or all the demonstration sites should have been required to conduct the type of rigorous evaluation of their interventions—akin to the evaluation requirements of many other agencies' waiver programs—described in chapters 6 and 7. Such evaluations require that sites design and implement their interventions so that they are amenable to research, and that a rigorous research design be followed. Unfortunately, this was not done.

Instead, research goals play no part in the sites' design and implementation decisions. The research plan is restricted to a general monitoring of the key activities and outcomes in all sites; the counterfactual—what would have happened without the MTW intervention—will be addressed through comparisons of demographic characteristics of tenants in study sites to those in HUD administrative records on other PHAs not participating in MTW. Although this research design is an improvement over those applied to the earlier HUD self-sufficiency initiatives described in chapter 5, it will still leave many questions about the *impacts* of the MTW interventions on work behavior unanswered, particularly if these impacts are not large. After more than a decade of missed opportunities to learn about the effects of housing programs on dependency, this latest and, in many ways, richest demonstration will come and go with the prospect of only a modest contribution to our understanding. While we may learn something about which strategies are feasible to implement, this information alone will have little utility in the absence of information on which strategies are most effective.[15]

The context in which MTW was generated unfortunately doomed its knowledge development prospects from the start. MTW was launched primarily as an effort to "block grant" housing programs and devolve authority to the local level. The demonstration route was chosen mainly as a political compromise in Congress between those calling for the block granting of housing programs and those resisting this massive change. Reaping one of the major rewards of demonstration and research programs properly conceived—to systematically test an idea and, thereby, develop new knowledge—was not on the radar screen. In fact, the research that is being conducted on the program is funded by the Office of Public and Indian Housing. HUD's research arm, the Office of Policy Development and Research, decided to devote its limited staff and resources to the three major initiatives with more promising research potential—Jobs-Plus, Moving to Opportunity, and Bridges to Work—"not this broad, bottom-up block grant in which researchers had no authority to impose any structured intervention on the MTW sites" (Turner 1998).

The history of MTW is disturbing for anyone interested in understanding the role of assisted housing in welfare reform and, ultimately, improving the effectiveness of housing policy. Whether politics over-took research, or whether HUD's research functions are too discon-nected from the operating departments, the story of MTW—like those of Project Self-Sufficiency, Operation Bootstrap, and Family Self-Sufficiency before it—says that knowledge development is not an in-tegral part of HUD's culture. It will be very difficult for the housing sector to meet the challenges of welfare reform until this changes.

FROM THE PRACTITIONERS' MOUTHS TO THE RESEARCHERS' EARS

The implications of welfare reform for housing appears to be a subject for which the world of reality is not in conflict with the world of research. Practitioners and researchers agree on the fundamental housing policy question of the day, namely, whether housing assis-tance helps or hurts a family's ability to achieve economic indepen-dence. And they also generally agree on the factors most likely to act as incentives or disincentives for achieving this goal.

What most researchers have missed or ignored, however, is the substantial variation in the implementation and administration of housing programs. While this variation represents a significant com-plication for research on the effects of housing programs on outcomes for recipients, ignoring it risks uninterpretable or misleading results. At the same time, this variation itself is worthy of study, though few such studies have been done since the 1970s. At least as important as the implications of administrative variation for research, however, are the implications for the development, regulation, and enforcement of housing policies. The multiplicity and complexity of programs, the ab-sence of an ongoing quality control system, and intermittent enforcement of policies established by law present major obstacles to achieving the ultimate goal—fair, efficient, and effective housing policy. While these issues are beyond the researcher's domain, research can play a role by documenting these problems and proposing alternatives.

OTHER IMPLICATIONS FOR RESEARCH AND POLICY DEVELOPMENT

Two additional and major challenges for housing research raised by welfare reform are (1) data inadequacies, and (2) accounting for the complex interaction across programs when estimating the housing program effect. Beyond the lack of measures of the variations in policy implementation and administrative variations in existing data sets is the poor validity of the standard survey questions on housing assistance receipt. Similar if not identical questions on housing assistance receipt are asked in the American Housing Survey (AHS), CPS, SIPP, National Longitudinal Survey of Youth (NLSY), and AFDC-QC. Yet, quantitative evidence from a comparison of address records of assisted housing units and survey responses (Casey 1992; Newman and Schnare 1997) and qualitative evidence from cognitive interviews (Rucinski and Athey undated; Shroder and Martin 1996) indicate that many respondents do not answer these "standard" assisted housing questions accurately. These findings seriously limit research on housing assistance programs.[16] To remedy this problem, the standard approach to collecting data on housing program participation will have to be improved.[17] Fortunately, the three major studies now under way that hold the most promise for improving our understanding of the role of housing assistance in economic self-sufficiency—Jobs-Plus, research on the Moving to Opportunity program, and the study of Housing Assistance and Long-Term Dependency—do not have either data problem.[18]

Even with accurate data, however, estimating the impact of housing assistance on work behavior is methodologically difficult. Other safety net programs, such as AFDC or food stamps, are entitlements, for which it is the eligible person's choice whether to receive welfare or engage in work activity. There are well-tested statistical approaches to modeling such choices among eligibles. Because housing assistance is not an entitlement, its effects on work behavior cannot be modeled using the same framework. The alternatives are less well-developed, complex, prone to error, and require panel data with relatively large case counts of those in assisted housing. These factors have so far stymied efforts to study the effects of housing assistance on labor force participation for those participating in multiple safety net programs (Keane and Moffitt 1995) and, in fact, for those participating only in housing programs.

* * *

Welfare reform poses the most significant challenge to safety net programs that they have faced in the last 50 years. This applies with extra force to housing assistance programs, which are struggling with their own transformation. But the challenge also presents opportunities. The message of this volume is for the housing assistance system to seize this opportunity to build action on the basis of ideas that have been well tested empirically.

Notes

1. This chapter draws on a symposium panel featuring Rick Gentry, then Executive Director of the Richmond, Virginia, Housing Authority; John White, then Executive Director of the Philadelphia Housing Authority; and Greg Duncan, Professor at Northwestern University. Ophelia Basgal, Executive Director of the Alameda County, California, Housing Authority, also provided substantial input.

2. More specifically, PHAs typically are responsible for the administration of public housing and the Section 8 certificate and voucher programs. These two programs account for roughly 45 percent of all rental housing units receiving subsidy from the federal or state governments (Newman and Schnare 1997). The third prong of assisted housing, privately owned and subsidized developments, does not usually fall under the PHAs' purview.

3. Although the QC program is no longer required under Temporary Assistance for Needy Families, all states are required to provide annual reports to the Department of Health and Human Services (HHS) that include performance measures. Some states are planning to use some version of their sample-based QC monitoring to fulfill this obligation.

4. Pub. L. No. 101-625, S. 515(b), 104 Stat. 4199 (Nov. 28, 1990). In addition to this set of mandatory disregards, PHAs may also elect to implement optional disregards.

5. Although JTPA is administered by the Department of Labor, not HUD, it has a provision approved by Congress stating that payments made under this act have to be disregarded.

6. Operating subsidies are proposed to increase to 100 percent in fiscal year 1999.

7. In particular, all or some of the difference in subsidies before and after the disregard.

8. The requirements governing disregards for those in HUD-funded programs were published in 1987.

9. Detailed rules on the 18-month disregard were published in 1998 (Bryson 1998b).

10. As this book was being prepared for publication, this provision became law.

11. For recent evidence of dissension, see *Journal of Housing and Community Development* 1998.

12. These include public housing operating subsidies, modernization funds, and certificate and voucher funds.

13. Some rules remain. For example, the number and sizes of families served must remain the same, they must be low income, and their housing must meet housing quality standards. While MTW provides an unusual degree of latitude for a HUD demonstration program, waiver programs with comparable flexibility have operated in other agencies for years (e.g., HHS's welfare reform waivers; the Health Care Financing Administration's home- and community-based care waivers).

14. An excellent overview of the MTW plans can be found in National Housing Law Project (1998b). Note that the statute refers to "up to 30 public housing agencies," but 6 PHAs are participating in Jobs-Plus, which is also authorized in this legislation, and one of these six is participating in both. Therefore, 24 sites are participating in MTW.

15. Even though current plans for the research call for quasi-experimental methods for at least some of the MTW sites, data will come from administrative records only. Therefore, it will be difficult if not impossible to follow those who leave assisted housing, leaving the researchers with a sample of unknown bias.

16. Chapter 2, which relies on one of these databases, the AFDC-QC, indicates how response errors are likely to affect the estimates.

17. Based on the results of the cognitive interviews, the 1998 AHS questions were modified somewhat. Without a validation study, however, it will be impossible to determine if these modifications improve validity. The best approach would be to ascertain program participation from accurate administrative data and attach this information to the records of sample members.

18. For more information on these initiatives contact James Riccio at the Manpower Demonstration Research Corporation (Jobs-Plus), HUD's Office of Policy Development and Research (Moving to Opportunity), and Sandra Newman at Johns Hopkins University (the Housing Assistance and Long-Term Dependency Study).

References

Bryson, David. 1998a. Personal communication, June 12.

Bryson, David. 1998b. "Setting Rents for Welfare Recipients in Public and Assisted Housing: An Historical Overview." Paper presented at the Center on Budget and Policy Priorities–Fannie Mae Foundation Housing Roundtable, Washington, D.C., June 26.

Casey, Connie. 1992. Characteristics of HUD-Assisted Renters and Their Units in 1989. Washington, D.C.: U.S. Department of Housing and Urban Development, Office of Policy Development and Research.

Journal of Housing and Community Development. 1998. "Bricks and Mortar or Helping Hands? An H/CD Debate." Vol. 55, No. 3, May/June.

Keane, M., and R. Moffitt. 1995. "A Structural Model of Multiple Welfare Program Participation and Labor Supply." University of Minnesota and Brown University, mimeo.

National Housing Law Project. 1998a. Housing Law Bulletin 28(January).

————. 1998b. Housing Law Bulletin 28(April).

Newman, Sandra, and Ann Schnare. 1997. "'. . . And a Suitable Living Environment': The Failure of Housing Programs to Deliver on Neighborhood Quality." Housing Policy Debate 8(4): 703–741.

Nightingale, Demetra. 1998. Personal communication, June 9.

Rucinski, Dianne, and Leslie Athey. Undated. Identifying Recipients of Housing Assistance through Survey Questions. Chicago: National Opinion Research Corporation, mimeo.

Shroder, M., and M. Martin. 1996. *New Results from Administrative Data: Housing the Poor, or, What They Don't Know Might Hurt Somebody.* Washington, D.C.: U.S. Department of Housing and Urban Development, Office of Policy Development and Research.

Turner, Marjorie. 1998. Personal communication, July 1.

INDEX

Sandra J. Newman is the interim director of the Institute for Policy Studies at Johns Hopkins University and a research professor teaching in the Master's Program in Policy Studies. Her research focuses on the nature and effects of housing assistance policy for the poor; and the housing problems and needs of vulnerable populations, including persons with severe mental illness, the homeless, welfare families, the frail elderly, and persons with physical disabilities.

Neil Bania is the associate director for community analysis and a senior research associate at the Center on Urban Poverty and Social Change at Case Western Reserve University. His current areas of interest include the effects of welfare reform on low-skill labor markets, the effect of education on labor market outcomes, and the importance of access to suburban labor markets for low-skill workers.

Amy S. Bogdon is director of housing research at the Fannie Mae Foundation. She also serves as co-editor for the *Journal of Housing Research* and assistant editor for *Housing Policy Debate*. Before joining the Fannie Mae Foundation, she was a senior research economist at Fannie Mae and, before that, was a research associate at the Urban Institute. Her published research addresses issues in housing economics, including multifamily housing, housing affordability, housing policy, and government housing programs.

Claudia Coulton is the Lillian F. Harris Professor at the Mandel School of Applied Social Sciences and codirector of the Center on Urban Poverty and Social Change. Through the Center she works with community-based organizations and their initiatives to address poverty and related conditions in urban neighborhoods. Her program of research includes the effects of community environments on children and families, measuring community change, evaluating community initiatives, analyzing the concentration of poverty and affluence in metropolitan areas, and studying the impact of welfare reform on poor communities.

Joseph Harkness is a research statistician in the Housing Research Group of the Institute for Policy Studies at Johns Hopkins University. His research focuses on housing economics, housing policy for vulnerable populations, and location theory.

Pamela M. Jones, formerly a research analyst at Mathematica Policy Research, has completed work in the areas of housing policy, welfare reform policy, health policy, and child care policy.

G. Thomas Kingsley is the former director of the Urban Institute's Center for Public Finance and Housing, which addresses policy issues in housing, local community and economic development, transportation, infrastructure, and local public finance. His current research includes testing the market of the National Neighborhood Indicators Project, an initiative to expand the development of advanced data systems for local policy analysis and community building. He has advised HUD on strategy guidelines for the Empowerment Zone and Consolidated Planning Programs, and assisted former HUD Secretary Henry Cisneros in developing a series of essays on the future of American cities.

Laura Leete is an assistant professor of economics in the Weatherhead School of Management at Case Western Reserve University. Her research has focused on the distribution of wages and employment across the labor force. She is currently studying the implications of welfare reform for low-skill labor markets. She has also written on the increasing polarization in working hours, the increasing disparity in career mobility patterns, gender- and race-based wage differences, and the relationship between wage equity and worker motivation, particularly in the context of for-profit and nonprofit organizations.

James Riccio is a senior research associate at Manpower Demonstration Research Corporation (MDRC), a national nonprofit research institute in New York City. He specializes in the study of work-related programs and policies for welfare recipients and other disadvantaged groups. He is currently the research director for MDRC's Jobs-Plus initiative, a new seven-city research demonstration project attempting to achieve large increases in employment and earnings and improvements in the quality of life among residents in public housing developments. He recently directed a long-term evaluation of California's GAIN program, the nation's largest welfare-to-work program of its type, and has studied welfare reform in Britain as a recipient of an Atlantic Fellowship in Public Policy.

Peter Tatian is a research associate with the Urban Institute's Public Finance and Housing Center. He is the author of the latest version of the Institute's Housing Needs Assessment Model; he participated in the national evaluation of Native American housing programs, and contributed to the Institute's USAID-sponsored technical assistance program in Eastern Europe.

Craig Thornton is a senior fellow at Mathematica Policy Research, specializing in evaluation design and disability policy. His evaluations have examined a wide range of social policy topics, including supported housing, employment and training, welfare reform, offender rehabilitation, long-term care, and health care financing. A major focus of his work has been the development and implementation of social experiments using random assignment. He has also focused on using benefit-cost analysis as a tool for synthesizing research results to be used in policy decisionmaking.

Robert G. Wood is a senior researcher at Mathematica Policy Research, specializing in welfare and education policy. During his tenure at Mathematica, as well as at his previous position at Manpower Demonstration Research Corporation, Dr. Wood has worked on several large policy evaluations designed to measure program impacts, using both experimental and nonexperimental techniques. His most recent work has focused on the job retention of welfare recipients and teenage parenthood.